D1554073

*Law, Legend,
and Incest
in the Bible*

Law, Legend, and Incest in the Bible

LEVITICUS 18–20

Calum M. Carmichael

Cornell University Press ITHACA AND LONDON

THIS BOOK HAS BEEN PUBLISHED WITH THE AID OF A GRANT FROM
THE HULL MEMORIAL PUBLICATION FUND OF CORNELL UNIVERSITY

Library of Congress Cataloging-in-Publication Data

Carmichael, Calum M.
    Law, legend, and incest in the Bible : Leviticus 18–20 / Calum M.
  Carmichael.
      p. cm.
    Includes bibliographical references and indexes.
    ISBN 0-8014-3388-6 (cloth : alk. paper)
    1. Bible. O.T. Leviticus XVIII–XX—Criticism, interpretation,
  etc. 2. Law (Theology)—Biblical teaching. 3. Incest—Biblical
  teaching. 4. Jewish law. I. Title.
  BS1255.2.C36 1997
  222′.1306—dc21   96-52609

First published 1997 by Cornell University Press.

Printed in the United States of America.

Cornell University Press strives to utilize environmentally responsible
suppliers and materials to the fullest extent possible in the publishing
of its books. Such materials include vegetable-based, low-VOC inks
and acid-free papers that are also either recycled, totally chlorine-free,
or partly composed of nonwood fibers.

Cloth printing   10 9 8 7 6 5 4 3 2 1

Contents

Preface

In this volume I expand my theory about the methods and intent of biblical lawgivers, begun in my earlier work (*The Origins of Biblical Law* [Ithaca, 1992] and *Law and Narrative in the Bible* [Ithaca, 1985]) concerning the rules in the Book of the Covenant (Exod 21—23:19) and those in Deuteronomy 12—26, by applying it to the Priestly rules in Leviticus 18—20 about incest and other matters. I claim that a single thesis explains how every law in the Pentateuch came to be formulated and why the Pentateuch is a unique combination of law and narrative.

In quoting biblical texts I have relied on the King James Authorized Version of 1611, but I made changes where these were called for. I used this version because it is almost always a more literal rendering of the Hebrew original than any other translation. It also has the merit of reminding the reader of something I consider to be very important, that biblical literature is a product of the past and hence of a quite different culture from our own.

CALUM M. CARMICHAEL

Ithaca, New York

Abbreviations

AB	Anchor Bible
ABD	*Anchor Bible Dictionary*, ed. D. N. Freedman (New York, 1992)
AJCL	*American Journal of Comparative Law*
AnBib	Analecta Biblica
ANET	*Ancient Near Eastern Texts Relating to the Old Testament*, ed. J. B. Pritchard, 3d ed. (Princeton, 1969)
AOAT	*Alter Orient und Altes Testament*, ed. K. Bergerhof, M. Dietrich, and O. Loretz (Neukirchen-Vluyn: Neukirchener Verlag)
AV	Authorized Version
BAR	*Biblical Archaeology Review*
BBB	Bonner Biblische Beiträge
BDB	F. Brown, S. R. Driver, and C. A. Briggs, *A Hebrew and English Lexicon of the Old Testament* (Oxford, 1906)
BCOT	Biblical Commentary on the Old Testament
Bib	*Biblica*
BSC	Bible Student's Commentary
BWANT	Beiträge zur Wissenschaft vom Alten und Neuen Testament
BZAW	Beihefte zur Zeitschrift für die alttestamentliche Wissenschaft
CB	Century Bible
CBC	Cambridge Bible Commentary

CBQ	*Catholic Biblical Quarterly*
CBSC	Cambridge Bible for Schools and Colleges
CD	Cairo (Genizah text of the) Damascus (Document)
CH	Code of Hammurabi
D	The Deuteronomic literary strand in the Pentateuch
EPC	Expositor's Bible Commentary
ET	English Translation
H	The Holiness Code
HAR	*Hebrew Annual Review*
HAT	Handbuch zum Alten Testament
HL	Hittite Laws
HTR	*Harvard Theological Review*
IB	Interpreter's Bible
ICC	International Critical Commentary
IDB	*Interpreter's Dictionary of the Bible,* ed. G. A. Buttrick (Nashville, Tenn., 1962)
ILJ	*Indiana Law Journal*
JBL	*Journal of Biblical Literature*
JE	The Y(J)ahwistic and Elohistic literary strand in the Pentateuch
JITE	*Journal of Institutional and Theoretical Economics*
JLR	*Journal of Law and Religion*
JLS	*Journal of Legal Studies*
JPS	Jewish Publication Society
JPSC	Jewish Publication Society Torah Commentary
JR	*Juridical Review*
JSOT	*Journal for the Study of the Old Testament*
JSS	*Journal of Semitic Studies*
LCL	Loeb Classical Library
LQR	*Law Quarterly Review*
LXX	The Septuagint
Mekhilta	A second-century CE Rabbinic commentary on the Book of Exodus
MT	The Masoretic Text
NCBC	New Century Bible Commentary
NEB	New English Bible

NICOT	New International Commentary on the Old Testament
OTL	Old Testament Library
P	The Priestly literary strand in the Pentateuch
pr	*Principium* (the first, unnumbered part of a text in some Roman legal sources)
RB	*Revue Biblique*
RJ	*Rechtshistorisches Journal*
RSV	Revised Standard Version
SVT	*Supplement to Vetus Testamentum*
TDOT	*Theological Dictionary of the Old Testament,* ed. G. J. Botterweck and H. Ringgren (Grand Rapids, Mich., 1980)
TOTC	Tyndale Old Testament Commentaries
VT	*Vetus Testamentum*
WBC	Word Bible Commentary
WC	Westminster Commentary
WMANT	Wissenschaftliche Monographien zum Alten und Neuen Testament
ZAW	*Zeitschrift für die alttestamentliche Wissenschaft*
ZSS	*Zeitschrift der Savigny-Stiftung für Rechtsgeschichte*

*Law, Legend,
and Incest
in the Bible*

Introduction

FROM the world of the Near East, the incest rules of the Bible—
in particular those found in the two chapters of Leviticus 18 and
20—have had greater effect on Western law than any comparable
body of biblical rules.[1] The Levitical rules, with the addition of rules
from Roman law in some instances, became the law governing incestuous relations in those countries where the Church's writ ran
large. For centuries not only were the rules of Leviticus 18 and 20
in force but also a great many others that were derived from them.
One reason for the expansion was that later authorities judged the
Levitical lists to be only a limited set of examples of the marital and
sexual relationships that should be banned. One of the best-known

---

1. It would be interesting to study which biblical rules did in fact have some im-
pact on Western legal systems. Despite much talk about the Judeo-Christian heritage
in American society, the ideas that went into the Constitution of the United States
came from the enlightenment and hence from classical antiquity. Even in regard to
the construction of the canon law of the Catholic Church (from 1100 to 1600 CE),
Richard Helmholz shows how difficult it is to judge whether or not the Bible exercised real force; "The Bible in the Service of the Canon Law," *Chicago-Kent Law Review* 70 (1995), 1557–81. On the other hand, even the commandment from the decalogue to honor one's parents, which can hardly be described as a legal provision, found
its way into Napoleon's *code civil* and the *Burgerlijk Wetboek*, the Dutch civil code.
See Alan Watson's comments in "From Legal Transplants to Legal Formants," *AJCL*
43 (1995), 474.

examples of an expanded list is the Table of Levitical Degrees set
out by the Church of England in 1603. This list contained rules that
were construed (by the "Parity of Reason" interpretation of Leviticus) to apply to relatives who were equivalent to those cited in Leviticus. A relative by marriage such as a sister-in-law was to be treated
as equivalent to a relative by blood such as a sister. However out of
touch with the intent of the original lawgivers, this mode of interpreting and expanding on a biblical text is common in all legal systems. Interpreters view the rules as consisting of both explicit and
implicit norms.

One indication of how powerful the incest rules have been is the
fact that only in this century have many of them, especially those
involving affinal relationships (those that come into being through
marriage) been put aside as no longer constituting a bar to marriage.
In England, for example, the Deceased Wife's Sister Marriage Act of
1907, permitting marriage to a deceased wife's sister—the prohibition had been added to the biblical ones—began a trend away from
upholding other rules in the 1603 Table of Levitical Degrees. The
result is that today even the marriage of a brother and a half-sister
is, if the trend in Sweden is an indicator, not inconceivable.[2] Should
brother-sister marriages come to be permitted we shall have a precedent in Roman Egypt. Detailed evidence shows that for at least
two hundred years in that part of the world such marriages between
full brother and sister were publicly celebrated, with wedding in-
vitations, and entailed marriage contracts, dowries, children, and
divorces.[3]

2. Consanguinity is still listed as an impediment to marriage in Sweden, but a
brother and his half-sister may marry if they receive a special license from the government. Although the government's declared position is that the genetic risk for offspring born to a brother and his half-sister is the same for the offspring born to a full
brother and sister, they will grant a dispensation if the parties have been brought up
in separate homes. (See Fariborz Nozari, *The 1987 Swedish Marriage Code* [Washing-
ton, 1989], 11–13.) This position suggests that the genetic factor is not the primary
consideration and that other unrecognized factors are playing a role. Why not, one
would want to ask, grant the dispensation to half-siblings who have been brought up
in the same household?

3. See Keith Hopkins's major study, "Brother-Sister Marriage in Roman Egypt,"
Society for Comparative Study of Society and History 22 (1980), 303–54. In his entry
"Inbreeding in Human Populations" (*Encyclopedia of Human Biology* [San Diego,

The existence of incest rules at all times and places has exercised a compelling fascination among thinkers of all kinds—anthropologists, ethnographers, historians, lawyers, novelists, philosophers, sociologists, and theologians. The drive to explain them has been one of the most compelling in the history of thought and is associated with, among others, Philo, Plutarch, Augustine, Maimonides, Jeremy Taylor, Hugo Grotius, David Hume, Francis Hutcheson, Charles Montesquieu, Jeremy Bentham, John McLennan, Lewis Morgan, Edward Tylor, Emil Durkheim, James Frazer, Sigmund Freud, Bronislaus Malinowski, A. R. Radcliffe-Brown, Edward Evans-Pritchard, and Claude Lévi-Strauss.[4]

A number of theories account for the origin of incest rules, but in scholarly circles bafflement more than enlightenment increasingly prevails. Keith Hopkins's study of brother-sister marriage in Roman Egypt leads him to state:

> The frequent practice of brother-sister marriage in Roman Egypt over a period lasting at least two centuries and perhaps much longer suggests that all the universal quasi-explanations (the demographic theory about the unavailability of marriageable siblings, the indifference theory that siblings do not feel lust for each other, the repression theory that in human development incestuous desires are necessarily repressed, and the evolutionary theory that man as the most developed mammal has somehow replaced genetically transmitted checks against incest with cultural prohibitions

---

Calif., 1992], 4:431–41), L. B. Jorde stresses how difficult it is to reach firm conclusions about the deleterious effects of inbreeding. His unexamined assumption, nonetheless, is that at all periods incest rules testify to the belief in such effects. He wrongly thinks that all the relationships prohibited in Lev 18:6–18 are consanguineous ones (note that marriage to a wife's mother, to a brother's or uncle's wife, or to two sisters are not consanguineous relationships). He suggests that in ancient Egypt brother-sister marriages among the upper classes resulted in reproductive problems: "Cleopatra VII was the product of a brother-sister mating, and she in turn married her two younger brothers but produced no children by these marriages (her relations with Mark Anthony and Julius Caesar were both fertile, however [431])." Jorde is not familiar with the long history of brother-sister marriages among other classes of Egyptians in the Roman period.

4. I cite Sybil Wolfram's list of experts past and present on the topic in her *In-Laws and Outlaws: Kinship and Marriage in England* (New York, 1987), 161.

of incest), as usually put, need to be modified in the light of the single exception, the repeated practice of brother-sister marriage in Roman Egypt.[5]

Sybil Wolfram is a trenchant and persuasive critic of the various theories put forward to explain the origin and existence of incest rules.[6] One of her major contributions is to highlight how twentieth-century anthropologists revived most of the theories devised by seventeenth- and eighteenth-century lawyers and theologians. She categorizes three such types of theorizing: (1) "those that attribute the prohibitions to some feature of the household" (for example, keeping the family sexually unimpassioned as a curb on jealousy and to discourage extramarital intercourse); (2) "those maintaining that sexual unions are forbidden between relatives to avoid conflict with or destruction of previously existing relationships" (social-roles theories); and (3) "those which claim that relatives are forbidden to marry in order that alliances by marriage should be created between otherwise separate persons or groups" (alliance theory). She makes the further point that the elaboration of and the disputes about the various theories of the seventeenth and eighteenth centuries revolved around the question as to whether the positions adopted were in accord with the prohibitions set out in Leviticus.[7] In other words, the thinking underlying these theories all focused on the biblical prohibitions.

In this book my aim is to show that interpreters throughout the centuries were and are not aware of how the Levitical rules came to be formulated in the first instance, and that their automatic assumption that the rules necessarily governed the society of the time is a wrong one. Once the process of how and why the rules come to be set down is explained, we have, I submit, many new insights about the biblical rules. Further, there are implications for contemporary theorizing about the past.

Some traditions in the Old Testament might well have been

5. Hopkins, "Brother-Sister Marriage," 311.
6. See Wolfram, *In-Laws*, 161–206.
7. See ibid., 162, 168–69.

viewed at some point as, potentially at least, offering a license for incestuous unions. I refer to the remarkable number of liaisons between close kin in the early narratives of the Bible. For example, in the books of Genesis and Exodus the daughters of Lot produce sons by their father; Abraham marries his half-sister Sarah; Jacob marries two sisters who are his first cousins; Nahor marries his niece (that is, his brother's daughter); Judah's daughter-in-law, Tamar, seeks a remedy for her childless state by having intercourse with her father-in-law; Moses's father marries his aunt (that is, his father's sister). In 2 Samuel, David's daughter Tamar tells her half-brother, Amnon, who is sexually harassing her, that he should go to their father so that David can find a proper way by which the two siblings can marry.

Abraham, Jacob, Judah, Moses, and David were outstanding figures in Israelite tradition. It surely mattered to the lawgiver that the issue of incest arose with them. My contention is that it mattered very much. The patriarchs' incestuous involvements are the key to the case I will make for a new way of understanding how the incest rules of Leviticus 18 and 20 came to be formulated. Let us note right away that these rules treat the relationship that Abraham has with Sarah, the union of brother and half-sister, as incest, hence too the relationship that Tamar discusses with Amnon. A relationship with a daughter-in-law is ruled out. So too is marriage to two sisters while both are alive. These Levitical rules also prohibit the union that Moses' own parents contracted, the union of a man and his aunt. On the other hand, the lists do not prohibit a union between first cousins or a union between a man and his niece.

A pressing question is this: How do we relate the biblical rules about incest to the incest of the founding fathers of the nation? The biblical lawgiver justifies the rules by saying that the Israelites must not imitate the practices of the Egyptians and the Canaanites. All later commentators have readily accepted these reasons. One must wonder, however: Were the compilers of the rules not aware of the conduct of some of their ancestors? The general view is that we have to reckon with historical development. A relationship acceptable in an early period was not acceptable at a later time.

My view is different. I see a direct link between patriarchal sexual conduct and the existence of the incest rules in Leviticus 18 and 20: the Priestly lawgiver disapproved of what he found in some of his nation's traditions because these traditions condoned incestuous relationships. I do not hold that biblical laws reflect the social history of the times when they were formulated, the standard assumption among scholars who interpret biblical laws.[8] Instead, I believe that the laws take up issues that appear in the stories and legends in, for example, the book of Genesis. My assumption is that the biblical lawgivers set out to tackle the ethical and legal problems they encountered in their reading of these tales. Biblical laws consequently constitute commentary on matters arising in the national folklore. In Chapter 1 I discuss the notable fact that the Priestly lawgiver lashed out at the Egyptians and the Canaanites for incestuous practices but not at their own ancestors who did the same things.

The lists of incest rules in Leviticus 18 and 20 present some peculiar features. It is puzzling, for example, to find that a prohibition—the first in the list—against a son's violation of his father or the son's intercourse with his mother should be set down at all. By and large, lawgivers addressing societal problems are not motivated to set down in writing what no one questions, just as no university has rules stating that those giving lectures should not come dressed in spacesuits.[9] Everyone takes for granted that relationships such as

---

8. In regard to the incest laws, the titles of studies reveal this bias; for example, S. F. Bigger, "The Family Laws of Leviticus 18 in Their Setting," *JBL* 98 (1979), 196; in his recent commentary, *Leviticus*, WBC 4 (Dallas, Tex., 1992), 280, J. E. Hartley has the heading "Laws Governing the Extended Family"; Baruch A. Levine has an excursus, "Family Structures in Biblical Israel," in his commentary, *Leviticus*, JPSC (Philadelphia, 1989), 253–55.

9. On this characteristic aspect of ancient law codes in particular, and also of language—there are no words, for example, for those who do not murder; and until 1892, with the introduction of the word "heterosexual" (to indicate a negative feature: "a morbid sexual passion for one of the opposite sex," *Merriam-Webster's New International Dictionary*), for those who are sexually active only with partners of the opposite sex; see David Daube, "The Self-Understood in Legal History," *JR* 85 (1973), 126–34; David Daube, *Ancient Jewish Law* (Leiden, 1981), 123–29; David Daube, "The Contrariness of Speech and Polytheism," *Festschrift Judge John T. Noonan*, *JLR* 11 (1995), 1601–5.

a son with his father or a son with his mother are forbidden.[10] They are so taboo that they do not even come to consciousness, except, for effect, to modern filmmakers. Yet we find this peculiar formulation at the head of a list of incest prohibitions.

The list contains no express prohibition against intercourse with a full sister. Nor is there a prohibition against intercourse with a son or a daughter—that is, where the father, not the child, is the target of the prohibition. We must take this seriously and ask why the initial rule is addressed to the child of a family as though he, or she, would be the instigator of an incestuous liaison.[11] After all, the sexual abuse of a son or daughter by a parent (or a sister by a brother) is much more likely in the world of experience at any time.[12] No one, so far as I am aware, has bothered to ask why the child and not the parent is the target of this particular rule. The concern with a child who initiates an incestuous liaison and the lack of any rule about more commonly occurring liaisons within a family suggest that the usual attempt to read these rules against the social practice of ancient Israel is the wrong approach to understanding them.

---

10. On such unwritten laws in ancient Athens, see Plato, *Laws*, 838, and Xenophon's *Memorabilia* 4.4.19–22. See David Cohen's discussion, *Law, Sexuality, and Society: The Enforcement of Morals in Classical Athens* (Cambridge, Eng., 1991), 225–27.

11. In the Hittite laws (189) both a son (with a mother; cp. CH 157) and a father (with a daughter; cp. HL 189, a father with a son) are targeted; *ANET*, 196.

12. Consider the impressionistic reporting of a Mrs. Christian Annersley, "magistrate and Chairman of the Bench," in an East Anglian village in the twentieth century. "There was more incest in the past and it was always fathers and daughters, never brothers and sisters. It happened when mother had too many children, or when mother was ill, or when mother was dead. And very often it didn't matter a bit. The daughter usually proved to be very fond of the father and there would be no sign of upset in the family. No, I think it was quite an understood thing that a daughter would take on the father when the mother was ill or dead. It would always happen in a 'basic' family, of course. Then somebody would give them away. Or it would come out when the daughter became pregnant. You would then come up against a strange form of innocence. Not ignorance, innocence. You would hear all about it from police notebooks, pages and pages and pages, and you'd wonder why the man didn't look like a monster. Then you'd realize that what he'd done and what we were saying he had done seemed to be two quite different things. We had strayed into the dark, into the deep—the hidden ways of the village"; from Ronald Blythe, *Akenfield, Portrait of an English Village* (New York, 1969), 244.

Rules other than incest prohibitions appear in Leviticus 18–20. The famous rule about loving one's neighbor as oneself (Lev 19:18) is followed—one interpreter comments that the sequence is like going from the sublime to the ridiculous[13]—by rules prohibiting certain mixtures (breeding two kinds of cattle, sowing two different seeds in a field, and wearing two different kinds of clothing [Lev 19: 19]). Why are rules about incest set down among rules that have nothing to do with the topic? A rule prohibiting intercourse with a menstruant woman comes in between a rule prohibiting the union of a man and his half-sister and a rule prohibiting the union of a man and his aunt (Lev 20:17–19).

Even the most casual reading reveals the lack of any apparent logical order in the arrangement of the rules. A related problem is that so many of the rules turn up again at different points throughout Leviticus 18–20. A rule, differently expressed each time, aimed at those who consult the dead recurs no less than three times (Lev 19: 31; 20:6, 27). If penalties are given at all, they are often bewilderingly varied: "their blood is upon them," burning, stoning, or the threat of divine punishment. Why the variation, and why are the penalties sometimes quite specific but other times general in nature? Similar to the variation in penalties is the variation in language when the lawgiver characterizes the nature of the same offenses and their penalties.

We have to ask whether it really is the case that additions over time can account for the seemingly disorganized arrangement of the rules in Leviticus 18, although it is easy to understand why this view has become so embedded in scholarly approaches. Two rules about intercourse with a half-sister—one rule more general than the other—are separated by a rule prohibiting intercourse with a granddaughter. A rule about the worship of Molech seems out of place in a series of rules involving sexual offenses.[14] And how do we explain the sequence menstruation, adultery, and then Molech wor-

---

13. Gordon J. Wenham, *Leviticus*, NICOT (Grand Rapids, Mich., 1979), 269.

14. Angelo Tosato thinks that intercourse with a foreign woman is at issue in the Molech rule, so intent is he to introduce some homogeneity into the list of rules in Lev 18:18–23. His view underlines the problem rather than solves it; see "The Law of Leviticus 18:18: A Reexamination," *CBQ* 46 (1984), 206.

ship? Can we solve these problems without resorting to the assumption that biblical scribes went in for redactions of existing lists of rules unaware that their insertions and additions were so badly done?

The single thesis I put forward encompasses every one of the above puzzles and yields solutions that avoid the conventional, rather depressing view, exemplified by one scholar, that "the compilations of laws and customs [come] from different sources, all brought together without any real attempt at editing or correlation."[15] Although the rules do seem at times to be chaotically placed, in fact what is really before us is one of the most remarkable exercises in composition in the history of law and literature. Once one sees how the lawgiver worked there emerges a process of editing and correlation on a grand scale. The thesis that explains why a rule about menstruation comes between two incest rules also explains even the most detailed differences in the language of the rules (for example, why the verb *karat* "to be cut off" is commonly used in many rules, but a synonymous, rare word *'ariri* "stripped, cut off" is used instead in one of them [Lev 20:18]). The thesis thus addresses and explains, in a way not possible before, matters major and minor pertaining to the Levitical laws.

The lawgivers of the Pentateuch formulated biblical laws in relation to biblical narratives.[16] They examined the historical traditions of Israel and set down rules in response to events or issues that arose in these traditions rather than in response to problems in their own time.[17] Viewing the material in this light can explain

15. N. H. Snaith, *Leviticus and Numbers*, CB (London, 1967), 137. See also Martin Noth: "A book of laws obviously without much plan, and brought into being by loosely stringing together existing complexes of precepts"; *Leviticus*, OTL (Philadelphia, 1965), 146.

16. Mary Douglas seems to share a similar view but does not spell out her reasons for it. She links the dietary rules in Lev 11:9–19 to Genesis 1: "The dietary laws systematically pick up the order of creation in Genesis"; "The Forbidden Animals in Leviticus," *JSOT* 59 (1993), 16–18. (She has the Earth created on day one instead of day three, a sequence, in turn, she erroneously attributes to the texts in Gen 1:11–13 instead of to Gen 1:9–13.)

17. The thesis I develop received serious and positive discussion at the turn of the century, as reported in S. R. Driver's masterful commentary, *Deuteronomy*, ICC, 3d ed. (Edinburgh, 1902), 213: "Unless, indeed, the other alternative be adopted, and

the archaizing presentation of biblical laws, that is, their attribution
to the legendary figure of Moses, who judges matters past, present,
and future. The primary impetus in the composition of the laws
was to create for the nation of Israel its own ancient legal tradition,
with the laws explicating the epics of the past. The process that accounts for the presentation of the narratives is the same process that
accounts for the presentation of the laws. The narratives do two
major things: they reflect the compilers' interest in universal and
Israelite origins (from the origin of the world in the book of Genesis
to the origin of kingship in the book of Samuel), and they record
matters that recur throughout succeeding generations (from the
problems of the first family in the book of Genesis through the problems of the kings in the historical books). The compilers of the laws
did likewise. They took up problems that first presented themselves in the biblical narrative history and addressed comparable
problems that recur in succeeding generations of that history.[18]

The Deuteronomic and Priestly writers compiled all the laws in
the Pentateuch and they proceeded in identical fashion.[19] Their
rules reflect a special mode of ancient law teaching that to date has
gone unnoticed. For example, frequently a narrative tradition that
recounts a dispute in which the deity plays a decisive role is taken
up in a law, and a legal rather than a divine judgment arbitrates

the author of Dt. 17:14–20 [law of the king] be supposed to have been influenced, as
he wrote, by his recollections of the narrative of Sam. (so Budde, *Richter und Samuel*,
p. 183 f.; Cornill, *Einl.* par. 17.4). As the nucleus of 1 S. 8; 10:17–27a 12 appears to be
pre-Deuteronomic (L.O.T. *l.c.*,) the latter alternative is not the least probable one."

18. Many modern investigators of customary or legal rules—for example, anthropologists and inquirers such as Freud—adhere to Emil Durkheim's procedure: "In
order to gain a proper understanding of a practice or institution, a moral or legal rule,
one must go back as nearly as possible to its first beginnings"; Sybil Wolfram's translation (in *In-Laws*, 171) of Durkheim's "La prohibition de l'inceste et ses origines,"
L'année sociologique 1 (1897), 1. This return to beginnings is remarkably similar to
the procedure of the biblical lawgivers and narrators. As these biblical authors judged
matters, what happened at the beginnings of things set a pattern for future developments. In effect, however, they too, like their modern counterparts, sought understanding of issues in their own time.

19. For the laws of the Book of the Covenant (Exod 21:1–23:19) as the product of
the Deuteronomist, see Calum Carmichael, *The Origins of Biblical Law: The Deca-
logues and the Book of the Covenant* (Ithaca, 1992).

some equivalent dispute.[20] Similarly, the deity's judgment in a narrative tradition often translates into a rule that applies to an approximately corresponding situation in the world of experience.[21]

In their review of this epic material both D and P did what we have always attributed to them, but to an extent not before realized. It has long been recognized that as literary editors they followed through on the doings of their ancestors' generations, laying out the successive histories, inventing some of them, seeking out parallel developments, and conveying, either by arrangement of the material or by comments integrated into the histories, moral and religious judgments. What has not been recognized is that their laws are an extension of this process. Their evaluative work with the narrative epics is both continued and extended, with the result that their law codes are separate compilations of legal and moral judgments. A striking aspect of their mode of working is that they did not revise narratives to bring them into line with their own judgments. By and large they allowed problems to stand and expressed, much more extensively than in their redactional activity, opposition or criticism in the laws. It is this fundamental link between the laws and the narratives of the Bible that accounts for the unique integration of law and narrative that is the Pentateuch, and also for the unique nature of biblical law.

Meir Malul stresses that the Near Eastern codes represent a literary tradition that was not necessarily used to inform the practice of law in the real world.[22] I wish to emphasize that the links between the laws and the narratives in the Bible represent Israelite literary activity equivalent to that found in the broader Near Eastern cultural

20. For example, God's judgment on Onan's failure to meet his levirate obligation to his dead brother in Genesis 38 has its legal equivalent in the rule about the levirate in Deut 25:5–10. See Calum Carmichael, *Law and Narrative in the Bible* (Ithaca, 1985), 295–97.

21. God's opposition to Sarah's going from her husband, Abraham, to another man and back to Abraham in Genesis 20 becomes a rule against the renovation of a marriage when the legal machinery of divorce has been used for the first husband's gain. See Calum Carmichael and David Daube, *The Return of the Divorcee* (Inaugural Jewish Law Fellowship Lecture, Oxford Centre for Postgraduate Hebrew Studies, Oxford, 1992), 15–28.

22. See Meir Malul, *The Comparative Method in Ancient Near Eastern and Biblical Legal Studies*, AOAT 227 (Neukirchen-Vluyn, 1990), 105–7 n. 13.

world. I do not exclude the possibility that the Israelite lawgivers gave the Mosaic equivalent of laws from the Near Eastern codes by asking themselves what, in light of Israelite and patriarchal history, Moses's judgments would have been in the same situation.

The lawgivers did not set down a rule that corresponded exactly to some obvious offense committed in the narrative. Presumably there was no need for them to do so because the narrative communicated the wrongdoing well enough. Rather, the lawgivers came up with a problem related to the one that dominates the story. A parallel to this procedure appears in the hypothetical cases that the prophets sometimes constructed in response to actual offenses. For example, King Ahab fails to kill King Ben-hadad of Syria when he ought to have done so after defeating him in battle (1 Kgs 20:26–43). Instead, Ben-hadad, hiding in the city of Aphek, sends messengers to Ahab to see if he will spare his life. Ahab responds positively and receives Ben-hadad well, especially after Ben-hadad promises to restore some cities that his father captured from Ahab's father and authorizes the Israelites to set up bazaars in Damascus. A member of a prophetic guild goes in disguise to Ahab and presents him with a fictitious case that concerns an offense analogous to Ahab's: "Thy servant [the disguised prophet] went out into the midst of the battle; and, behold a man turned aside and brought a man unto me, and said, 'Keep this man; if by any means he be missing, then shall thy life be for his life, or else thou shalt pay a talent of silver.' And as thy servant was busy here and there, he was gone" (1 Kgs 20:39, 40).[23]

Ben-hadad was not given over to Ahab with an instruction to guard him, whereas in the fictitious case someone gives the soldier an enemy to guard. The soldier is under no obligation to kill his ward, but is simply warned not to lose him. Ahab, on the other hand, is, it is understood, under an obligation to kill Ben-hadad. When the

---

23. Compare how the prophet Nathan presents King David with a made-up case for judgment about the theft of a ewe lamb (2 Sam 12:1–6), and the woman of Tekoah with one about a widow threatened with the loss of her one remaining son because, this son having killed his brother, other family members seek vengeance for the killing (2 Sam 14:4–7). David's adultery with Bathsheba and Absalom's exile from his father, David, because he had his brother Amnon slain inspired the two hypothetical constructions.

king hears the case about the soldier he judges that the soldier has been derelict in his duty. In so judging, Ahab condemns himself for his analogous offense, as the prophet, revealing himself, spells out: "Thus saith Yahweh, 'Because thou hast let go out of thy hand a man whom I appointed to utter destruction, therefore thy life shall go for his life, and thy people for his people'" (1 Kgs 20:42).

There is no question, then, that the made-up offense derives from Ahab's situation. The offense that the prophet invents is comparable to Ahab's offense but is not the same, presumably because it is crucial that the prophet not address Ahab too directly lest he be struck down on the spot. The way that biblical lawgivers constructed legal formulations from narrative accounts of ancestral offenses is very similar to the prophet's procedure. Indeed, the lawgivers probably identified themselves with these prophetic guilds, not only adopting their method of constructing judgments but also, when judging Israel's ancestors, taking the same religious, moral, and legal perspective. The lawgivers' motivation in judging their ancestors is in one way strikingly similar to these prophets when they judge monarchs: the lawgivers only indirectly attacked ancestral conduct.

In analyzing the laws in Leviticus 18–20 I have arbitrarily created chapters, as if there are natural breaks in the flow of the material which merit separate discussions of different sequences of laws. I do so only for the convenience of the reader. At every turn I recognize that the reader is faced with the demanding, double task of going not just from one law frequently unconnected to another, but from a story to a law, then back to the story—even to a related one—and then on to another, often quite different law. If the interweaving of law and narrative which I describe is accurate, we are unraveling the strands of thought which belong to the major enterprise engaged in by those ancient scribes who devised the Pentateuch. Insofar as critics have propounded the view that the Pentateuch consists of an elaborate exercise in composition, I am building on their insight.

CHAPTER 1

The Incest Laws of Leviticus 18

ONCE we recognize the link between the rules in Leviticus 18 and certain narratives in the book of Genesis the puzzling arrangement and formulations of the rules are not puzzling at all. The reason that the prohibition about sexual relations with parents is the first in the series in Leviticus 18, and that it was formulated at all, is because legends in the book of Genesis determined the lawgiver's concerns. Moreover, because the Levitical rules were formulated as a reaction to what went on in these legends, and not to what went on in ordinary life, it becomes understandable why many of the rules strike us as implausible. There is, for example, in Lev 18:17 a quite extraordinary rule against a man's having a relationship with three different generations of women: a woman, her daughter, and her granddaughter.

Interpreters do draw attention to the fact that patriarchal history provides examples of unions that are prohibited by the incest laws of Leviticus 18 and 20,[1] but they do not go far enough in their observations. If, as is universally agreed, the Priestly (P/H) writer not only knew but worked with the ancient traditions of his people

---

1. See "Marriage," *IDB* suppl. (Nashville, Tenn., 1976), 574; also Baruch A. Levine, *Leviticus*, JPSC (Philadelphia, 1989), 253.

which are contained in the Pentateuch, it can occasion no surprise that much, to him, objectionable behavior became the focus of his concern. It is precisely this kind of analytical and critical response to his sources—largely Genesis, but also Exodus—that accounts for both his setting down the rules in Leviticus 18 and the order in which he arranged them. After all, many of the relationships cited in Genesis and Exodus involve kinship ties.

After presenting my analysis of the incest rules in Leviticus 18, I shall address a few of the other puzzling features about them. H—the designation commonly used for Leviticus 17–26 (the Holiness Code) or its redactor—first took up three examples of incestuous or near-incestuous conduct in primeval and patriarchal times, and then responded to both actual and hypothetical situations involving incest or related sexual matters posed by the stories about Abraham, Isaac, Jacob, and Judah. Although he gives no reasons for his assessment, Malcolm Clark is correct to characterize Leviticus 18–20 as "a purely ideal literary construct without institutional realization."[2]

Leviticus 18:6, 7

None of you shall approach to any that is near of kin to him, to uncover their nakedness: I am Yahweh. The nakedness of thy father, or the nakedness of thy mother, shalt thou not uncover; she is thy mother; thou shalt not uncover her nakedness.

The two earliest incidents of incestuous conduct in the book of Genesis involve drunkenness, first Noah's and then Lot's. The two incidents have much in common: the role of wine, the initiative

---

2. See his contribution, "Law," in *Old Testament Form Criticism,* ed. J. H. Hayes (San Antonio, Tex., 1974), 128. All lists of rules about incest have something of this character. The philosopher John Locke expresses the matter as follows: "To know whether his idea of adultery or incest be right will a man seek it anywhere among things existing? Or is it true because anyone has been witness to such an action? No; but it suffices here that men have put together such a collection into one complex idea that makes the archetype and specific idea, whether ever any such action were committed in *rerum natura* or no"; "Names of Mixed Modes and Relations," in *An Essay Concerning Human Understanding,* ed. A. C. Fraser (Oxford, 1894), 2:44.

toward the parent from the son or daughter taking advantage of the drunken father, and the concern with future generations. The lawgiver looked at the two incidents together and used them to set down the first rule of his series of rules on incest.

The first incident in the Bible which raises the issue of incestuous conduct is Ham's offense against his father, Noah (Gen 9: 20–27).[3] Ham looks upon Noah's nakedness and informs his two brothers, Shem and Japheth, who carefully walk backward and cover their father with a garment. When Noah finds out that Ham has violated him (in some way that is not clear to us), he curses Ham to a life of enslavement to his brothers. Whatever the precise nature of the offense,[4] the Priestly lawgiver used the incident to reflect on the potential sexual offense of a son against his father (cp. Ezek 22:10).[5]

The second incident pertinent to the rule occurs when Lot's daughters get their father drunk and lie with him in order to produce offspring by him (Genesis 19). The lawgiver sets down the equivalent male offense, a son's intercourse with his own mother. This move on the part of the lawgiver is an example of how the link between a rule and a narrative can be of an indirect nature. It is also an understandable move because the lawgiver addresses males, as the rules in Lev 18:18 and 19 indicate (prohibitions against taking a

3. The account is confusing. Ham is the offender, but his son, Canaan, is cited in Noah's condemnation. It is as if there is a reversal of actions. Ham, who is explicitly cited as the father of Canaan, offends against his father, Noah, and Noah in turn acts against Ham's son, Canaan. The lawgiver concentrated on Ham's offense.

4. It is safe to assume that sexuality is involved, that Ham is looking not at his father's left ear or right toe, but at his genitals. In light of Canaan's punishment—he loses his status as a member of Noah's line and becomes a slave to his brothers—the offense seems to be disrespect of a progenitor's status. Noah's drunkenness is not considered relevant to the matter.

5. For those who think the incident between Ham and Noah involved a homosexual act, see Anthony Phillips, "Uncovering the Father's Skirt," *VT* 30 (1980), 39, 40. They speculate—wrongly, I think—that because the act was so abhorrent the biblical author did not spell it out. My view is that a lawgiver found the narrative *suggestive* of the topic of sexual encroachment on a father. See the comments of S. D. Kunin in *The Logic of Incest: A Structuralist Analysis of Hebrew Mythology* (Sheffield, 1995), 173–75. Anthropological evidence suggests that in many cultures fathers make every effort to ensure that they do not reveal their genitals to their sons. See Stanley Brandes, *Metaphors of Masculinity: Sex and Status in Andalusian Folklore* (Philadelphia, 1980), 99.

woman as a rival wife to her sister and approaching a woman during her menstrual period).

The rules are addressed to males, but we should be alert to the distinct possibility that in certain instances the masculine second-person pronoun, "thou," may include the feminine.[6] I am claiming that the lawgiver moved from Noah's situation, in which a son offends against his father, to Lot's situation, in which daughters offend against their father. There is thus merit in reading the first part of the rule about the father to include an offense by either a son or a daughter. The language of the law is most appropriate if the lawgiver was considering the two offenses in the legends together. Ham looks upon, and wants his two brothers to look upon, a father's nakedness, and Lot's daughters uncover their father's nakedness. In expressing an offense against a father in terms of nakedness, the lawgiver encapsulates both offenses well. I think it likely that the use of the expression "to uncover nakedness" in the sense of sexual intercourse came first from the Priestly writer's focus on these two incidents.

If the language of the rule includes a daughter, then we have a rule prohibiting a daughter from instigating a relationship with a father. Ordinarily, it is the father's sexual advances on a daughter which are the problem, but no such formulation is found in the code.[7] The story about Lot's daughters would account for the implicit reverse formulation in this rule, namely, a daughter's sexual interference with a father.[8]

---

6. To cite but one example, the rule in Deut 12:18: "Thou, and thy son, and thy daughter, and thy manservant, and thy maidservant . . ."; the first "thou" includes the man's wife.

7. Karl Elliger (who first introduced me to the study of biblical law) feels compelled to introduce it. It had, he believes, inadvertently dropped out; see "Das Gesetz Leviticus 18," *ZAW* 67 (1955), 2. Note that he assumes the rules to have been set down with a view to governing social and family life.

8. Recent translations—for example, RSV and JPS—interpret the rule as solely about intercourse with a mother. They choose to read not the literal "The nakedness of thy father, or the nakedness of thy mother, shalt thou not uncover" but instead place on the connecting particle *waw*, "and," the weight of a circumstantial clause: "The nakedness of thy father which is [=*waw explicative*] the nakedness of thy mother." While it is a possible, if a rather free, translation, it is an awkward one that badly overloads the sentence, as interpreters who accept the translation point out;

The rule gives more attention to an offense against a mother than to an offense against a father because the language describing the offense against her contains the added emphasis: "she is thy mother; thou shalt not uncover her nakedness." The increasingly common attempt to read the rule as solely about sexual violation of a mother has doubtless been encouraged by the emphasis on her in the rule's formulation. The reason for the bias in the rule may well be the fact that in the narratives the offense against the father is not in doubt, it is spelled out. In making a rule, however, the lawgiver had to postulate a corresponding offense against a mother. It is important to emphasize that the lawgiver used the tradition less to condemn conduct described in it—after all, the tradition itself takes care of the obvious offense—than to bring out analogous conduct. The relationship between the law and the narrative is not a slavish one-to-one correspondence. It is rather a sensible exploration of the pertinent issues that the narrative raises.

Leviticus 18:8

The nakedness of thy father's wife shalt thou not uncover: it is thy father's nakedness.

The lawgiver next takes up another offense from the patriarchal history. Reuben, Jacob's oldest son, lies with his father's wife Bilhah (Gen 35:22). Again, as in the legends about Noah and Lot, the child violates a parent, in this instance it is said to be the father. The

---

see, for example, S. F. Bigger, "The Family Laws of Leviticus 18 in Their Setting," *JBL* 98 (1979), 196. Usually the lawgiver is more explicit when he makes the point that uncovering the nakedness of one person uncovers a related person's nakedness. For example, in the immediately following rule in Lev 18:8, we have: "The nakedness of thy father's wife shalt thou not uncover: it is thy father's nakedness." In Lev 18:14 ("Thou shalt not uncover the nakedness of thy father's brother, thou shalt not approach to his wife"), uncovering an uncle's nakedness does indeed mean intercourse not with him but with his wife. There is no use of the *waw explicative*. Phillips also opposes the transferred meaning: "It is much more natural to understand Lev xviii 7a in its present form as prohibiting sexual relations with either of one's parents"; "Uncovering the Father's Skirt," 39, 40.

lawgiver generalized from this patriarchal incident to include any wife of the father, even if the father has divorced his wife or is dead. The rule readily follows the previous one because the first one also focuses on a father's wife, specifically, a man's own mother. The reason that the lawgiver would have set down the offense even though it is explicitly cited in Gen 35:22 is that from his point of view Jacob's condemnation is too mild. (All the text says is that Jacob heard about it.) Only at the end of Jacob's life does Reuben learn of a negative consequence, that he has lost the right of the firstborn (Gen 49:4). The comparable rule in Lev 20:11 lays down a death sentence, as does Jub 33:1–17, whose author also links both rule and story and raises the issue of Reuben's not receiving a capital sentence.

The rule describes the son's intercourse with the wife of his father as an uncovering of the father's nakedness. This focus on the father and not on his wife may well have come from Reuben's father's own description of the incident. Jacob tells Reuben that it is against him that Reuben has offended when at the end of his life he assembles his sons together and addresses each in turn. In speaking to Reuben he takes up the matter of Reuben's sexual offense but, interestingly, states it in a way that makes it appear that Reuben violated him. Thus Jacob says, "Thou wentest up to thy father's bed; then defiledst thou it: he went up to my couch" (Gen 49:4).[9] Jacob does not refer to the fact that a woman was involved.

In moving from the earliest history of the biblical ancestors to Reuben's escapade, the lawgiver typically ranged over the history of the generations. Where he found a comparable example in a later generation, he would switch to that example, then return to the chronological sequence of events.

---

9. A major reason that intercourse with a father's wife is thought of as uncovering the father's nakedness has to do with the near universal use of clothing to indicate the marital relation. As well illustrated in Deut 22:30 ("A man shall not take his father's wife, nor shall he uncover his father's skirt"), a husband and wife, for both protective and sexual purposes, cover each other as if each is a garment. The Koranic statement that wives are "raiment for you and ye are raiment for them" (Q.2:187) well describes the biblical position also. See Calum Carmichael, *Law and Narrative in the Bible* (Ithaca, 1985), 198.

Leviticus 18:9–11

The nakedness of thy sister, the daughter of thy father, or daughter of thy mother, whether she be born at home, or born abroad, even their nakedness thou shalt not uncover. The nakedness of thy son's daughter, or of thy daughter's daughter, even their nakedness thou shalt not uncover: for theirs is thine own nakedness. The nakedness of thy father's wife's daughter, begotten of thy father, she is thy sister, thou shalt not uncover her nakedness.

The next three rules pose a very obvious puzzle. There is first a prohibition against intercourse with a half-sister, either a daughter of the same father or a daughter by the same mother from a previous marriage. There is next a prohibition against a man's relationship with a granddaughter. The third prohibition is again intercourse with a half-sister, this time more narrowly defined: she and her brother have the same father but a different mother.

Why would a lawgiver set down the same prohibition about a brother and a half-sister almost side by side? Why too, for that matter, does a rule about a man and his granddaughter come between these two almost identical rules about a half-sister? The conventional view is that we are reckoning with a code of laws patched together from different sources at some time in the history of ancient Israel.[10] There is another, more interesting solution—and, I might add, one more complimentary to the ability of ancient authors to set out rules in a way that made sense to them.

Patriarchal history continues to be the focus of these three rules. In the first, a man must not have intercourse with the daughter of his father's wife—a father's wife was the focus of the preceding law—or a daughter by his mother's previous marriage. This rule and the two following ones about grandfather-granddaughter rela-

---

10. For various attempts to delineate such sources, see H. G. Reventlow, *Das Heiligkeitsgesetz formgeschichtlich Untersucht*, WMANT 6 (Neukirchen, 1961), 65–78; Rudolph Kilian, *Literarkritische und formgeschichtliche Untersuchung des Heiligkeitgesetzes*, BBB 19 (Bonn, 1963), 57–65; Christian Feucht, *Untersuchungen zum Heiligkeitsgesetz* (Berlin, 1964), 37–42; Alfred Cholewinski, *Heiligkeitgesetz und Deuteronomium: Eine vergleichende Studie*, AnBib 64 (Rome, 1976), 44–54.

tions and brother and half-sister relations look at actual and hypo-thetical aspects of the history of Abraham.[11]

The lawgiver first focuses on Abraham's marriage to Sarah. Abra-ham encounters problems during a sojourn in Egypt (Gen 12:10–20). On the occasion, Abram (his name at this point in time) says to his wife: "Say, I pray thee, thou art my sister" (v. 13). Abram is attempt-ing to deceive the pharaoh in order to conceal that Sarai (Sarah's name at this time) is in fact his wife, because he fears that the Egyp-tians will kill him, as a husband, to appropriate her. The hypothet-ical issue of a man's marriage to his sister arises from the story in the sense that a man who can say that his wife is his sister, even if she is not, poses the question, can a man marry his sister?[12]

This issue of marriage to a sister thus would have arisen even if we did not know from a later notice, in Gen 20:12, that Sarai is indeed Abram's half-sister, the daughter of his father. In the first of his rules about the half-sister, the lawgiver generalized from Abram's remark to the pharaoh, and he thinks of both the half-sister from the father and the half-sister from the mother. August Dill-mann points out that the statement in Gen 12:13 regarding Sarai as Abram's sister does not necessarily imply what we are told in Gen 20:12, that Sarah is the daughter of Abraham's father but not of his mother.[13] Nor does the genealogical notice in Gen 11:29 about Abraham's father's lineage give this information. In other words, the lawgiver had the statement in Gen 12:13 in focus, and he simply

11. On the role of hypothetical constructions in legal culture ancient and modern, see, for ancient Near Eastern codes, F. R. Kraus, "Ein zentrales Problem des altmeso-potamischen Rechts: Was ist der Codex Hammurabi?" *Genava* 8 (1960), 283–96; for Roman law, H. F. Jolowitz, *Historical Introduction to Roman Law* (Cambridge, Eng., 1952), 93, 95. For contemporary America, there is the role of the Restatements of the Law by the American Law Institute. Judges typically treat its formulations with re-spect, and some even regard them as the "law." See R. S. Summers, "The General Duty of Good Faith—Its Recognition and Conceptualization," *Cornell Law Review* 67 (1982), 810–40; also A. J. Jacobson, "Death of the Hypothetical," *Stanford Litera-ture Review* 9 (1992), 125–38 (made-up cases flourish when there is a transition from oral to written judicial culture).

12. The lawgiver must have been all the more impelled to address the issue of brother–half-sister marriage because a similar incident occurs in the generation after Abraham. To protect himself from the men of Gerar, Isaac falsely claims that the woman (Rebekah) to whom he is married is his sister (Gen 26:6–11).

13. August Dillmann, *Die Genesis* (Leipzig, 1892), 227.

covered the two possibilities: marriage to a sister who is the daughter of one's father, and marriage to a sister who is the daughter of
one's mother. Of the daughter by the mother the lawgiver states
that the prohibition applies to a daughter who has been born to the
mother at home or abroad. Gen 11:31 indicates that Abram's father,
Terah, moved with Abram and Sarai from his home in Ur of the
Chaldees to go abroad. Because we learn in Gen 20:12 that Sarah's
father is also Terah, her mother would presumably have been from
Ur. The point, however, is not Sarah's genealogy. It is the contrast
between home and abroad, which the Genesis narrative brings out,
that has prompted the geographical statement in the rule.

Why do we find the additional rule about the half-sister in the instance where she is solely the daughter of a father's wife? Why this
prohibition again, which the lawgiver has included in the preceding
rule but one? The answer is that he had under scrutiny the specific,
later notice in Gen 20:12 about Abraham's relationship to Sarah.
Abraham (his name and Sarah's have been altered by this time) is
again sojourning in foreign parts, the kingdom of Gerar this time,
and again he fears that he will be killed so that his wife can be ap-
propriated. He resorts to the same ruse he tried in his previous visit
to Egypt, and again the ploy comes undone. The foreign king, Abimelech, finds out that Sarah is Abraham's wife. In response to the
king's discovery, Abraham informs Abimelech that Sarah is indeed
his half-sister as well as his wife: "the daughter of my father, not
the daughter of my mother, and she became my wife." It is precisely this relationship that the lawgiver prohibits, having laid out
in his previous law but one the more general prohibition against
marriage to a daughter of one's father or a daughter of one's mother.
The lawgiver's method of examining from a later ethical and legal
stance information brought out in the narrative sequence explains
why he repeats the prohibition.[14]

---

14. I might add that it is my contention that the legal material in the Bible constitutes the substance of the redactional activity that the Graf-Wellhausen theory
claims is responsible for the makeup of the Pentateuch with its different strands: Jahwistic, Elohistic, Deuteronomic, and Priestly. See K. H. Graf, *Die geschichtlichen*

In Genesis, the verses describing Lot's daughters lying with their father appear between the two episodes about Sarah's relations with the pharoah and Abimelech. That incident was pertinent to the first rule prohibiting intercourse with a parent. The lawgiver looked at the incident again and used it to derive his prohibition against a sexual relationship between a man and his granddaughter. This time he scrutinized the incident in its wider context as part of the history of Abraham.

Lot is Abraham's nephew (the son of his brother Haran), so Lot's daughters are Abraham's grandnieces. Lot and his daughters are saved from the destruction of Sodom and Gomorrah because of Abraham's good standing with the deity (Gen 19:29). Their future husbands are not saved because they refuse to depart the threatened city. As a consequence of the destruction wrought on Sodom, the daughters reckon that they need their father for procreative purposes: "Our father is old, and there is not a man in the earth to come in unto us after the manner of all the earth" (Gen 19:31).

The lawgiver had reflected on the reasoning of the daughters of Lot. There is no man on earth to impregnate them, they reckon. That is not true. If they mean only that men from their kinship group are not available, that is not true either; there is their granduncle Abraham. To be sure, he is even more aged than their father, but as we learn from the account of Abraham's life at this time, he is perfectly capable of performing sexually at an advanced age (Gen 18: 9–15; 21:1–3). In their old age he and Sarah produce their son, Isaac. Abraham, then, could have come in to these daughters of Lot "after the manner of all the earth."

The lawgiver condemns out of hand the action of the daughters in resorting to intercourse with their father. The very fact that they get him drunk to begin with is an indication that they know their

---

Bücher des Alten Testaments: Zwei historisch-kritische Untersuchungen (Leipzig, 1865), and Julius Wellhausen, *Prolegomena zur Geschichte Israels* (Berlin, 1883). The relationship between the Deuteronomic and Priestly rules, on the one hand, and, on the other, the Jahwistic and Elohistic narratives is such that the strands form a much greater unity than critics have hitherto realized.

action is improper. For the lawgiver, on the other hand, the daughters' intercourse with their granduncle Abraham would presumably have been acceptable. Just as the lawgiver does not prohibit a union between a man and his niece—a relationship Abraham's brother Nahor had with his niece Milcah—so he would not prohibit a union between a man and his grandniece. As in Roman law, the relationship is too distant to trigger a prohibition.[15]

My submission is that the lawgiver derived his prohibition against a man's having a relationship with a granddaughter from his examination of the episode of Lot's daughters. He has made the following move. He condemns a relationship of a daughter with a father but would not condemn one between a man and his grandniece. He does, however, consider the relationship in between these two relationships. Can a man have a sexual relationship with his granddaughter? The lawgiver, prohibiting daughter and father, likewise prohibits grandfather and granddaughter. The rule is another example of one that is derived indirectly from the narrative.

Two other features of the material may also have been suggestive of a relationship between a man and his granddaughter. First, Lot is very old when the incident with his daughters occurs. Second, Lot's own father, Haran, died before Abraham and Lot migrated to Canaan. As Lot's uncle, Abraham took on the role of father to Lot. In this light Abraham is very close to being a grandfather to these daughters. What we should primarily keep in mind is that the tradition highlighting Abraham's sexual activity when he is very old would understandably bring up the issue that a sexually active aged male might seek sex with a female relative two generations removed from him.

There is no explicit prohibition against either a brother's intercourse with a full sister or a father's intercourse with a daughter, where the father is the target of the prohibition. There is, however, a prohibition against a man's having intercourse with his daughter-

15. If S. A. Naber's emendation of "sister" into "niece" is correct, Plutarch cites a prohibition in Roman law for marriage with a niece (but not, I repeat, between a man and his grandniece). See F. C. Babbitt, *Plutarch's Moralia*, LCL 4 (Cambridge, Mass., 1962), 16 n. 2.

in-law (Lev 18:15). The reason that the prohibitions about a sister and a daughter are omitted is not solely that the lawgiver does not raise issues that no one questions, although this universal feature of early law codes is a factor.[16] The main reason for the absence of express prohibitions against intercourse with a full sister and a daughter is that the relationships in question were not ones that the lawgiver felt pressed to extrapolate from his scrutiny of the narrative material he worked with. The omission of a rule prohibiting a father's intercourse with a daughter may be surprising.[17] In that the incident involving Lot and his daughters is about the daughters' initiative and Lot's lack of it because of age and drink, the lawgiver has not bothered to look at the offense in terms of a father's initiative.

The inclusion of a rule about a man's having intercourse with his granddaughter when there is no rule about a father's intercourse with his daughter presents a major problem for those inquirers who automatically apply sociohistorical considerations to an understanding of biblical legal material.[18] J. E. Hartley, for example, proposes that "the reason for its [the rule about a daughter] absence may have been socio-economic; that is, an Israelite would not think of severely reducing the marriage price his daughter could command by having relations with her."[19] It is difficult to believe that a father's lust for a daughter would be deflected by thoughts of his bank account. Sexual passion just does not work that way. Hartley admits that his proposal does not explain the absence of a law against a brother–full-sister union. Approaching these laws primarily in terms of social history is not a fruitful strategy. The laws were not set down to govern society, even though some of them may in fact have done so.

16. So David Daube, "The Self-Understood in Legal History," *JR* 85 (1973), 126–34. It is a factor for a sister. Thus in Lev 18:11 the reason given for prohibiting a relationship between a man and his father's daughter by a wife other than the man's own mother is that "she is thy sister." It follows that there is a bar to a relationship with a full sister.

17. CH 154 has the prohibition: "If a seignior has had intercourse with his daughter, they shall make that seignior leave the city"; *ANET,* 172.

18. These inquirers are well represented by Frank Crüsemann, *Die Tora: Theologie und Sozialgeschichte des altestamentlichen Gesetzes* (Munich, 1992).

19. J. E. Hartley, *Leviticus,* WBC (Dallas, Tex., 1992), 287.

Leviticus 18:12, 13

Thou shalt not uncover the nakedness of thy father's sister: she is thy father's near kinswoman. Thou shalt not uncover the nakedness of thy mother's sister: for she is thy mother's near kinswoman.

The preceding rule, prohibiting a union between a brother and his half-sister, was set down because of Abraham's marriage to his half-sister Sarah. The next rule, in Lev 18:12, 13, prohibits a union between a nephew and his aunt—the sister of his father or of his mother. Why do we find this particular rule at this point? The shared interest in a sister is too weak a link. What again proves to be the determining factor is a quite remarkable feature of the Genesis narrative. Before we turn to it, some background information about Abraham and Sarah's son Isaac is in order.

Difference in age (between a grandfather and a granddaughter) is a feature of the preceding law but one. A major interlude in the narration of the destruction of Sodom and Gomorrah is the problem of Sarah's inability to procreate because of her age. It is a problem comparable to the one that prompts Lot's daughters to have sex with an aged relative. When the deity informs Sarah that the extraordinary will occur, that she will produce a child by Abraham, she laughs at the idea. The reason is: "Now Abraham and Sarah had entered into the days"—that is, they are of an advanced age. It has "ceased to be with Sarah after the manner of women" (Gen 18:11). The extraordinary does occur and Isaac is born, his name reflecting Sarah's laughter.[20]

A possible explanation for the setting down of this rule against sexual relations with an aunt might run as follows. In prohibiting sexual relations with her, the lawgiver had in focus women well on in years, sexual relations with whom might be out of the ordinary but could occur.[21] In regard to these particular women, however,

20. See David Daube's discussion of Bar Kappara's boldness about Abraham and Sarah at this stage in their life; "Bar Kappara," *RJ* 12 (1993), 403–4.

21. A considerable age difference between a man and his aunt would be most likely, but no doubt in a polygamous society the difference might not be so great in some instances.

they must not occur because of the tie of kinship. In other words, Sarah's sexual history raised the topic of sex with older women. Equally to the point, her unlikely sexual activity at an advanced age with a kinsman, her half-brother Abraham, might have prompted the lawgiver to turn to such activity as was to be prohibited, namely, a man having a sexual relationship with a kinswoman who was relatively advanced in years.

There is, however, one remarkable or, better, bizarre (from our perspective) feature of the situation in Genesis which is a major factor in the lawgiver's proscription of the union cited in the rule. Isaac's relationship to Sarah is not just son to mother. She is also his aunt because she is his father's sister.[22] It is this decidedly curious relationship between Isaac and Sarah that primarily determined the topic of the rule. Although it was never a possibility that Isaac would have a sexual relationship with Sarah,[23] the lawgiver nonetheless took up the issue of a nephew's relationship to an aunt. After all, Isaac's parents had an odd relationship, which the lawgiver took up in the preceding prohibition against marriage between a brother and a half-sister.

If the idea of a union between Isaac and Sarah is not in any way suggested in the tradition, why did the lawgiver nonetheless proceed to bring up the union of a nephew and his aunt? The reason is that future developments among Abraham and Isaac's descendants furnish him with an example of just such a union. In keeping with the overall approach of biblical authors when they recorded history, the lawgiver turned to the first generation after Isaac's which presented him with the marriage of a man and his aunt. He found it in the generation between the patriarchs of the book of Genesis and Moses of the book of Exodus. The relationship is that of Moses's own parents: "And Amram took Jochebed his aunt to wife" (Exod 6:20). The term *dodah* "aunt" can refer to either a father's brother's wife

22. Compare how in some societies a son is related not to his father or mother but to members of their families. For the Trobriand Islanders, see Bronislaus Malinowski, *The Sexual Life of Savages in North Western Melanesia* (London, 1953).

23. The lawgiver, of course, did not steer away from explicitly prohibiting a union between a son and his mother (Lev 18:7).

or a father's or mother's sister.[24] As we learn from Num 26:59, Jochebed in fact is Amram's father's sister.[25] That is, Amram's relationship to Jochebed is the same as Isaac's to Sarah.

The narrator in Exodus himself links the generations stretching from Abraham to the parents of Moses. Thus he gives his genealogical information when relating how the pharaoh oppresses the Israelites and how the Israelite god acts on their behalf because he promised to give the land to Abraham and his descendants (Exod 6: 2–4). The union of Moses's parents takes place during the period of the pharaoh's oppression, just as the matter of Abraham's marriage to his sister Sarah (the union that elicits the presentation of a preceding rule against a relationship with a half-sister) comes up at a time when Abraham expected trouble from the pharaoh (Gen 12:12).

In his incest rule, then, the Priestly lawgiver (H) has taken stock of this marriage between Amram and Jochebed[26]—the genealogy in Exod 6:2–4 is attributed to H—because he ranged over matters that arise in succeeding generations. The rule covers both a father's sister and a mother's sister because the reference to Amram's aunt in Exod 6:20 is indeterminate. If we go by the notice in Exod 6:20 alone, either his father's sister or his mother's sister could be meant, or, for that matter, a father's brother's wife—the relationship in focus in the next rule.

Leviticus 18:14

Thou shalt not uncover the nakedness of thy father's brother, thou shalt not approach to his wife: she is thine aunt.

It is again an important question why this particular union, involving this time an aunt through an uncle's marriage, should come

24. See BDB, 187. The term *dodah* "aunt" occurs only in Lev 18:14 (=Lev 20:20) and in Exod 6:20 (cp. Num 26:59).

25. Amram's father is Kohath, son of Levi (Exod 6:16). Jochebed is a daughter of Levi (Num 26:59); that is, Kohath and she are brother and sister. Hence Amram marries his father's sister.

26. On the relevance of this union to the narrative about the virgin birth in Matt 1: 18–25, see Dale C. Allison, *The New Moses* (Minneapolis, Minn., 1993), 146–50.

into consideration after one about a man and his aunt, where she is the sister of a man's father or mother. The explanation lies in the indeterminacy of the notice in Exod 6:20. As just noted, the term *dodah* "aunt" can refer to either a father's or mother's sister—or, as in this rule, to a father's brother's wife. The lawgiver set down another rule about an aunt which corresponds to the preceding rule about the father's or mother's sister.

The two rules (about the father's or mother's sister and the uncle's wife) correspond in another and, to us, surprising way. Just as Isaac's relationship to Sarah is that of nephew to aunt (his father's sister), so his relationship to Abraham is not just that of son to father but also nephew to uncle, because Abraham is his mother's brother. She is also his uncle's wife. This strange set of relationships contains the one of nephew to uncle's wife which is cited in the rule under review.

The lawgiver, then, has taken stock of Isaac's relationship to his uncle's wife, noted that there was not the slightest possibility of a union between them, and turned to later Israelite history, to the indeterminate notice in Exod 6:20 which led to the preceding rule about the father's or mother's sister: "And Amram took Jochebed his aunt [*dodah*] to wife." To be sure, the lawgiver knew from elsewhere (Exod 6:16, Num 26:59) that Jochebed is in fact Amram's father's sister. He nonetheless lays out another of the possibilities inherent in the statement in Exod 6:20, that is, *dodah* as the wife of a father's brother.[27] The genealogical information implies no bar to a relationship between a man and his uncle's wife, but the lawgiver prohibits it.

A digression follows. Why does the lawgiver single out the wife of the father's brother as against the wife of the mother's brother? A possibility is that another part of the tradition about Isaac's kinship ties had come under his scrutiny. Apart from Isaac's marriage to Rebekah and his dual relationships with Sarah as his mother and aunt and with Abraham as his father and uncle, one, and only one, other

27. Recall how the lawgiver formulates the prohibition against marriage to a half-sister who is from a father or a mother (Lev 18:9) from the indeterminacy of the narrative in Genesis 12 (unlike the narrative in Genesis 20, which gives Abraham's precise relationship to Sarah).

kinship tie to a woman comes into the account of Isaac's life at the
point when he is in a position to marry. That tie also involves a dual
relationship. Milcah is the wife of his father's brother, Nahor. She is
therefore Isaac's aunt. It is the relationship cited in the rule. As it
happens, Milcah is also Isaac's first cousin (and Nahor's niece) because she is the daughter of Abraham's other brother, Haran (Gen 11:
29). Just as Isaac has an odd relationship to Sarah (son and nephew),
so too he has an odd relationship to Milcah (first cousin and nephew),
which is worth looking at more closely.

Isaac's birth very late on in the lives of his parents explains why
this odd tie to Milcah exists. One consequence of his birth is that
his position relative to his own generation is a singularly anomalous
one, especially as regards marriage. Abraham arranges for him to
marry one of his kin. The narrative begins with a statement about
Abraham's age (Gen 24:1), which is the cause of his urgency about
finding a wife for Isaac. The concern with age, I suggested, may have
been a factor in the preceding prohibition against a union between
a man and his aunt when the birth of Isaac himself comes into focus (cp. Gen 24:1 about Abraham's "entering into years" with 18:11
about both Abraham and Sarah's "entering"). Isaac marries Rebekah.

Rebekah is the granddaughter of Isaac's uncle Nahor and Nahor's
wife Milcah.[28] The rule speaks initially about uncovering the nakedness of a father's brother. Thus it takes up a relationship between a
nephew and an uncle, which is Isaac's relationship to Nahor. Abraham's concern with the woman his son marries shows up in the narrative. Isaac is not to marry a Canaanite woman (Gen 24:3). When
introducing his incest rules (Lev 18:3), the lawgiver similarly prohibits relationships with Canaanites. Abraham's servant is sent to
Mesopotamia and there he meets Rebekah. In Gen 24:15 Rebekah's
father is "Bethuel, son of Milcah, the wife of Nahor, Abraham's
brother."[29]

Isaac marries into the generation not of his cousins—he might

---

28. Because they uncovered their father's (Lot's) nakedness, the granddaughters of
Abraham's other brother, Haran, came into the lawgiver's scrutiny in Lev 18:7.

29. Dillmann points out that the designation "son of Milcah" here (and in Gen 24:
24) to refer to Isaac's uncle's wife is surprising, because elsewhere it is the father's
name that is given, not the mother's; *Die Genesis*, 303.

well have done so in the normal way of things—but of a cousin's (Bethuel's) offspring and of a cousin's (Milcah's) offspring's offspring. The age gap between Isaac and Milcah would have been considerable. The point is, however, that if Isaac had not been born so late into the lives of his parents, Milcah, as his first cousin, might well have been a possible marriage partner for him, especially in light of the tendency among the patriarchs to marry within their kin group. Isaac's son, Jacob, marries two of his first cousins. What the lawgiver contemplated was the more normal situation when a man and his uncle are in competition for the same woman because there is not the great gap in age which is the idiosyncratic feature of the situation in Genesis. Should the uncle acquire her and then divorce her, the judgment is that his nephew cannot marry her.

There is, then, a rule against a sexual relationship with an uncle's wife but no rule against a relationship either with a cousin once removed or with one's niece (Nahor's union with Milcah), or, even more to the point, with a first cousin, as in Jacob's marriages to the daughters of his mother's brother Laban. The lawgiver does not make the distinction that is commonly made between degrees of consanguinity and degrees of affinity.[30] In that our assumption is that consanguineous relationships are, as a rule, prohibited ahead of affinal ones, we are left puzzled why there is the prohibition about the affinal relationship, an uncle's wife (Lev 18:14), but no prohibition for the consanguineous relationships that Jacob's marriages to Rachel and Leah presented.

We should be careful not to read back into the biblical material our notions about incest. We might note, for example, that this lawgiver readily sets down prohibitions about nonincestuous sexual offenses—or even nonsexual ones, as in the rule forbidding Molech worship (Lev 18:21)—alongside rules that we characterize as constituting the topic of incest. Why then is there the rule about the uncle's wife but none about cousins? Presumably, in regard to marriages involving cousins, they were common in the real world of the lawgiver and he could think of no reason to prohibit them.

---

30. Levine views this distinction as a fundamental one in the rules in Leviticus 18; *Leviticus*, 117–18, 121.

In regard to the prohibition about the uncle's wife the matter is more complicated. Is its basis solely the close tie between a nephew and an uncle? I think not. Another factor may be the issue of the difference in age between the younger man and the older woman, in particular, the problem of procreation that a sexual relationship with an older woman presents. Note how there is no bar to an uncle's marrying his niece.[31] Nahor's own marriage to Milcah is an example. She produces eight children by him (Gen 22:23).

I am suggesting that the two prohibitions against unions to aunts may owe something to a consideration of age and that interest in the topic came from the lawgiver's dwelling on the problem of Sarah's becoming pregnant late on in life. The lawgiver could not anticipate supernatural intervention (as in Sarah's case) to bring about fertility among later generations of Israelites should they marry older women. He might have reasoned that although Abraham was successful in obtaining progeny by the aged Sarah, no such expectation should come into consideration for any future Israelite. The deity's intervention in human affairs was not helpful to the lawgiver.[32] He had to pay attention to normal conditions and prohibit unions where the difference in age between the man and the woman would be a problem in producing progeny. In that the lawgiver's thinking was dominated by what happens from generation to generation it is not surprising that he would have had concerns about the problems a union between two different generations might present when the woman is from the older generation.

We have a rule prohibiting a man's relationship with the wife of the father's brother but no rule for the wife of the mother's brother.

31. I am assuming that the lawgiver would have set one down if he had been opposed to Nahor's union with Milcah.

32. On the topic of the negative aspect of divine intervention, see Calum Carmichael, *The Origins of Biblical Law* (Ithaca, 1992), 123, 128, 135, 144–45, 202–3. The problem became an acute one in later Rabbinic jurisprudence when a deeply religious culture had to deny regulative force to examples held out by God. See *Collected Works of David Daube*, vol. 1, *Talmudic Law*, ed. Calum Carmichael (Berkeley, 1992), 205–11. Compare how in *Republic* 326B Plato desires the relationship between kingship and philosophy to come about "by divine dispensation"; in his *Laws* 709E–12 he has the king rely on a perfect lawgiver.

Yet in the preceding rule, in regard to marriage to an aunt (Lev 18: 12, 13), the lawgiver spells out both the sister of a father and the sister of a mother. Why is one rule comprehensive in scope but the other not? The notice in Exod 6:20 about Amram's marriage refers to his aunt without further specification. Hence the lawgiver, I argued, may be spelling out the two possibilities when prohibiting a union with an aunt. The puzzle is why does he not do likewise in regard to the rule about the uncle's wife because the indeterminacy of the notice in Exod 6:20 should have similarly encouraged him to do so. After all, he had the two examples, the wife of a mother's brother (Sarah as Abraham's wife and sister) and the wife of a father's brother (Milcah as Nahor's wife), before him in the traditions. One possibility to explain why the rule confines itself to the father's brother may have been that the lawgiver focused solely on Isaac's relationship to Nahor's wife. His reason for doing so would have been that if the birth of Isaac had occurred at a much earlier time in the lives of his parents, he had the hypothetical prospect of Milcah as a possible partner for him in marriage should Nahor have died or divorced her. No such prospect presented itself for Isaac's marriage to his own mother should Abraham have died or divorced her.[33]

There follows a sequence of rules beginning with a prohibition against a man's having a relationship with his daughter-in-law, which is followed by a rule prohibiting a man from taking his brother's wife. Then follows the extraordinary rule about a man's having sexual relations with a woman, her daughter, and her granddaughter.

Leviticus 18:15–17

Thou shalt not uncover the nakedness of thy daughter in law: she is thy son's wife: thou shalt not uncover her nakedness. Thou shalt not

---

33. One can see why in the Church's later use of the Levitical incest rules there developed the "Parity of Reason" interpretation: "Relatives thought of as equivalent to those specified in Leviticus were considered to be implicitly included as forbidden"; so Sybil Wolfram, *In-Laws and Outlaws: Kinship and Marriage in England* (New York, 1987), 26.

uncover the nakedness of thy brother's wife: it is thy brother's nakedness. Thou shalt not uncover the nakedness of a woman and her daughter, neither shalt thou take her son's daughter, or her daughter's daughter,
to uncover her nakedness; for they are kinswomen: it is wickedness.

These three rules, I submit, were formulated in response to the
story of Judah and Tamar in Genesis 38. In the preceding rule Isaac's
marriage to Rebekah was one tradition under scrutiny. She is Abraham's daughter-in-law, and the history of sexual relationships in
Abraham's time had dominated the lawgiver's attention. H turned
to the later generation of Jacob's sons in setting down this prohibition against a man's having intercourse with his daughter-in-law,
because the generation of Jacob's sons presented an example of just
such a union.

Judah, one of Jacob's twelve sons, separates himself from his
brothers and, living in Canaan, marries a Canaanite woman. Judah
produces three sons by her. He marries the first of his sons, Er, to
Tamar. God strikes Er down for some wickedness. There is no child
by the union, and the second son, Onan, is obliged by the levirate
custom (then thought to exist) to help Tamar conceive so that she
may raise up a child to his dead brother. Presumably for reasons of
greed (Onan stands to gain if no son becomes heir to his dead elder
brother), Onan avoids his obligation by ejaculating outside Tamar.
Onan too is struck down by the deity. The obligation to fulfill the
levirate duty then falls upon the youngest son, Shelah. But Shelah
has not yet reached puberty. Moreover, from Judah's vantage point
it appears that Tamar is the sinister force causing the deaths of his
sons. Therefore when Shelah reaches sexual maturity, Judah, fearing
for Shelah's life, does not involve him with Tamar. Tamar takes the
matter into her own hands. She dresses as a prostitute and, with her
face covered, seduces Judah as he is on his way to a sheep-shearing
festival. After some months, Judah is told that his daughter-in-law
is pregnant by harlotry and he pronounces a sentence of death by
burning for her offense. As she is being led out to be burned, Tamar
in her own defense produces objects that Judah gave to her at the
time of their sexual transaction. Judah then acknowledges the right-
ness of her action: producing an heir to her dead husband by a mem-

ber of his family. By keeping Shelah from Tamar, Judah failed to fulfill this duty to his dead son Er. The story ends with Tamar producing twins.

The lawgiver sets down his rule against a sexual relationship with a daughter-in-law in response to Judah's dealings with Tamar: "Thou shalt not uncover the nakedness of thy daughter in law: she is thy son's wife, thou shalt not uncover her nakedness." At the time of Tamar's ploy she is not actually married to any of Judah's sons. The point is, however, that whether or not Judah permits Shelah to consummate a marriage with her, Tamar is affianced to Shelah by the custom of levirate marriage. That is why she can be accused of harlotry.

The story itself brings out the taboo inherent in a relationship between a man and his daughter-in-law. Tamar does not approach Judah openly to obtain seed from him, but instead disguises herself as a harlot and seduces him. The story, moreover, tells us that after that one encounter they never again have a sexual relationship. There is, then, a sense in which all the lawgiver does is spell out a rule that is implicit in the narrative. The narrative, after all, itself contains ethical and legal judgments.[34] The lawgiver would simply have been extending this process of judgment. He would have been further encouraged to do so because the story in fact gives an ambiguous message. Judah states that Tamar, in getting seed from him, is "more righteous than I, inasmuch as I did not give her to my son Shelah." Judah's statement might actually imply that in some circumstances it is acceptable for a daughter-in-law to have a sexual relationship with her father-in-law. The lawgiver opposes any such relationship.

The next rule, against a sexual relationship with a brother's wife, also comes from reflection on the Judah and Tamar story. "Thou shalt not uncover the nakedness of thy brother's wife: it is thy

---

34. Using methods of analysis derived from the contemporary study of law and economics, Geoffrey P. Miller does not view biblical narratives as mere stories or national epics but as themselves having a degree of legal force. See "Contracts of Genesis," *JLS* 22 (1993), 15–45, and "The Legal-Economic Approach to Biblical Interpretation," *JITE* 150 (1994) 755–62. For his discussion of the Adam and Eve, Cain and Abel material, see "Ritual and Regulation: A Legal-Economic Interpretation of Selected Biblical Texts," *JLS* 22 (1993), 477–501.

brother's nakedness." The story presupposes the custom of levirate marriage, in which a man in certain circumstances is obliged to have a sexual relationship with his dead brother's widow. Onan is unwilling to meet his obligation and conceals his unwillingness in an offensive way. Either the lawgiver opposed any union between a man and his brother's wife no matter the circumstances, thereby canceling the levirate custom, or the lawgiver viewed Onan's unwillingness as wholly appropriate for all Israelite men, except in regard to the levirate custom. I cannot decide which view prevailed although I tend to think that the lawgiver was opposed to levirate marriage. The Deuteronomic law about the custom acknowledges that it might fall into disuse because D devised a ceremony of disgrace for a brother who refuses to take on the obligation (Deut 25: 5–10).

There follows the extraordinary rule prohibiting a man from having sexual relationships with two or three generations of women in the same family: "Thou shalt not uncover the nakedness of a woman and her daughter, neither shalt thou take her son's daughter, or her daughter's daughter, to uncover her nakedness; for they are kinswomen; it is wickedness." The rule is not just narrow in that it contemplates such extraordinary relationships but also in that it concerns a man who marries a woman who already has children from a previous marriage.

Again the story of Judah and Tamar is the key. A central feature of the story is that Tamar has several sexual relationships within the same family. Although this story features a woman, in his rules the lawgiver addresses males. He therefore discusses a set of relationships for a man which approximates Tamar's experience. (Recall that Lot's daughters' intercourse with their father prompted a rule prohibiting a son's intercourse with his mother.)

Tamar has a sexual relationship with a man of her own generation, but also with his father; that is, she has relations with two generations of men belonging to the same family. Thus Tamar has a sexual relationship with a man who has already been married to a woman (the daughter of Shuah, Gen 38:2) by whom he has had children. The lawgiver thought of a set-up similar to Tamar's: a man's taking a woman who has been married before and who has had children by the previous husband, in particular, a daughter with whom the man also has a sexual relationship. There is nothing improbable about such a development. What is remarkable is that the lawgiver should have proceeded to contemplate the man's having an additional sexual relationship with the woman's granddaughter (her son's daughter or her daughter's daughter). Why should such an improbable development have come up for consideration?

Tamar contemplates a sexual relationship with yet another member of Judah's family, Shelah, but he has not yet reached puberty. There is a sense, then, in which from a sexual point of view Shelah's youth puts him into a different generation from his dead brothers. Sexual status is central in defining what it means to belong to a generation. Both the English term "generation" and the Hebrew term *toledhoth* "generations" focus on the aspect of procreation.[35] Greek sources indicate that boys incapable of emitting semen were thought of as not truly male. In many societies a prepubescent, uninitiated male is essentially female.[36] I suggest that it is Shelah's different sexual status from his brothers' which prompted the lawgiver to come up with the example of the third generation in his rule. Unlike prepubescent boys, prepubescent girls married.[37]

Even after Shelah reaches sexual maturity, Tamar nonetheless skips him—hence the generation to which he belongs—and seeks intercourse with the by-now-aged father. In this light the narrative does bring up the issue of a woman's having intercourse with a man far removed in age from his son. The lawgiver translates the situation in Genesis 38 into a rule about a man's relationship with a woman and the very much younger daughter of her son or daughter. Tamar's actual or potential sexual liaisons with what amounts to three generations of men in the same family inspired the lawgiver to set down a rule that prohibits a man from having sexual relations

35. In belonging to the generation he is born into, Isaac in effect belongs to a generation after the one we would expect him to be born into.

36. See Aristotle, *Generation of Animals* 728a, *Problems* 879a, and David Cohen's discussion for the position in ancient Greece and the literature he cites for other societies; *Law, Sexuality, and Society: The Enforcement of Morals in Classical Athens* (Cambridge, Eng., 1991), 192–93.

37. The Mishnah's definition of a virgin is: "Whoever has never seen [menstrual] blood even though she is married" (*mishnah Niddah* 1:4).

with three generations of women in the same family. The rule first prohibits a man from having sexual relations with both a woman and her daughter and then prohibits a relationship with her son's daughter or her daughter's daughter.[38] The rule is divided into two parts because the lawgiver has worked with the two distinctive developments in the story involving Judah's three sons.

If the rule is in any way meant to apply to real life, we must ask how realistic it is. In the world of antiquity such a mother could have been around forty, her daughter around twenty-five, and her granddaughter, like Shelah, around the age of puberty. Such short intervals between generations would have been quite exceptional, however.[39] When we take into account the proposition that a man would have sought a sexual relationship with all three generations, I think we have to reckon that the dramatic developments in the legend rather than a real-life situation have triggered the lawgiver's thinking.

Interpreters have been puzzled by the use of the term; *ša'ra*, "relative," and typically read it as "[they are] her kin." The problem with this reading is that it states the obvious and we have to wonder why the lawgiver felt it necessary to use the term. The LXX is probably more accurate: "they are your [the male addressee's] kin." The law's background may again prove illuminating. The reference to kinship may reflect the fact that Judah's relationship to Tamar was that of father-in-law to daughter-in-law.

I conclude by considering the problem I set aside earlier. In introducing the sequence of rules I have just discussed, the biblical lawgiver expressly condemns the conduct of the Egyptians and the Canaanites, but says nothing about the similar conduct of his own

---

38. The rule speaks of uncovering the nakedness of the woman and her daughter but of taking (to wife, *laqaḥ*) the granddaughter. Tamar would not have lain with her father-in-law if he had done his duty by her and arranged for Shelah to fulfill the levirate marriage. It would then have been appropriate to have spoken of Shelah taking Tamar (to wife) for this purpose. As just indicated, for the lawgiver, a granddaughter is equivalent to Shelah in Judah's family.

39. See Martha T. Roth for marital ages in Babylonia and Assyria of the first millennium BCE: "Age at Marriage: Ancient Babylonia and Assyria," *Comparative Studies in Society and History* 29 (1987), 715–47. Her tentative conclusion is that "a bride will be in her middle or late teens . . . and a mother in her early to mid forties" (747).

ancestors. In the prologue to the rules in Lev 18:1–3 the Priestly lawgiver warns: "After the doings of the land of Egypt, wherein ye dwelt, shall ye not do: and after the doings of the land of Canaan, whither I bring you, shall ye not do." In the warnings that follow the presentation of the rules (Lev 18:24–30), the lawgiver again returns to the unacceptable conduct of the Canaanite inhabitants of the land and insists that the Israelites should not imitate it when they occupy the land of Canaan. One problem about these warnings is the difficulty of finding any evidence in the pertinent Near Eastern sources that the liaisons prohibited in Leviticus constituted a major feature of Egyptian and Canaanite life.[40] Further, it is hard to believe that Canaanite and Egyptian children were known for initiating sexual encounters with their parents or that men frequently had relationships with three generations of women in the same family. I know of no scholar who addresses the discrepancy between the vices that Moses attributes to Egypt and Canaan and the actual social practices in those lands. Presumably the tacit view is that if we knew more about these societies revelations of their outrageous ways would be forthcoming. I am skeptical, however, about the common assumption that these nations were indeed notorious for decadent behavior and that the Israelites were reacting against them in the regulation of their own social life.

In every time and every place, it is typical for one group to blame another for sexuality that is deemed damnable. The Germans blamed syphilis on the French, the French on the Spanish, and the Spanish on Native Americans. Homosexuality has been termed the English disease; the term "bugger" means that it was the Bulgarians who engaged in homosexuality; and the word "Sodomite" refers to the homosexual activity of the natives of Sodom. AIDS has been blamed on Africa. In a pre-Socratic Greek source we are told that the "Persians think it seemly that not only women but men should adorn themselves, and that men should have intercourse with their daughters, mothers and sisters, but the Greeks regard these things as

---

40. Harry Hoffner points out how sparse, for example, is the evidence for bestiality and homosexuality (prohibited in Lev 18:22, 23, 20:13, 15, 16) in Syro-Palestine and Mesopotamia; see "Incest, Sodomy, and Bestiality in the Ancient Near East," in *Orient and Occident*, AOAT 22 (Neukirchen-Vluyn, 1973), 82.

disgraceful and against the law."[41] According to the Bible, (sexual) harlotry started with the Canaanites (Genesis 34).

My scrutiny of the incest rules suggests that it was the behavior of the ancestors of the Israelites, not Egyptian or Canaanite behavior, that the lawgiver condemned.[42] This conclusion should not be so unexpected when we recall that some of the rules do prohibit relationships actually found among the patriarchs. Why, then, did the lawgiver point the finger at the Egyptians and the Canaanites instead of at them? The answer is that the lawgiver had to view the behavior of the ancestors in light of their milieux. Such judgments are a universal phenomenon. Conduct barely acceptable in Denver is considered good enough in San Francisco.[43] The patriarchs did not have the laws of Moses by which to live,[44] but instead were influenced by their Canaanite or Egyptian environment. That environment had to be taken into account in an assessment of their behavior. The lawgiver inferred, in a way that I indicated is typical at all times and places, that Canaanite and Egyptian ways were beyond the pale and that the activities of the ancestors were more understandable as a consequence.

Abraham is married to his half-sister. The lawgiver probably inferred that such a union, offensive to him, simply reflects Abraham's deficient social and cultural setting, Mesopotamian in this particular instance. He and Sarah were married before they migrate to

41. Cited by R. N. Frye, "Zoroastrian Incest," *Orientalia I. Tucci memoriae dicata,* ed. G. Gnoli and L. Lanciotti (Rome, 1985), 448. According to the much later *babylonian Berakhoth* 8b the Zoroastrians were chaste in sexual matters.

42. In his *Logic of Incest,* 92, 266, Kunin argues that a mythological—but, he stresses, only a mythological—analysis of the Genesis narratives suggests that in some of the instances of incest there is positive assessment in order to resolve some of the fundamental issues that the redactors of the material confronted.

43. Philonic, New Testament, and Talmudic ethical judgments sometimes take into account the influence of a harmful milieu. For example, the reference in Gen 6:9 that Noah was "just and perfect in his generation" has occasioned much debate as to whether he possessed absolute virtue or whether he stood out only among his contemporaries (Philo, *De Abrahamo* 7.36–40; *Genesis Rabba* on 6:9). See David Daube, "Neglected Nuances of Exposition in Luke-Acts," *Principat* 25 (1985), 2329–56.

44. Angelo Tosato forgets this fact, hence his difficulty when he states, "It is hard to believe that such personages [the patriarchs] were made into breakers of the Law"; "The Law of Leviticus 18:18: A Reexamination," *CBQ* 46 (1984), 212. See Chapter 2, n. 3.

Canaan. Abraham himself sees the need for his son Isaac to avoid a Canaanite marriage (Gen 24:3). Abraham's awareness of such an undesirable union would have been evidence for the lawgiver that already in Abraham's time the Canaanites represented a harmful influence. Judah's relationship with his daughter-in-law occurs in Canaan, after he himself has married a Canaanite in Canaan. Moses prohibits the very union that his own parents had contracted—in Egypt (Num 26:59). For the lawgiver, then, it was the host cultures in which the ancestors lived, not the ancestors themselves, that his people must be warned about.[45]

The consensus of scholarly opinion has it that the Levitical lawgiver was himself living in a host culture, Babylon. If he was, it may be significant that he does not cite Mesopotamia as one of the cultures he deplored. To have done so would have been unwise. At the same time, however, if this historical context is relevant to the rules, the lawgiver was in a coded way telling his fellow Israelites to avoid Babylonian ways. The reference to the Egyptians and the Canaanites would have directed attention to the Babylonians just as, later, "Edom" was a code word for Rome among the Jews who lived under the Romans.[46]

The Sequence of Topics in the Narratives for the Laws in Leviticus 18:7–17

Although the rules in Lev 18:7–17 constitute a series about incestuous relationships, it is still important to work out why one rule follows another and why particular though often idiosyncratic

45. Without realizing just how important is the connection, commentators have long drawn attention to the notices about the iniquity of these cultures in Genesis (13:13, 18:20, 21, 19:1–29, 20:11) and the similar ones in Lev 18:24–28; 20:22–24. See Dillmann, *Die Genesis,* 251; also M. A. Fishbane, *Biblical Interpretation in Ancient Israel* (Oxford, 1985), 420, which states that while Abraham, on divine authority, would inherit the land defiled by the Amorites (Gen 15:7, 16), Abraham's descendants would forfeit it if they defiled it with those sins decried by Ezekiel. Fishbane then cites Ezek 33:25, 26 and Lev 18:20, 26–30.

46. See G. F. Moore, *Judaism in the First Centuries of the Christian Era* (Cambridge, Mass., 1966), 2:115, 116.

relations are discussed but not others. I explain their order and contents by looking at the incidents the lawgiver has drawn on in the books of Genesis and Exodus. The sequence of incidents begins with one involving Noah in Genesis 9 and ends with one involving Judah's family in Genesis 38. In between come incidents from Genesis 12, 19, 20, and 21. In general, then, the lawgiver progressed through the traditions about his ancestors.

Primeval history came under the lawgiver's scrutiny first. Ham abuses his father's, Noah's, sexuality, and an initial rule prohibiting a son's interference with his father is set down. (In passing, I should point out that the rules in Leviticus 17 which precede the first of the incest rules in Leviticus 18 concern the eating of meat and forbidding the consumption of the blood of an animal. The narrative material in Genesis 9 which precedes the incident about Ham's abuse of his father permits Noah and his family to eat meat but only on condition that they do not consume any blood. One can see the possibility that the apparently disjointed arrangement of the laws in Leviticus may somehow be linked to the arrangement of the material about Noah and his family in Genesis.)

Although the lawgiver usually proceeded sequentially through biblical traditions, another factor has also played a role. An incident involving Abram's passing his wife off as his sister in Genesis 12 gave rise to the rule about the half-sister in Lev 18:9. The lawgiver has set down two rules before this one, and each involves incidents that appear not in the material between Genesis 9 and 12 but in Genesis 19 and 35 respectively. This sequence does not reflect an orderly progression through the narratives.

The explanation is that the lawgiver was abreast of the entire range of traditions extending from the primeval history in Genesis through the period of the monarchy in 2 Kings. Where he found in a different generation a development parallel to the one that had his attention he incorporated it in his scheme of presentation. The two incidents in Genesis 19 (daughters' sexual abuse of a father) and Genesis 35 (a son's abuse of a father by having intercourse with his father's wife) were later but parallel to Ham's abuse of his father. In each instance the child abuses the parent. The lawgiver constructed two rules in response to these two later incidents and attached them to the rule forbidding abusing a father sexually (arising from the incident about Ham's abuse of Noah). One of these two rules prohibits a son from having sex with his mother—the rules are addressed to males, and sex with a mother is the equivalent male offense to Lot's daughters' sex with their father—and the second prohibits sex with a father's wife. The lawgiver then resumed his progression through the narrative histories (Genesis 12) and set down the rule against a relationship with a half-sister. The laws are ordered not only by the linear flow of history but also by the recognition of *similar* events in some other generation.

The arrangement of the biblical narratives themselves reveals the same features. There is a progression from one event to the next within the same generation, but now and again a future development from a quite different time is brought into view. Two examples in the book of Genesis are the references to the much later enslavement of the Israelites in Egypt in the account of the life of Abraham (Gen 15:13–16; compare the similar reference in Gen 46:1–5 in the account of the life of Jacob), and to the later problems Judah encounters in Canaan in the account of the history of Joseph's youth (Genesis 38).

Beginning with the rule about a half-sister, the lawgiver looked at a succession of events in the life of Abraham's family. He turned from the episode in which Abram passes his wife off as his sister in Egypt to the episode in which Lot's daughters complain that there was no man other than their father to give them conception to the episode in which Abraham again passes off Sarah as his sister in the kingdom of Gerar. The three laws about the half-sister, grandfather and granddaughter, and the half-sister again are set down in response to these three incidents.

The lawgiver proceeded to the birth of Isaac, who, for him, is the product of an incestuous union. Isaac's relationships to his own parents are such that his mother is an aunt to him on two counts. Taking up Isaac's relationships to Sarah, the lawgiver found that Moses's father, in a later generation, married his aunt. Because the notice about this union in Exod 6:20 does not specify what kind of aunt Moses's mother was, the lawgiver lays out prohibitions against unions both between a man and his father's sister and between a

man and his uncle's wife. The lawgiver has kept to the sequence of
the narratives but also expanded his horizon to take in from a later
generation a relationship in the book of Exodus which presents a
parallel to Isaac's relationships to Sarah.

Returning to the sequence of narratives in Genesis, the lawgiver
next encountered incestuous unions in Genesis 38. Tamar has sexual relationships with Judah's son, the son's brother, and with Judah
himself. She also seeks a relationship with another son but he has
not yet reached puberty. Although the narrative tells of Tamar's
unions, the lawgiver chose to focus on the male equivalent, and
he set down rules prohibiting a man to have relations with his
daughter-in-law, his brother's wife, a woman *and* her mother, and
the daughter of that woman's son or daughter. The setting down of
these rules concludes the series of incest rules in Lev 18:7–17.

Chapter 2

Other Laws of Leviticus 18

WHEN the lawgiver set down his rules, the link between the topic of one rule and the topic of the next is often bewilderingly unconnected. For example, a prohibition against sexual relations with a menstruant woman comes after a prohibition against marrying two sisters during the lifetime of one them. How does one explain this lack of logical connection between the subject matter of one rule and the next? What we should not do, I submit, is what scholars typically do. They look at the two rules together and try to puzzle out a link despite the gulf in substance between them. This approach proves a fertile breeding ground for observations that wrongly attribute to the ancients concepts and beliefs that these modern scholars think are peculiar to the ancient Near Eastern world, for example, that these ancients made no distinction between moral and ritual rules.[1] The error in this approach is like the error of a modern reader who turns to an index of topics in a scholarly treatise and relates one entry, say, "carnivore," to the one that comes before it, say, "carnival." A modern reader who did this would come up with

---

1. The article "Law in the Old Testament," *IDB*, 83, states, "Distinction is often made between cultic, moral, and juridical types of law. Such a distinction may be useful in the present day, but it is not a distinction which ancient man knew or would recognize."

the strangest of notions. One should relate, of course, each index entry to the appropriate place in the body of the book—so too in puzzling out why one biblical law follows another. We should not read them in their immediate context but relate each rule back to the issue that the lawgiver picked up from the body of biblical narratives he was working with.

Leviticus 18:18

Neither shalt thou take a woman as a rival wife to her sister, to uncover her nakedness, beside the other in her lifetime.

The lawgiver sets down a rule that is not about incest. A man must not marry two sisters while both are alive.[2] It is easy to relate this rule to patriarchal history. Jacob is married to the sisters Rachel and Leah. The rule uses the verb *laqaḥ*, "to take [as wife]." These women are also his first cousins, but that particular degree of consanguinity is plainly not the reason for the prohibition. Presumably the lawgiver permitted marriage between first cousins. The reason for the rule is the problem of rivalry between the sisters. The notable feature of Jacob's marriages to Rachel and Leah is precisely the rivalry between them in competing for his sexual services. On one occasion one sister even hires him out to the other for a night's lovemaking (Gen 30:14–18).[3]

2. S. D. Kunin states that the rule is about incest because a man who marries one sister automatically creates a kin relationship with the other; *The Logic of Incest: A Structuralist Analysis of Hebrew Mythology* (Sheffield, 1995), 265 n. 2. If this were the case, however, there would have been no need for the lawgiver to bring up the issue of rivalry as the ground of the prohibition. Kunin's view seems to come from the history of the interpretation of the Levitical incest rules in English law (see next note). The word *'alehah* "upon her," in the sense of beside the other sister as a wife, occurs also in Gen 28:9 (Esau's acquiring other wives) and Gen 31:50 (Jacob's acquiring wives in addition to Leah and Rachel).

3. I do not accept the view of Angelo Tosato that this rule has been properly interpreted by the Dead Sea community; "The Law of Leviticus 18:18: A Reexamination," *CBQ* 46 (1984), 199–214. CD 4:20–21 paraphrases the rule as prohibiting bigamy, not as prohibiting marriage to two sisters while both are alive. English law also reads the rule as prohibiting polygamy, but this interpretation derived from the "Parity of Reason" interpretation of Leviticus 18 on which English law came to be based. I agree

The history of patriarchal sexual relationships accounts, I contend, for the setting down of the series of rules in Lev 18:6–18. Where these relationships raise issues of incest, the lawgiver duly recorded his judgment. Where the stories raise related issues but ones that do not involve incest, the lawgiver also proceeded to give his judgment. The lawgiver's method, then, accounts for the mixing together of laws to do with incest and laws not to do with incest. Any hypothesis about the nature of these rules has to account for such combinations of topics.

The lawgiver turned from Tamar's story to Jacob's when he followed a rule about a man's sexual relations with three generations of women with a rule about a man's marriage to two sisters. How do we account for this switch from one story to another? The lawgiver's fundamental procedure is to move back and forth between the histories of the generations. What prompted him to do so was that time and again he found that what occurred in one generation also occurred in a later or earlier generation.

Tamar is married to first one brother and then, after he dies, to another brother. The lawgiver logically turns to a comparable marital setup in the preceding generation, Jacob's. Jacob is married to two sisters, Rachel and Leah. Unlike Tamar's consecutive marital unions to two brothers, Jacob is married to each sister during the lifetime of the other. There are other features shared by the two stories. Tamar's marriages to the two brothers are disastrous. Jacob's own marriages founder—he hates Leah because he was tricked into marrying her, and Rachel, the one he loves, is barren. Onan's father

---

with Tosato that we should not introduce the notion of incest into this rule—a major part of his argument—but his interpretation that the rule is a general prohibition of bigamy still does not follow. He finds himself in considerable difficulty when he argues against the usual view that the rule is about two sisters. Thus he comments (212): "One cannot forget that Jacob-Israel had at the same time two sisters as wives. . . . It is hard to believe that such personages were made into breakers of the Law on account of incest, with the counterproductive consequence for these 'sons of Israel' of portraying themselves as a people irremediably unclean (just the opposite of the holiness sought!)." Not incest, to be sure, but on other grounds the lawgiver condemns marriages comparable to Jacob's marriages. One wonders what Tosato would have to say about Abraham's marriage to Sarah in light of the Levitical prohibition against that incestuous union, and also about Moses' rule in Lev 18:12, 13 legislating against the union his parents contracted.

instructs him, because of the levirate custom, to take Tamar as a wife. Onan spurns her. Leah is instructed by her father, because of the custom to marry off the elder daughter before the younger, to become Jacob's wife. Jacob spurns her. Onan would never voluntarily have taken Tamar, nor Jacob Leah.

The narrative about Jacob's marriages takes for granted that it is permissible to marry two sisters while each is alive. The narrator nonetheless recognized two complications in the marriages. First, Jacob does not wish to marry both sisters but is tricked into doing so because of his prospective father-in-law's cunning. On his wedding night, Laban substitutes his elder daughter, Leah, for his younger daughter, Rachel, whom Jacob assumes is about to become his wife. Darkness and drunkenness combine to dupe Jacob into marrying a woman he does not want. Second, the marriages to the two sisters turn out to be less than satisfactory, one reason being the rivalry between them. The lawgiver rejected the position assumed in the narrative, the acceptability of marrying two sisters at the same time, and prohibited such a marital set-up. The very fact that Jacob wants one sister but not the other indicates that he does not want to be married to these two sisters. The narrative can therefore be used to raise the issue in general: should a man, or rather an Israelite, a son of Jacob/Israel marry two sisters? The fact that Jacob's marriages are foisted on him in a foreign setting raised the issue more sharply for an Israelite lawgiver. What compelled the lawgiver to prohibit such a double marriage is the problem of rivalry between the two sisters. On the one hand the lawgiver went against what he found presupposed in the narrative; on the other hand he was influenced to do so because of features in it.

The link between the law and the narrative is not in question. The only question is what moral or legal consideration in his own personal make-up or in his cultural background compelled him to take the stance he did. And that we cannot know because we lack the means of understanding the time and culture to which he belonged.

I turn again to the very real puzzle of how the lawgiver moved from one topic to another that is often quite unrelated to it. No two rules better indicate the problem than the prohibition against a man marrying two sisters during each other's lifetime and the rule that follows it, a prohibition against approaching a menstruant woman.

Leviticus 18:19

Also thou shalt not approach unto a woman to uncover her nakedness, as long as she is put apart for her uncleanness.

A central feature of the story about Jacob's marriages to the two sisters, Leah and Rachel, is the pursuit of all three by their father when Jacob seeks to return to his own land surreptitiously. When Laban catches up with the fugitives, he accuses Jacob of the theft of his household gods. Rachel in fact is the culprit. Her father searches for them, but she conceals them in a camel's saddle and sits on it, and does not perform the usual courtesy of rising before a father because "the custom of women is upon me" (Gen 31:35). In other words, she has, she claims, her menstrual period. The two topics of marriages to sisters and the menstrual uncleanness of one of them are found in this patriarchal narrative.

The narrative does not link Rachel's menstrual condition with Jacob's having sex with her at this point in time. It is, however, noteworthy that the language of the rule about not approaching a woman to uncover her nakedness could describe what Rachel does not want to happen to her. Only her concern is with her own father, not with her husband. When she tells her father that she cannot rise, we are perhaps to understand that she does not wish to reveal her menstrual blood to him.

I do not wish to claim, however, that what happens between Rachel and her father prompts the formulation of the rule prohibiting sexual contact with a menstruant. Nothing in this narrative about Laban and his daughters suggests the topic of sexual intercourse during menstruation. How then does the lawgiver arrive at the topic?

It happens that in one other instance, in an earlier generation, the topics of menstruation and sexual activity come together in most peculiar circumstances: in an incident in the life of Jacob's grandparents, Abraham and Sarah. What happens to Rachel has its parallel in what happens to Sarah. Each experiences the problem of barrenness, each is in competition with a co-wife—Hagar in Sarah's case—and, most relevant for my purposes, the topic of menstruation comes to the fore at an important point in their lives. The lawgiver's turn from Rachel's situation to Sarah's is not a fortuitous move but a move determined by his historical method.

The narrator states of the barren and aged Sarah that "it ceased to be with Sarah after the manner of women" (Gen 18:11); that is, she no longer experiences her menstrual periods. Immediately after giving this information the narrator reports that when Sarah overhears Yahweh's promise of a future pregnancy she laughs to herself and says, "After I am waxed old shall I have pleasure, my lord [Abraham] being old also?" (Gen 18:12). She means sexual pleasure. In the story menstruation and anticipated sexual activity are linked. Because the ancient author was well aware of the connection between menstruation and childbearing,[4] we can presume that in order for Sarah to become pregnant she will resume menstruating. That is not to say that in response to Sarah's enthusiasm she and Abraham would have sex the day her period begins.[5] Nonetheless we are getting very close to the topic that is in the rule, namely, the link between sexual activity and menstruation. A feature of rule making at all times is that an untoward happening or development, not what commonly occurs, can prompt the rule.[6]

To account for the prohibition against intercourse during menstruation I suggest that the examples of Rachel and Sarah together have brought up the topic. Rachel presents an example of a menstruating woman with whom a man must not come in contact. Sarah, in turn, brings up the link between menstruation and sexual intercourse with a husband, even if it is not expressly the topic of intercourse at the time of menstruation. The highly idiosyncratic aspects of the two stories prompted the lawgiver to turn to an ordinary human situation and pose the question, should menstruation be regarded as a barrier to intercourse? The lawgiver affirms that it is.

The placement of a prohibition about sexual activity during menstruation just after incest prohibitions might appear surprising. It is less so in that the topic of menstruation in the traditions comes up in the context of relationships between a father and his daughter and, in the case of Abraham and Sarah, not just a husband and a wife but a brother and his half-sister.

4. The reference to Bathsheba's cleansing herself from her menstrual impurity is to convey that she is not pregnant (2 Sam 11:4).

5. It does not follow that postmenopausal women did not have sexual relations. Rather, the story focuses solely on the postmenopausal and aged Sarah who had ceased having intercourse.

6. See the examples I cite in my Conclusion.

Leviticus 18:20

And thou shalt not lie carnally with thy neighbour's wife, to defile thyself with her.

When formulating his rule about the menstruant, the lawgiver had in mind both Rachel and Sarah. He now took up another problem in Sarah's story. The preceding rule but one is about Jacob's marriages to two sisters (Lev 18:18). Sarah is in fact Abraham's half-sister. This sisterly aspect of his marriage plays a crucial role in the rule about adultery.

Why does a rule about adultery follow a rule against intercourse with a menstruating woman? One cannot determine any intelligible link between them by considering each rule by itself in relation to the other. The lawgiver's method of examining ancestral sexual history, in this instance Sarah's, provides an explanation. Just after the notice in Gen 18:11 about Sarah's postmenopausal state, she laughs: "After I am waxed old shall I have pleasure, my lord [Abraham] being old also?" (Gen 18:12). The next incident involving Sarah is Abimelech's near adultery with her (Genesis 20), not her anticipated intercourse with her husband.[7] She goes along with her husband's plan to let the men of Gerar think that she is a free woman, that she is Abraham's sister and not his wife. The consequence is that the king of Gerar, Abimelech, takes her into his harem. Only the intervention of the deity prevents adultery. Indeed, initially God pronounces judgment on Abimelech for the offense of adultery: "Behold, thou shalt die, because of the woman whom thou hast taken; for she is a man's wife" (Gen 20:3). Only after the king protests his ignorance of her true status does the deity relent and decide not to proceed with the punishment appropriate to the offense.

---

7. As we read the narratives, Sarah is transformed from an old woman to an attractive, presumably much younger woman when King Abimelech receives her at his court. To be sure, unlike the description of Sarah at the pharaoh's court in Gen 12:10–20, there is no reference to her beauty, a feature that presumably betokens her youth. (According to later Rabbinic tradition Er did not wish to make his wife, Tamar, pregnant because he wished to preserve the beauty of her body; see M. M. Kasher, *Encyclopedia of Biblical Interpretation* [New York, 1953], on Gen 38:5.) Such apparent awkwardness in the chronological narration of events seems to be of no significance for either the narrator or the lawgiver.

I noted earlier that the lawgiver was not inclined to formulate a rule for an obvious offense in a narrative. The narrative about the king of Gerar is, however, quite clear in its condemnation of the offense of adultery. Why then did the lawgiver choose to spell out such an offense at this point in his code? The explanation is that it was necessary for him to oppose the attitudes shown by Abraham and Sarah on this occasion. They actively encourage adultery, and after the king realizes that they are a married couple, Abraham attempts to justify what has occurred by saying that Sarah is indeed his half-sister. The lawgiver did not accept Abraham's defence of his action. For him, Sarah's relationship to Abraham as a half-sister does not supersede her relationship to him as a wife.[8] A wife may not under any circumstances have sex with a man that is not her husband. Because of Abraham's and Sarah's ruse the prohibition against adultery gives that notice to future generations of Israelites.

The law speaks of the adulterer's defiling (*ṭmʾ*) himself because of his adultery. This is an unusual way of speaking about the offense. The narrative about Abimelech illuminates why the lawgiver introduces the notion of defilement. A plague of sterility falls upon Abimelech's house (Gen 20:17, 18) because of his (supposed) adultery. The Levitical lawgiver elsewhere classifies such a plague as "uncleanness" (*ṭmʾ*), because for him all diseases and infections come under this category (Leviticus 13–15).[9]

Leviticus 18:21

And thou shalt not let any of thy seed pass through [the fire] to Molech, neither shalt thou profane the name of thy God: I am Yahweh.

A rule about the sacrifice of children follows, bewilderingly, a rule about adultery. After the narrative about Abimelech's near adultery

8. He has already prohibited the kind of marriage that Abraham contracted with his half-sister (Lev 18:11).

9. Jacob Milgrom is wrong to draw such a sharp distinction between the use of the term in Leviticus 1–16 (P) and its use in rules in Leviticus 17–26 (H); *Leviticus 1–16*, AB 3 (New York, 1991), 37. He states, "The term *ṭame'* in P strictly denotes 'ritually impure,' referring to the three sources of impurity—corpse or carcass, scale disease *ṣaraʿat*, and genital discharge (*zab/zaba*)—and their derivatives, while H employs this term metaphorically in nonritualistic contexts, such as adultery (18:20). . . ."

with Sarah, she doubtless has her sexual pleasure with Abraham and she bears their son Isaac (Gen 21:1–5). The next episode concerns the near death of this son: Isaac is almost sacrificed as a burnt offering because God requires Abraham to do so (Gen 22:1–19).

Abraham is living among the Canaanites at the time. The lawgiver focused on Isaac's near fate and, alert to the history of succeeding generations, linked it to later Canaanite practice of offering children by fire to the Canaanite god Molech. Lev 18:27, 28 presupposes that the Israelites knew Canaanite practices: "For all these abominations have the men of the land done, which were before you. . . ." The rule describes how it is wrong "to let any of thy seed pass through," namely, fire as in the similar rule in Deut 18:10.

A hypothetical question posed because of Abraham's previous conduct with Sarah may underlie the presentation of this prohibition against giving offspring to Molech. Under pressure because he was entering foreign territory, Abraham gave over his wife to become the wife of a foreign king. Might he or future descendants—the context of Genesis 22 concerns Abraham's descendants—in response to Canaanite pressure proceed to give over any seed born to them to the foreign god Molech, whose name signifies "[divine] king"? The Israelite deity establishes with Abraham—in dramatic circumstances that first suggest that Isaac should be given over as a burnt sacrifice to him—that in fact Abraham's offspring should not be given over in this way. All the more so, the lawgiver infers, should no child born to a descendant of Abraham be given as a burnt sacrifice either to Yahweh or to the Canaanite deity Molech. To confuse Yahweh with Molech would be, in the language of the law, to profane the name of the Israelite god.[10]

Leviticus 18:22

Thou shalt not lie with a male [as it were] the lying with a woman: it is abomination.

10. Fritz Stolz argues that Gen 22:1–4 is indeed to be related to the Molech cult. As part of his argument, he notes that in accordance with 2 Chron 3:1 Mount Moriah, where Isaac was to be burned as a sacrifice, is placed in Jerusalem, the place of

The focus on offspring continues into this rule, procreation and homosexuality being antithetical. The reason, however, that we move from a rule about Molech worship to one about homosexuality is again owing to the lawgiver's typical procedure. On account of their homosexuality, God destroys the inhabitants of Sodom and Gomorrah—by means of fire. The incident, which is related in the context of the history of Abraham, provides an example of how God removes some human beings by fire—in contrast to God's eventual nonremoval of Isaac by fire, which is the tradition underlying the preceding prohibition.

David Daube has argued that the curious formulation of the rule may well have a particular form of intercourse in focus, that is, anal. The language is not "to uncover the nakedness" or "to give one's lying," or simply "to lie," but "to lie with a male [as it were] the lying with a woman." [11] The only similar way a man can penetrate another man as he might a woman is by anal intercourse. The prohibition applies to men, with no corresponding prohibition against female homosexuality, whereas the next rule specifies both sexes in condemning intercourse with animals. If anal intercourse is what the lawgiver had in mind, the practice envisaged is inapplicable to women. [12] Daube suggests that the view of male homosexuality in Israelite society may have been similar to the Greek condemnation of anal intercourse but not of other forms of homosexual activity. [13]

---

the Molech cult; *Structuren und Figuren im Kult von Jerusalem*, BZAW 118 (Berlin, 1970), 207–12. John Day, too readily perhaps, discounts this view but thinks that there were those who worshiped both Yahweh and Molech and believed that Yahweh approved of the Molech sacrifices; *A God of Human Sacrifice in the Old Testament* (Cambridge, Eng., 1989), 23.

11. David Daube, "Old Testament Prohibitions of Homosexuality," *ZSS* 103 (1986), 447–48.

12. To be sure, there are other reasons why we find no rules about lesbian sex. For example, a woman would not be asked about her sexual preference when the issue of a marital arrangement came up between a prospective husband and her father or guardian. In the Talmud, lesbian conduct comes under its notion of licentiousness (similar to heavy petting by a woman outside matrimony and to women's joining in when men sing). See *b. Yeb.* 76a; *b. Sot.* 26b, 48a. A major reason that we find no rule about lesbian sex in the Bible is that the traditions the biblical lawgivers worked with do not bring up the topic.

13. For views on homosexuality in ancient Greece, see Kenneth J. Dover, *Greek Homosexuality* (New York, 1985), 60–68, 81–109; and David Cohen, "Law, Society, and Homosexuality in Classical Athens," *Past and Present* 117 (1987), 6–21.

The conduct of the homosexual mob in the Sodom story would confirm that the law refers to anal intercourse. The mob is intent on raping Lot's visitors. Also noteworthy for understanding the language of the rule is that Lot offers these men of Sodom two women (Lot's daughters) to enjoy sexually, but they decline them (Gen 19: 8, 9). In other words, in this tradition the men, declining to lie with the women, seek instead to lie with men.

Marvin Pope pays much attention to the view of D. S. Bailey that the interpretation of the sin of Sodom as being homosexuality is not found in the Old Testament, the Apocrypha, or the Talmud but was a reinterpretation developed by Pseudepigraphists, Josephus, and Philo, which was then accepted by the Church.[14] Bailey regarded it as significant that none of the biblical condemnations of homosexual practices (Lev 18:22; 20:13; Rom 1:26, 27; 1 Cor 6:9, 10; 1 Tim 1:10) mentions the Sodom story. On the basis of the text of Gen 19:5, Pope rightly rejects Bailey's view. I would add that the condemnation of homosexuality in Lev 18:22 takes up directly from the Sodom story. I would further add, in support of the homosexual character of Sodom's sin, that the story is an etiological myth that attempts to explain why that particular region of the world is sterile by attributing to its inhabitants the offense of homosexuality.[15] The etiological basis of the story also explains why all of the male inhabitants are homosexual. Homosexuality at all times and places is a minority activity. (It is precisely on this account that it meets with so much condemnation. If the eating of meat had been a minority activity it too would probably have been condemned.) The rule in Lev 20:13 is, as I shall note, differently based.

Leviticus 18:23

Neither shalt thou lie with any beast to defile thyself therewith: neither shall any woman stand before a beast to lie down thereto: it is confusion.

14. See Marvin Pope, "Homosexuality," *IDB* suppl. (Nashville, 1976), 415; and D. S. Bailey, *Homosexuality and the Western Tradition* (New York, 1955).

15. The link between the distress of a land and a human offense is a feature of many Deuteronomic laws, for example, Deut 21:1–9 (a man found slain on the land causes a blemish to it) and Deut 24:1–4 (renovating a marriage brings sin upon the land).

One possible link with the preceding two rules (seed to Molech, homosexuality) may be a focus on offspring. None comes from intercourse with animals. The story, however, that has suggested the topic of bestiality is Shechem's union with Dinah (Genesis 34). He was the son of the Ass (Hamor in Hebrew), and she was the daughter of the Ox, that is, Jacob/Israel (Gen 49:6, where the hamstrung ox stands for the weakened house of Jacob/Israel in Gen 34:30).[16] The Levitical lawgiver translated the figurative use of an animal for a human in the Shechem story into a literal relationship between an animal and a human—specifically, the son of an ass (Hamor) lay with Dinah.[17] A factor that might have motivated him to do so, apart from the suggestibility of the material, is the fact that Canaanites celebrated their god Baal's intercourse with a heifer.[18]

I assume that the biblical author's use of the name Hamor (Ass) for the head of the Canaanite tribe, the Hivites, is derogatory. Referring to the ass as the proverbial beast of burden was the Israelite way of giving expression to the view that the original Ham-Canaan had been destined to become a servant to his brothers Shem (the Israelites) and Japheth because of his unnatural sexual gesture (Gen 9: 18–27). I think it is unlikely that the animal name was indeed Canaanite and reflected the role of animals in Canaanite religion. The suggestion has been made that because in the Mari texts the killing of a donkey betokens the concluding of a covenant the expression "the sons of Hamor" refers to those who are bound together by a covenant.[19]

16. See Calum Carmichael, *Law and Narrative in the Bible* (Ithaca, 1985), 195, 196. For further evidence that bulls, oxen, and the like were symbols of fighting strength, see J. G. Janzen, "The Character of the Calf and Its Cult in Exodus 32," *CBQ* 52 (1990), 597–607.

17. Compare the interplay between the literal uncleanness of the plague of sterility, which struck the inhabitants of Gerar because of the problem of adultery (Genesis 20), and the metaphorical uncleanness attaching to the adulterer in Lev 18:20. The two rules that take up from the same incident in Genesis 34 retain the figurative use of the animals: Deut 22:10 (against plowing with an ox and an ass together) and Exod 22:19 (against lying with a beast). See Carmichael, *Law and Narrative*, 193–97, and *The Origins of Biblical Law* (Ithaca, 1992), 164–67.

18. See G. R. Driver, *Canaanite Myths and Legends* (Edinburgh, 1977), 72, lines 17–22.

19. See W. F. Albright, *Archaeology and the Religion of Israel* (Baltimore, Md., 1953), 113; also J. M. Myers, *Judges*, IB (Nashville, Tenn., 1953), 752; N. M. Sarna, *Genesis*, JPSC (Philadelphia, 1989), 233.

Why did the Levitical lawgiver move to the story of Dinah from the story of Sodom and Gomorrah? Jacob and his group set up camp beside the Canaanite city of Shechem. With surprising initiative Dinah pays a visit to the Canaanite women, and during her visit one of its inhabitants, Shechem ("shoulder [of an ass]") sexually violates her. This episode parallels that of the two visitors to Sodom—the inhabitants of that city, having declined Lot's invitation to violate his daughters, sought to violate these visitors. The lawgiver turned from this attempted violation of males, which was accompanied by an invitation to violate two women instead, to the successful violation of a woman, in this instance, the daughter of Jacob/Israel. In each story there is an almost wholesale extermination of the city's inhabitants on account of these sexual offenses.

The lawgiver's turning to unnatural sexual activity between humans and animals is consistent with his interest in the homosexual conduct of the Sodomites and the unnatural gesture of Ham's (Canaan's) looking at his father's genitals (in the rule in Lev 18:7). The Canaanite Shechem is a descendant of Ham.

Unlike the preceding prohibition against homosexuality, this rule against bestiality considers both males and females. The reason is that in Genesis 34 Dinah's culpability for the sexual offense comes into reckoning because she shows such boldness in visiting the Canaanite group. She approaches these "asses." Her conduct is reminiscent of other types of dubious conduct by girls in Mediterranean society past and present. For example, by lingering at fountains or returning late to their homes, they compromise their honor and become the objects of gossip and slander.[20] We cannot tell from the narrative how willingly Dinah responds to Shechem's overtures ("He loved the maiden and spoke tenderly to her" [Gen 34:3]). The mere fact, however, that she goes to the Canaanites would have

20. See J. K. Campbell, *Honour, Family, and Patronage* (Oxford, 1964), 86, 199–201. Sarna thinks that the verb *yaṣaʾ*, "to go out," draws attention to Dinah's unconventional behavior: "Like its Akkadian and Aramaic equivalents, the verb can connote coquettish or promiscuous conduct"; *Genesis*, 233. *Genesis Rabba* on 34:1 already interpreted "And Dinah went out" (Gen 34:1) as reminiscent of "And Leah went out" (to meet Jacob for her hired time of lovemaking [Gen 30:16]): both women were angling. Dinah visits the "daughters of the land." In other texts the phrase indicates disapproval (Gen 24:3, 37; 27:46; 28:1, 6, 8).

been sufficient for the lawgiver to have come up with the case of a woman's approaching an animal for sexual purposes.

If the rule does indeed refer to literal intercourse with beasts, a woman would have to initiate the contact. Presumably in ancient Israelite society, as in all societies, bestiality was and is common enough.[21] In other biblical material there are perhaps two places where the topic of bestiality might have come into reckoning. A curious feature of the Adam and Eve story is that before a suitable partner for him is conjured up, Adam tries to find a partner among the animals (Gen 2:18–25). Robert Graves and Raphael Patai suggest that bestiality is implied.[22] Nathan's parable in 2 Samuel 12:1–6 has the poor man's ewe lamb lying in his lap and being like a daughter to him. In his excellent analysis of the parable, Uri Simon thinks that the statement about how the lamb eats of its owner's morsel, drinks from his cup, and lies in his bosom recalls Uriah's words about eating, drinking, and lying with his wife.[23]

It might be worthwhile to summarize the sexual and family matters in the books of Genesis and Exodus which came under the lawgiver's scrutiny in his rules in Leviticus 18: Ham-Canaan's looking upon his father's nakedness (Gen 9:18–27); Abraham's passing his wife off as his sister to both the pharaoh and Abimelech (Gen 12:10–20; 20); Sarah's sexual pleasure in old age (Gen 18:1–15); menstruation as it affected Sarah and Rachel (Gen 18:1–15; 31); the homosexuality of the inhabitants of Sodom (Genesis 19); Lot's daughters' seduction of their father (Gen 19:30–38); Abimelech's near adultery with Sarah (Genesis 20); the near sacrifice of Isaac (Genesis 22); Isaac's marriage into his father's family (Genesis 24); Jacob and his wives (Genesis 29; 30:1–24); Shechem's seduction of Dinah (Genesis 34; 49:5–7); Reuben's intercourse with his father's concu-

21. On bestiality, see Midas Dekkers, *Dearest Pet: On Bestiality* (London, 1994); Joyce E. Salisbury, *The Beast Within: Animals in the Middle Ages* (New York, 1994); and C. J. Sanders, "Ninth Life: An Interpretive Theory of the Ninth Amendment," *ILJ* 69 (1994), 759, 822 n. 267 (discussing why there are rules outlawing intercourse with animals).

22. Robert Graves and Raphael Patai, *Hebrew Myths: The Book of Genesis* (London, 1964), 67.

23. Uri Simon, "The Poor Man's Ewe-Lamb: An Example of a Juridical Parable," *Bib* 48 (1967), 229.

bine (Gen 35:22; 49:3, 4); Judah's relationship to Tamar and Onan's relationship to Tamar (Genesis 38); and the marital union that produced Moses (Exod 6:20). All in all, the lawgiver's survey of sexual matters in patriarchal times is thorough, even exhaustive. The survey represents a profound evaluation of existing traditions that already constituted a history of the generations.

A recurrent feature of the laws and the traditions they relate to is the theme of procreation. Although this topic, in laws relating to sexual and family matters, can hardly occasion surprise, it is nonetheless interesting to observe just how extensive interest in the topic is. Such a concern links up with the Priestly writer's intense interest in the continuing life of the properly constituted Israelite community. Time and again, for example, the person offending against the ritual and moral order is to be cut off from his people.

The stories that inspire the initial rules in Lev 18:7 (Ham-Canaan's offense against his father and the daughters' offense against Lot) had future offspring in focus. Behind the rule in Lev 18:8 about a father's wife stands Reuben's offense against his father: in Gen 49:3, 4 Jacob denies this firstborn son, whom he describes as the firstfruits of his virility, the right of this primary role in the future life of his family because he misused his virility. In the corresponding judgment by Moses in Deut 33:6 the judgment on Reuben is that his descendants should be few in number. Of the several rules in Lev 18:9–14 that took up from Abraham's marital history, one (vss. 10, 11) reflects again on the problem of procreation as experienced by his grandnieces (the daughters of Lot), and the others (vss. 9, 12–14) relate in particular to Sarah's problem of barrenness. The three rules in Lev 18: 15–17 took up from the problems in Judah's family history in which the central feature is the noncontinuation of Judah's family line. The rule in Lev 18:18 against marriage to two sisters in their lifetimes reacted negatively to the competing desires of the two sisters Rachel and Leah to produce children by Jacob. The rule about menstruation in Lev 18:19 takes us to Sarah's capacity to procreate after she was postmenopausal; and her near adultery with the foreign king Abimelech, when she had not yet become pregnant by Abraham, underlies the presentation of the rule against adultery in Lev 18:20. The rule about Molech in Lev 18:21 is about the sacrifice of offspring and had Abraham's near sacrifice of a son—the son whom God had just given—as the epic under consideration. The two rules about homosexuality and bestiality in Lev 18:22, 23 are directly concerned with sterile unions and had, respectively, the destruction of Sodom and the opposition to Canaanite marriages in focus.

The Sequence of Topics in the Narratives for the Laws in Leviticus 18:18–23

Although mainly dealing with sexual offenses—the rule about Molech worship is an exception—the series of laws in Lev 18:18–23 presents a motley assortment: marriage to two sisters, sex with a menstruant, adultery, Molech worship, homosexuality, and bestiality. Order can be introduced if we note the systematic way in which the lawgiver took up issues that arise in the narratives. I explained the sequence of the preceding series of incest laws in Lev 18:7–17 by noting that the lawgiver proceeded on two fronts. He worked his way through similar issues in successive narrative histories, but at points he deviated by looking at comparable developments in generations much later than the one with which he was concerned. Both features again characterize the lawgiver's method in Lev 18:18–23. He proceeded forward—or back—through the narrative histories, but if in one of them he found a similarly recurring matter in a different generation he switched to it before returning to his linear progression. The rule about marriage to two sisters in Lev 18:18 illustrates the method.

The last rule in the incest series (Lev 18:7–17) was derived from Tamar's fraught unions with two brothers and their father (Genesis 38). The lawgiver then proceeded back through problems in earlier marriages. He first turned back to Jacob's marriages to two sisters (Genesis 29, 30). The tensions between Rachel and Leah involving their rivalry over Jacob and Rachel's barrenness prompted the rule prohibiting unions to two sisters while each is alive. Continuing to move back through the generations, the lawgiver came upon the problem of Abraham's marriage to Sarah. It too has to do with remedying barrenness. Expecting to resume menstruation, Sarah anticipates renewed sexual pleasure for herself and her husband (Genesis 18). Their situation raised for the lawgiver the question whether or not it is acceptable for a man to have sexual contact with a woman during her menses. His rule on the subject forbids it.

The lawgiver stayed with Sarah's sexual history and noted that a tradition in Genesis 20 intervenes between her anticipation of sexual pleasure with her husband and its realization (Genesis 21). The tradition recounts that Sarah came very close indeed to committing adultery with Abimelech. A prohibition about adultery is set down. Sexual intercourse between Abraham and Sarah then occurs, Isaac is born (Genesis 21), and God requires Abraham to offer him up as a burnt sacrifice (Genesis 22). In any event, Isaac is not sacrificed. The incident, however, brought up for the lawgiver the later Israelite involvement in the Canaanite practice of sacrificing children by fire to the god Molech, and he sets down a rule prohibiting such a practice.

From what happened in a much later period in Israelite history (the worship of Molech), the lawgiver switched back to the history of Abraham's generation, but the topic is no longer marriage and procreation. Instead he took up a specific divine intervention in human lives, consummation by fire, because of the sexual unions they seek. If in the end God desists from taking Isaac as an offering by fire, he nonetheless at this time consumes all of the inhabitants of Sodom by fire because the homosexual mob in that city sought to abuse two visitors who had come to see Abraham's nephew, Lot (Genesis 19). The lawgiver sets down a rule condemning homosexuality.

The sexual abuse of a visitor continues as the lawgiver's focus. Lot offers his two daughters to the men of Sodom that they might sexually abuse them instead of his two male visitors. In a later generation Jacob's daughter Dinah visits a Canaanite city belonging to the Hivites and is sexually violated by Shechem, the son of its ruler Hamor (Genesis 34). The name Hamor means "ass." Jacob later comments on the incident and refers to his own family's involvement: his sons' extermination of all the male Hivites on account of Shechem's violation of Dinah weakened his house, the house of the Ox, because other Canaanite clans would seek vengeance (Genesis 49). The suggestion that Shechem's violation of Dinah is that of an ass's sexually violating an ox raised for the lawgiver the topic of human-animal intercourse. He sets down a rule against bestiality.

CHAPTER 3

Ethical, Ritual, and Social Laws: Leviticus 19:1–18

N̲o body of biblical laws is regarded as so representative of the spirit of these laws as the rules in Leviticus 19. Johannes Hempel refers to these rules as the "fundamental social ethical law" of Yahwism.[1] More explicitly than other interpreters, Arie Noordtzij states the standard view:

> To the Western mind, the content of this chapter [Leviticus 19] seems rather heterogeneous and gives the impression of being a more or less arbitrary assemblage of commandments that deal partly with religious, partly with moral, and partly with civic life. We are disposed to regard life as composed of various realms that, to our way of thinking, have little or no connection with one another. The perspective of the ancient Near Eastern world was more unified, however, for not only were the cultic and moral spheres considered to be two sides of the same concern . . . but civic and political life were also controlled by a religious outlook. The whole of life was thus religious in character.[2]

1. Johannes Hempel, "Das sozialethische Grundgezetz der Jahvereligion," *Gott und Mensch im Alten Testament*, BWANT 38 (Stuttgart, 1926), 18 n. 1.
2. Arie Noordtzij, *Leviticus*, BSC (Grand Rapids, Mich., 1982), 189.

The standard scholarly view assumes that the material in Leviticus 19 reflects the living reality of ancient Israelite society. Jacob Milgrom in his recent commentary does not doubt this relationship between law and life: the laws came into existence in response to real-life issues, and their content can consequently communicate the operating principles at work in that society. Thus, if the moral and ritual rules are bound together, this is because Israelite society did not distinguish between them in the way modern communities do.[3] Baruch Levine expresses similar sentiments: "Holiness, an essentially cultic concept, could not be achieved through purity and worship alone; it had an important place in the realm of societal experience. Like the Ten Commandments and other major statements on the duties of man toward God, this chapter [Leviticus 19] exemplifies the heightened ethical concern characteristic of ancient Israel."[4]

The view shared by these scholars is based on a misunderstanding of the nature of the material they are interpreting. My starting point is the same as theirs; namely, the perplexing arrangement of the laws in Leviticus 19, which invariably invites comment. On the one hand, scholars use the miscellaneous character of the laws as evidence that they have different sources, that they belonged to different times and places before they found a common location in Leviticus 19.[5] At the same time, however, scholars see the miscellany of the laws as evidence of the undifferentiated nature of all aspects of human affairs in ancient Israel. They infer that the sequence of the rules must have made ready sense to their recipients and that these ancient Israelites would not have found it jarring to hear

---

3. See Jacob Milgrom, *Leviticus 1–16*, AB 3 (New York, 1991), 26.

4. Baruch A. Levine, *Leviticus*, JPSC (Philadelphia, 1989), 257. Compare also J. E. Hartley, *Leviticus*, WBC (Dallas, Tex., 1992), 308; Jonathan Magonet, "The Structure and Meaning of Leviticus 19," *HAR* 7 (1983), 151; and Gordon Wenham, *Leviticus*, NICOT (Grand Rapids, Mich., 1979), 264.

5. For various attempts to delineate such sources, see H. G. Reventlow, *Das Heiligkeitsgesetz formgeschichtlich Untersucht*, WMANT 6 (Neukirchen, 1961), 65–78; Rudolph Kilian, *Literarkritische und formgeschichtliche Untersuchung des Heiligkeitsgesetzes*, BBB 19 (Bonn, 1963), 57–65; Christian Feucht, *Untersuchungen zum Heiligkeitsgesetz* (Berlin, 1964), 37–42; Alfred Cholewinski, *Heiligkeitsgesetz und Deuteronomium: Eine vergleichende Studie*, AnBib 64 (Rome, 1976), 44–54.

sequentially a rule about a sacrificial offering, a rule about leaving behind grain and olives for the poor at harvest time, and a rule about
stealing.

A different picture emerges once one takes stock of the process
of legal formulation I am describing. Once one understands why the
lawgiver moved from one topic to the next, one also understands
the sequence of the material. Real-life needs that were readily com-
municable in sequential fashion to the ancient recipients do not
come into the reckoning. The assumption that the ancients did not
differentiate between cultic and ethical matters, for example, is un-
warranted.[6]

My first task is to account for the switch from the last rule about
bestiality in Lev 18:23 to the rules in Leviticus 19, the initial ones
of which focus on Joseph—in particular, on his dreams about how
his brothers' sheaves bow down to his sheaf and how the sun,
moon, and stars bow down to him. In the introduction to his rules
in Lev 18:1-3 the lawgiver counsels: "After the doings of the land
of Egypt, wherein ye dwelt, shall ye not do: and after the doings of
the land of Canaan, whither I bring you, shall ye not do." At the
conclusion to his rules in Lev 18:24-30 the lawgiver returns to the
topic of the unacceptable conduct of the previous Canaanite inhabitants of the land and insists that the Israelites should not imitate it
when they occupy the land of Canaan. The last rule in Leviticus 18
about bestiality is very much concerned with the house of Jacob's
entanglement with a Canaanite group: after Shechem's seduction of
Dinah, there were negotiations—spurious, to be sure, on the part of

6. I might concur with the views of modern scholars about the integration of cult,
civic affairs, and the moral life if they attributed them to these ancient biblical authors. There is a vast difference at all times and places between the ideals of individual members of a society and the practice of that society. For example, it is well recognized among social anthropologists that native informants describing what goes on
in their societies will set out normative ideals as if they are describing how things actually are. See David Cohen, *Law, Sexuality, and Society: The Enforcement of Morals
in Classical Athens* (Cambridge, Eng., 1991), 152, 174. Often biblical scholars assess
the assumed reality of their own legal culture against myths about the biblical one in
order to affirm idealized biblical values. For illuminating comments about mythical
features of contemporary American law, see Walter O. Weyrauch, "Oral Legal Traditions of Gypsies and Some American Equivalents," *AJCL* 44 (1997).

Jacob's two sons Simeon and Levi—about a merger of the two groups (Gen 34:9, 10, 16). The punishment the lawgiver lays down for an Israelite who does what these foreign nations do—both the Egyptians and the Canaanites are meant—is that he will be cut off from his people (Lev 18:29). It is consequently not surprising that the initial laws of Leviticus 19 should turn to Joseph, who was forcibly taken from his family and exiled to Egypt.

The adventures of this son of Jacob/Israel constitute the beginnings of a long and significant episode in the history of the nation. Just as the narratives in the book of Exodus demonstrate profound reflection on the subsequent slavery of the entire nation of Israel in Egypt, so the laws reveal profound reflection on the sojourn in Egypt, which begins with Joseph's experiences.

Specifically, the lawgiver turned from the problem of Canaanite idolatrous influence to the problem of potential idolatry, which comes through in Joseph's dreams, the recounting of which was a major reason that he ended up in Egypt. Another link between Genesis 34 plus 49:5–7 (the joint traditions that prompted the rule about bestiality) and Genesis 37 (the tradition about Joseph to which the lawgiver turned) is that figurative language played a major role in the translation of problems in the stories into the subject matter of the laws. In Genesis 34 and Gen 49:5–7 the ass stood for the Hivites and the ox for the Israelites, and in Genesis 37 harvest sheaves and the sun, moon, and stars represent members of Jacob's family. Also noteworthy is that Jacob rebukes his sons Simeon and Levi in Genesis 34 and his son Joseph in Genesis 37. From the viewpoint of the narrator, however, these sons are to be commended. In other words, conflicting judgments within the family of Israel are characteristic of these traditions. The narrator's stance is one that the lawgiver shared. The lawgiver, however, worked with these stories in much greater depth, and his stance, as I shall observe, was a balanced and sophisticated one.

I can also account for the fact that the lawgiver moved from the sexual subject matter that almost totally dominated his rules in Leviticus 18 (the rule about Molech worship is the exception) to rules in Lev 19:1–18 which have no such subject matter. (The rules in Lev 19:19 about forbidden mixtures begin again to take up sexual matters.) The reason is simply that the lawgiver found many topics of a nonsexual nature that the traditions about Joseph bring up.

Leviticus 19:3

Ye shall fear every man his mother, and his father, and keep my sabbaths: I am Yahweh your God.

The focus here is on Joseph. One may expect the lawgiver's survey of Israel's experience in Egypt, which starts with Joseph's family experiences because of the notice in Lev 18:3: "After the doings of the land of Egypt, wherein ye dwelt, shall ye not do." Having turned from Jacob's rebuke of his two sons, Simeon and Levi (the climax of Genesis 34), to Jacob's rebuke of his other son, Joseph, the lawgiver took up the topic of respect for parents. His move explains why the contents of Joseph's second dream about the heavenly bodies came into the lawgiver's reckoning before the contents of the first dream about harvest sheaves, which is relevant to the next rule about the worship of idols. In Genesis 37, Jacob interprets Joseph's dream about how the sun, moon, and stars bowed down to him and acknowledged him to be superior to themselves as meaning that his parents should bow down and worship him. Rather than teach respect for one's parents, the dream communicates the opposite. Joseph's father rebukes him. For the Priestly lawgiver, the proper perspective, as set out in the decalogue (Exod 20:12) and taken up again by him here, is that a son acknowledge his parents as his begetters. Because the act of procreation is the one human activity in which human beings participate in God's creation (compare the notice in Gen 4:1, where Eve conceives and gives birth to Cain with God's aid), proper reverence is necessary. The rule cites the mother first because the Priestly writer's focus is on procreation. The mother gives birth to the child.[7]

---

7. Noordtzij (*Leviticus*, 193) says that the mother is cited first because in a polygamous society children have a more intimate attachment to their mother than to their father. That attachment, however, is true regardless of the society's structure. It is no accident that we refer to our "mother tongue."

The acknowledgment of God's creation is the focus of the rule about keeping the sabbaths, as the Priestly version of the decalogue (Exod 20:8–11) and the Priestly material in Exod 31:12–17 spell out. Joseph's dream that he was superior in status to the sun, moon, and stars requires a reminder that God is the creator of such entities and that Joseph should not compete for that honor. As in the decalogue, in Lev 19:3 the sabbath rule is juxtaposed with the rule about parents because procreation is linked to the original creation. Philo expresses the link thus: "Parents, in my opinion, are to their children what God is to the world, since just as he achieved existence for the nonexistent, so they in imitation of his power, as far as they are capable, immortalize the race" (*De spec. leg.* 2.225; cp. *Deter.* 54; *Mos.* 2.209).

Moshe Weinfeld thinks that the rules about parents, sabbaths, and idols in Lev 19:2–4 are based on the decalogue.[8] He mistakes analogy for influence. He speaks first of how all the laws in Leviticus 19 resemble the decalogue, but then of their dependence on it. The fact that two sets of rules share similar topics is no argument for one set's dependence on the other, especially when the rules in question deal with topics that recur frequently throughout biblical material. If the shared topics were of an arcane nature and were found only in these two places, there might be cause for considering a link other than resemblance.[9] Weinfeld explains away the difference between the formulation of the rule about fearing parents in Lev 19:3 and the formulation about honoring them in the decalogue by arguing that in Lev 19:3 one fears out of respect, and hence the verb meaning "to fear" (yr') parallels the verb meaning "to honor" (kbd), because each rule fundamentally insists on respect.[10] I account for the difference in formulation by arguing that

---

8. Moshe Weinfeld, *Deuteronomy 1–11*, AB 5 (New York, 1991), 250–53.

9. Weinfeld's claim (*Deuteronomy 1–11*, 242) that it is "clear that during the times of Hosea the prophet (eighth century BCE) it [the decalogue] was already existent (Hos 4:2; cf. Jer 7:9]" labors under the same error. Hos 4:2 refers to "swearing, and lying [with no reference to a witness as in the decalogue], and killing, and stealing, and committing adultery." These are offenses of such common occurrence that one cannot make the kind of claim that Weinfeld makes without further argumentation. The resemblance, moreover, tells one nothing about priority of composition.

10. Weinfeld, *Deuteronomy 1–11*, 310.

the rule in the decalogue is a response to Cain's act of dishonoring his parents by killing their son Abel,[11] whereas the rule in Lev 19:3 concerns the issue of Joseph's arrogance. It is not a question of one lawgiver's taking up an issue from another, but rather that the same method of formulating rules from different narrative sources applies in each instance.

Weinfeld's attempt to show that other rules in Leviticus 19 depend on the decalogue reveals how strained his position is. He thinks that the rule about adultery in the decalogue inspired what he thinks are similar rules in Lev 19:19–25, namely, laws about mixing kinds, intercourse with a slave-girl, and even a law about uncircumcised fruit. He further claims that the rules about idols, the sabbath, and parents in the decalogue inspired the three rules in Lev 19:30–32 about sabbaths, appealing to ghosts and soothsayers, and respect for an old man. (He puts "elderly" to suggest that both sexes are included, as in the rule about parents.) He speaks of the topics in the decalogue as recurring "with slight variation,"[12] but consultation with those expert in dealing with the dead is hardly a "slightly different" topic from the worship of idols.

Leviticus 19:4

Turn ye not unto idols nor make to yourselves molten gods: I am Yahweh your God.

With the topic of creation in focus, the lawgiver goes on to oppose the reliance on man-made gods. For him, the making of idols would have been an affirmation of human beings as supreme creators, in opposition to God as creator. Joseph's dream necessitates this objection to the exaltation of humankind. Viewed from a religious perspective, both dreams are problematic because they exalt Joseph to godlike status (cp. Gen 44:18, 45:8).[13] In the dream

---

11. See Calum Carmichael, *The Spirit of Biblical Law* (Athens, Ga., 1996), 94–95.

12. Weinfeld, *Deuteronomy 1–11*, 251.

13. Compare how Sennacherib is likened to a god in heaven to whom the sun, moon, and stars are subservient (Ahikar 6:16 in both the Syriac and Armenian versions). See

about the harvest, *'alumim,* "sheaves" (from *'alam* [*Piel,* "to bind";
Niphal, "to be dumb"]) bow down to another sheaf. In the rule, the
Israelite is not to bow down to *'elilim,* "idols" (the etymology is un-
certain but probably from *'al,* "nothingness"), possibly with the
sense that they are dumb idols.[14] If we set aside the possibility
of word-play, whereby *'alumim* influences the choice of the term
'elilim,[15] in the dream the sheaves behave like human beings, the
sons of Israel, but they do not speak; nor does the sheaf that is the
object of veneration. The dream conveys the idea of the veneration
of a dumb object.

Although the molten gods recall Aaron's golden calf (Exodus 32),
they especially recall Jeroboam's golden calves because of the plural
designation. Jeroboam was a descendant of Joseph (1 Kgs 11:26; *Gen
Rabba* on 37:6, 7). Aaron's molten calf is the earliest example of Israelite idolatry in the Pentateuch, and Jeroboam's activity represents the recurrence of the problem in a later generation. This recurrent feature explains the lawgiver's focus. The reason he turned
to Aaron's and Jeroboam's activity, however, is that Joseph's other
dream (in which the sun, moon, and stars bow down to him) also
raises the issue of idolatry. Deut 4:15–19 prohibits the worship of
the calf along with the worship of the sun, moon, and stars.[16] In his
rule, then, the lawgiver took into account successive developments
in different generations regarding the topic of idolatry. This kind of
survey is a prime characteristic of his procedure.

R. H. Charles, *The Apocrypha and Pseudepigrapha of the Old Testament* (Oxford,
1913), 2:759–60. Nabonidus is greeted by the moon, a star, and Jupiter (*ANET,* 310);
further, Pericles is compared to Zeus (Plutarch, *Pericles* 8.3). See D. B. Redford, *A
Study of the Biblical Story of Joseph, SVT* (Leiden, 1970), 204.

14. The expression *'elilim 'ilemim,* "dumb idols," occurs in Hab 2:18.

15. B. J. Schwartz suggests that in Lev 19:20a the unexpected selection of the term
shiphah and not *'imah* for "slave-girl" is a word-play reflecting the fact that she is not
hpsh, "free"; see "The Slave-Girl Pericope," *Scripta Hierosolymitana* 31 (1986), 244.

16. Gerhard von Rad, in *Genesis,* 3d ed. (London, 1972), 351, 352, is at pains to
stress that Joseph's dreams in no way signify a religious dimension. They are, he implies, just the vivid imaginings of a young boy. One wonders why he feels the need to
emphasize the lack of religious, mythological overtones. The issue that von Rad attempts to deny is precisely the one that lies behind the Priestly lawgiver's concern. I
am claiming not that the Priestly lawgiver read the dreams as idolatrous in character,
but that in light of his knowledge of Israel's religious history the dreams raised the issue of idolatry.

Leviticus 19:5–10

And if ye offer a sacrifice of peace offerings unto Yahweh, ye shall offer it for your acceptance. It shall be eaten the same day ye offer it, and on the morrow: and if any remain until the third day, it shall be burnt in the fire. And if it be eaten at all on the third day, it is abominable; it shall not be accepted. Therefore everyone that eateth it shall bear his iniquity, because he hath profaned the hallowed thing of Yahweh: and that soul shall be cut off from among his people. And when ye reap the harvest of your land, thou shalt not wholly reap the corners of thy field, neither shalt thou gather the gleanings of thy harvest. And thou shalt not glean thy vineyard, neither shalt thou gather every grape of thy vineyard; thou shalt leave them for the poor and the sojourner: I am Yahweh your God.

Continuing his focus on Joseph's dreams, the lawgiver considers how they come to fulfillment.[17] In his rule about a peace offering he first takes up the issue of worship that arose in the two dreams, and then, in his rule about leftovers from the harvest, he takes up the issue of sustenance raised by the dream about harvest sheaves.

If we follow the unfolding significance of the dreams in Joseph's later life, we see how, after a rule about idolatry, the lawgiver chose to take up the topic of an Israelite sacred meal (the peace offering) in reaction to a foreign, Egyptian meal at which Joseph and his brothers are present. In my previous attempts to analyze the rule about the peace offering, I failed to realize that the lawgiver was typically intent on contrasting native experience with foreign.[18]

Far from being treated with worshipful reverence as both his dreams anticipate, Joseph is humiliated; sold into slavery in Egypt and then cast into prison on a trumped-up charge that he had sexually assaulted Potiphar's wife.[19] Contact with his family is estab-

---

17. The statement in Gen 37:11 that Jacob kept the import of Joseph's dreams in mind is a pointer that their significance will unfold.

18. See Calum Carmichael, "Laws of Leviticus 19," *HTR* 87 (1994), 247–49; and *Spirit of Biblical Law*, 37–40.

19. Joseph is sold for twenty shekels of silver. In Lev 27:5 this is the valuation placed on a minor above five years old to release him from a vow dedicating him to the sanctuary. Dedication of a person to the sanctuary is the religious equivalent of the secular institution of slavery.

lished again only when they need food. When his brothers come to Egypt to obtain it Joseph knows who they are but they do not recognize him. Rather, they confront a disguised Joseph who has become an Egyptian dignitary second only to the pharaoh. On the occasion Joseph remembers his dream about his brothers (Gen 42:9). He accuses them of being spies, puts them in prison, releases them, arranges that one brother, Simeon, remain in prison while the rest return to Canaan, and demands that they bring back their youngest brother Benjamin. Faced with Joseph's demand for Benjamin the brothers recall what they did to Joseph and, in his hearing, confess among themselves their guilt (Gen 42:21). Although Joseph's aim is that they all be reconciled as members of the one family again, he contrives further to delay that reconciliation.

The brothers come again for food and, bringing Benjamin with them, also bring a present to appease Joseph. As before they "bowed down to him to the ground" (Gen 43:26, cp. 42:6). The term used for their present is *minhah*, which is a propitiatory gift to secure good will. (It plays a role in Levitical rules about sacrifices; for example, it accompanies a certain kind of peace offering [Lev 7: 11–14].) Joseph asks them about their welfare and the term used is *shalom* (v. 27, cp. 44:17), which is probably related to the word for peace offering (*shelamim*).[20] Joseph goes on to ask them how their father is faring—*shalom* again—sees his younger brother, Benjamin, and is overcome with emotion. Joseph, however, does not reveal himself at this point. Instead he provides his brothers with a meal. The brothers eat separately from the Egyptians, including Joseph, because an Egyptian rule about ritual purity excludes them: "the Egyptians might not eat bread with the Hebrews, for that is an abomination to the Egyptians" (Gen 43:32).

No reconciliation between Joseph and his brothers takes place during the course of the meal. Indeed, Joseph proceeds to trick them yet again by having his divining cup secretly placed in Benjamin's sack. The next day the brothers leave for Canaan but Joseph has them pursued and accused of the theft of his cup. They return to Joseph's house and "fall before him to the ground" (Gen 44:14). During the

---

20. On the sense of *minhah* and its role in the sacrificial system, and on the possible link between *shalom* and *shelamim*, see Milgrom, *Leviticus 1–16*, 196–97, 219–20.

examination of their alleged guilt for stealing the cup they recount the history of their family, including graphic details about Joseph's disappearance from his family. At the end of it, Joseph breaks down, reveals who he is, and accepts his brothers as his loved ones. Although they do not do so, it would have been appropriate for these brothers, the first sons of Israel, to celebrate an Israelite ritual feast in recognition of this happy outcome.

In any event, in response to the Egyptian meal the lawgiver set down his rule about a peace offering. This is an exalted and sacred occasion, one when Israelites who are not priests are allowed to consume the meat of a sacrifice.[21] The lawgiver, I submit, contrasts what should happen on an Israelite ritual occasion with what did happen on the Egyptian one. In his rule there is to begin with no problem about any Israelite's status in the meal company because of the issue of ritual purity. The food they eat together creates no barrier between one Israelite participant and another. Recall that when Joseph set up a festive meal with his brothers it would have been an abomination for him as an Egyptian to eat with them. In the rule, the Israelites are given a limit of two days to consume the sacrifice. On the third day, however, a situation does arise which is decidedly reminiscent of the Egyptian one. As at Joseph's feast, a rule about ritual purity attaching to food comes into play: should an Israelite partake of any of the food on the third day he is excluded from his community because he has committed an offense against his deity. The problem of sacred bonding within a community in the context of a meal showed up for the first time when the sons of Jacob/Israel, Joseph and his brothers, could not eat together because of an Egyptian requirement about ritual purity. The lawgiver has this history in mind when he lays down his rule for later sacred bonding among Israelites in their own land.

A humanitarian rule about leftovers from the annual harvest follows the ritual rule. Why should this be so? The reason is that, just as the lawgiver followed out the significance in Joseph's dreams of his brothers' reverential regard for him, as it plays out at the Egyptian meal at which Joseph eats separately from his brothers, so in the next rule the lawgiver followed out the significance in Joseph's dream

21. On this aspect and on the joyful character of the peace offering, see Milgrom, *Leviticus 1–16*, 218, 413.

of sheaves dependent on another sheaf, as it plays out in the brothers' dependency on Joseph to save them from starvation.[22] Like the ritual rule about peace offerings the harvest rule is about food, but in this instance it is about providing for the needy. The matter might appear to involve no sacred overtones. However, focusing on the consequence of Joseph's dream, namely, the agricultural policy he puts into effect in Egypt to relieve starvation, the lawgiver notes that Yahweh inspires the policy (Gen 41:33–57). Just as the role of food in the Exodus story came to be commemorated in the regulations of the Passover ceremony (Exodus 12), so the rule about provision of food for the needy looks back on Joseph's time in Egypt.

Joseph's dream about himself as the dominant sheaf of grain alludes to what is yet to be. His prediction to the pharaoh of bountiful harvests followed by famine leads to his appointment as overseer of food in Egypt, and he stores quantities of grain.[23] When his brothers come to Egypt seeking grain, they do not recognize Joseph but they acknowledge his dominance, just as his dream foretold (Gen 42:6, 43:26, 44:14). His elevation to power, however, had come only after years in prison, for the pharaoh's butler, a fellow prisoner whose dream he interprets, forgets to remember Joseph when he is released (Gen 40:23) and remembers him only when the pharaoh's dreams need interpretation (Gen 41:9–14). After he is remembered, Joseph brings relief to the hungry. The forgotten sheaf in the equivalent Deuteronomic law is like Joseph: if the harvester remembers the sheaf, it is used in the service of the needy, specifically, the sojourner, the widow, and the orphan (Deut 24:19–22). The Deuteronomic lawgiver commemorates Joseph's experience, sees how his harvest dream bridges the entire historical episode, and explicates its significance.[24]

22. The harvesting of sheaves in the dream explains why in the rule an injunction about the harvest precedes the injunction about the gleaning of grapes (Lev 19:9–10).

23. The term used for the grain that Joseph put in storage is *piqqadon*, "deposit" (Gen 41:36). Its only other occurrence is in Lev 5:21 (ET 6:2, cheating in regard to a neighbor's deposit).

24. See Calum Carmichael, *Law and Narrative in the Bible* (Ithaca, 1985), 278–88. Von Rad states (*Genesis*, 352), without giving any reason: "One ought not to see in it [the vision of the sheaves] a reference to Joseph's later policy of storage." Daphne du Maurier's *Rebecca* is an example of a later literary work that opens with a dream that points to the story's ending.

The Priestly lawgiver similarly turns to Joseph's life, takes over the Deuteronomic rule, but removes its eccentric, impractical feature about the forgotten sheaf. The Priestly rule's reference to the poor (along with the sojourner) is a typical attempt to categorize the two kinds of dependency cited in the Deuteronomic rule: the widow and the orphan.

The Deuteronomic rule is impractical because the poor will obtain something from the harvest only if the owner of the field should forgetfully leave a sheaf standing in his field. This would probably not be a frequent, or even likely, occurrence.[25] The Priestly rule, on the other hand, guarantees that the poor will receive food each year. If one is to assume that one lawgiver was aware of the other's rule, it seems obvious that the Priestly rule is the later formulation. Yet Moshe Weinfeld claims that the Deuteronomic formulation is the more pragmatic one and came after the Priestly rule. His reasoning is difficult to fathom. As evidence of the more pragmatic character of the Deuteronomic rule, he states that Deuteronomy presents it "in a more tangible manner and, characteristically, adds a religious-moral justification."[26] Whatever this statement means, it is not an argument about pragmatism. Weinfeld further postulates that ancient magical beliefs explain why the Deuteronomic rule avoids prohibiting the cutting of a corner of one's field (*pe'ah*): he believes (no evidence is cited) that Deuteronomy reacted against the Priestly formulation because the Israelites were leaving the corners of fields uncut to appease the spirits of the fields and demons. The weakness of the arguments arises from Weinfeld's commitment to the theory that Deuteronomy was written after the Priestly material.

Leviticus 19:11–12

Ye shall not steal, neither deal falsely, neither lie one to another. And ye shall not swear by my name falsely, neither shalt thou profane the name of thy God: I am Yahweh.

25. The Rabbis were rightly puzzled by the rule: "for if we seek to keep it deliberately, it cannot be kept, since it is ordained only for forgetfulness" (*tosephtah Peah* 3:8).

26. Weinfeld, *Deuteronomy 1—11*, 33.

The preceding rules place the initial focus on how Joseph came to be cut off from his people. His brothers stole him (Gen 40:15). The next series of laws explores aspects of their theft, and also aspects of theft in the history of Jacob/Israel.

Like the Deuteronomic lawgiver, the Priestly lawgiver, dealing with the origin and history of the nation of Israel, sought out the earliest example of a problem. The issue of theft involving brothers also arises in the generation previous to Joseph's when the original Israel (Jacob) stole the paternal blessing from his brother, Esau (Genesis 27). Esau's loss of the right of the firstborn son compares to Joseph's loss of sonship, particularly since Joseph's dreams portray him as the favorite son.

In order to carry out his theft, Jacob deals falsely with his father; he deceives blind Isaac with the clothes he wears when he brings him meat to eat. Jacob also lies about his identity when he claims to be Esau. There is a religious dimension to these two incidents which the next rule brings out. In the commission of his theft, Jacob claims that Yahweh his God—both names are used—had granted him success because he quickly obtains meat to give to his father (Gen 27:20). This is a falsehood—the use of God's name to cover up a duplicitous action. The Priestly lawgiver thus produced the cluster of five rules in Lev 19:11–12 in reaction to Jacob's cheating Esau out of his birthright.[27]

Leviticus 19:13

Thou shalt not defraud thy neighbour, neither rob him: the wages of him that is hired shall not abide with thee all night until the morning.

Aspects of theft continue to dominate the lawgiver's interest. Two links with the previous focus on Jacob's theft of Esau's birthright are noteworthy. First, the preceding rule about false swearing focused on Jacob's profanation of God's name in the commission of

27. There is a switch from the use of the second-person plural (you) to the second-person singular (thou) in the presentation of these rules, perhaps because the lawgiver was going back and forth between a judgment on individuals in Genesis to a judgment that is intended for all the people of Israel.

a theft. In the story on which the rule about defrauding a neighbor is based, Laban accuses Jacob of stealing his household gods (Gen 31: 30). Depending on his point of departure, the lawgiver was proceeding forward (from Jacob with Esau to Laban with Jacob) or backward (from Joseph back to Jacob) through the history of the generations. In light of this strategy, the order of the rules does not depend on the order of the narratives.

Second, the story about the theft of Laban's gods is part of a much wider issue. There is a claim and a counterclaim about fraud, for Jacob claims that Laban defrauded him (Gen 29:25, 31:7, 41).[28] An important aspect of the story brings out the link to the preceding rules (stealing and the false use of Yahweh's name) and their background: Jacob's cheating his blind father now meets with its own mirroring retribution when he in turn is cheated by his father-in-law, Laban. Instead of giving Jacob the younger daughter, Rachel, as his wife, Laban fraudulently substitutes the elder daughter, Leah, on the wedding night, when Jacob doubtless cannot see properly.[29] This act very closely mirrors Jacob's cheating his elder brother Esau out of the blessing of the firstborn son.[30]

In a later incident, Jacob claims that Laban would have robbed (*gazal*, as in the rule) him of both his wives (Gen 31:31). In the preceding rule about stealing (Lev 19:11), the theft of a person is also the issue because the brothers' theft of Joseph was under review.

Jacob also accuses Laban of arbitrarily changing his wages many times (Gen 31:7, 41); the incident readily explains why a rule about the wages of a hireling follows—most oddly, it would appear—a rule about robbery.

28. On theft as the leitmotif of the story of Jacob's relationship with Laban, see Ktziah Spanier, "Rachel's Theft of the Teraphim: Her Struggle for Family Primacy," *VT* 42 (1992), 404–12.

29. Deception by exploiting problems of sight is a factor in Jacob's fraud against his father, Laban's fraud against Jacob on his wedding night, and Rachel's concealment of Laban's household gods, the protectors of the family home. It is possible that the narrator intended Rachel's action as a mirroring retribution for her father's denial of her to Jacob on the night of their wedding; by substituting Leah for Rachel, Laban is denying Rachel the protection of a new home.

30. See David Daube's analysis, *Studies in Biblical Law* (Cambridge, Eng., 1947), 190–200, and the very similar analysis by Robert Alter, *The Art of Biblical Narrative* (New York, 1981), 42–46.

Leviticus 19:14

Thou shalt not curse the deaf, nor put a stumblingblock before the blind, but shalt fear thy God: I am Yahweh.

From a story in which a daughter treats her father with contempt by concealing his household gods (Gen 31:34–35), the lawgiver returned to an earlier instance of similarly contemptuous conduct, a son's (Jacob's) treatment of his blind father (Isaac). Both actions concern the rights of children. The verb *qalal* in both Exod 21:17 and Lev 20:9 has the same sense of treating someone with contempt, and in each rule the focus is abuse of a parent.[31] In Lev 19:14 the lawgiver uses the verb *qalal,* and again the issue is the abuse of a parent.

The lawgiver has picked up a topic from the narrative in focus, in this instance the contemptuous treatment of a parent. The choice is not arbitrary, however, because in his law about dealing falsely and lying (Lev 19:11) he had already come upon the topic of a son's contemptuous treatment of a father (Genesis 27). That similar conduct turns up in Rachel's treatment of her father impelled the lawgiver to formulate a rule on the subject.

Why does the law address offenses against the deaf? Probably the lawgiver wanted to offer a parallel to the offense against the disability found in the story, blindness. Deafness and blindness are parallel disabilities in Exod 4:11; Isa 29:18, 35:5, 42:18, 19, and 43:8. The offense against Isaac involves hearing as well as sight, for Isaac is also the victim of his wife's eavesdropping. Jacob's theft of the right of the firstborn begins when Rebekah, overhearing her husband's plan to bless Esau, tells Jacob how to get Isaac's blessing instead. Hearing, therefore, plays a crucial role in the story: "Now Rebekah was listening when Isaac spoke to Esau his son. . . . Indeed I [Rebekah] heard your [Jacob] father speak to Esau your brother" (Gen 27:5, 6).

The lawgiver, however, probably focused on a specific subsequent aspect of Jacob's shocking treatment of his father. When Jacob appears

---

31. See S. R. Driver, *The Book of Exodus,* CBSC (Cambridge, Eng., 1911), 217.

before Isaac to receive the blessing from him, Isaac asks him who he is. Jacob replies that he is Esau, a lie that the preceding rule in Lev 19:11 prohibits. Isaac has to rely on his sense of touch to determine, mistakenly, that it is Esau and not Jacob who stands before him. Isaac's hearing does function, since he recognized Jacob's voice. Looking for an offense parallel to Jacob's manifest deception of his blind father, however, the lawgiver could find in Jacob's lie an example of someone abusing another's sense of hearing. The implication is that Jacob thinks that he could use his own undisguised voice with Isaac and still not be found out. Or, alternatively, one can infer that although Isaac hears sounds that he thinks he recognizes, he nonetheless has to try other, more dependable faculties such as touch and smell (Gen 27:27) to determine the reality. Whatever the lawgiver's assessment, this particular aspect of the narrative illustrates how a son contemptuously treats a father in both matters of hearing and sight.

The admonition in the rule "Thou shalt fear thy God: I am Yahweh" is readily understood because, as with the rule in Lev 19:12, Jacob's treatment of his father involves the use of God's name to conceal cheating.

Jacob uses Esau's clothes and puts on animal skins in order to mislead his blind father. Jacob in turn will be deceived by Joseph's garment stained with animal blood (Gen 37:33).[32] The narratives themselves show an interest in the nature of justice, especially the variety now called poetic justice. Fraudulent conduct is thus the central issue behind the presentation of this rule about the deaf and the blind and the next rule.

Leviticus 19:15

Ye shall do no unrighteousness in judgment: thou shalt not respect the person of the weak, nor honour the person of the mighty: but in righteousness shalt thou judge thy neighbour.

32. This incident prompted the rules against treating a parent with contempt (the verb is *qalal*) in Exod 21:17 and Lev 20:9. See Calum Carmichael, *The Origins of Biblical Law* (Ithaca: 1992), 112, 113, and chap. 7 on Lev 20:7–9. Robert Alter identifies the link between the two episodes as the deceptive use of garments; *Art of Biblical Narrative*, 181.

Jacob's cheating causes his father to give the wrong judgment, to give the right of the firstborn to him instead of to Esau. The Priestly lawgiver next pursued a particular feature made explicit in the narrative: the contrast between the inferior, hairy hunter Esau and the superior, smooth tent dweller Jacob, and the father's partiality to the former and the mother's to the latter. In other words, the topics of partiality and the unequal standing of two parties show up in this tradition, just as these topics are the joint concern of the law about unrighteousness in judgment. A noteworthy issue in the struggle between Jacob and Esau, aside from Jacob's chicanery, is whether or not Esau deserves Isaac's bestowal of the birthright. Esau offends his parents by marrying Canaanite women (Gen 26:34–35), unions that particularly distress his mother (Gen 27:46). Although Isaac does admonish Jacob to avoid such marriages (Gen 28:1), he presumably would still have given Esau the birthright because his partiality for the game dishes Esau brings him would have prevailed over all other considerations.

In the next generation, similar problems of unrighteousness in judgment recur with Jacob's sons. Just as Jacob the son manipulates his father's judgment and causes him great anguish, so Jacob's own sons settle their dispute with their brother Joseph in an outrageously unfair way, bringing terrible anguish on their father. The brothers take it on themselves to avenge the wrong Joseph did to them in reporting their actions to Jacob (Gen 37:2). Their solution amounts to the theft of Joseph, the topic that dominates so many of the lawgiver's preceding laws. Joseph's dreams about his superior position as the top son further compound the brothers' dispute with him. As the head of the family, Jacob should arbitrate disputes between his sons, but he is biased in favor of Joseph.[33]

The brothers, with the exception of the oldest son, Reuben, who is responsible for Joseph's well-being in the absence of the father,

---

33. Both the Joseph tradition (relevant to the rule about unrighteousness in judgment) and the tradition about Isaac's blessing of Esau or Jacob (relevant to the preceding rules about swearing falsely and misleading the blind) contain a report about the doings of others. The Genesis narrator may have intended to link the two reports. Just as Jacob offends by wrongly acting on his mother's report about a father's love for a son (Esau), so Jacob in turn runs into trouble with his sons because he fails to act on Joseph's report about them, his failure also being motivated by love for his son (Joseph).

heed Judah's fundamentally unjust solution to their problem with
Joseph. Judah proposes that they sell Joseph and thus avoid slaying
their own flesh and blood (Gen 37:26–27). The appeal of the money,
especially to sons not independent of their father, and the false kind-
ness suggested by sparing Joseph's life, determine their support for
Judah's solution.

Joseph presents himself to his brothers as someone who is high
and mighty, but the lawgiver does not consider Joseph's superior
standing, as revealed in his dreams, a reason to overlook his possible
wrongdoing regarding the report about his brothers that he gave
to his father. The fact that Jacob favors Joseph over his brothers indicates that Jacob might have overlooked Joseph's talebearing—the
topic of the next law—had he moved to settle the dispute. The lawgiver draws out the wider issues that emerge in the history of the two
generations: in matters of judgment, neither sympathy for someone's inferior standing nor the inclination to honor (*hadar*) the
mighty should color one's judgment.[34]

The term *hadar* used in the sense of paying honor to a person is
found in only three places: here; in Lev 19:32, where Judah is the
focus of the lawgiver's concern (see Chapter 6); and in Exod 23:3,
where Judah and his brothers are the focus.[35] The noun *hadar*
"honor" is used by Moses in Deut 33:17 when he affirms Joseph's
elevated status by referring to Joseph's firstborn son as a noble bull.

Leviticus 19:16

Thou shalt not go up and down as a talebearer among thy people: neither shalt thou stand against the blood of thy neighbour: I am Yahweh.

The issue under scrutiny is again Joseph's report about his brothers. Because only his side of the story is presented to Jacob, Joseph's

---

34. It is not accurate to translate *dal* as "poor" and *gadol* as "rich," as Levine
claims that the context requires; *Leviticus*, 129. The word *dal* is usually paired with
'*ašir*, "rich" (Exod 30:15; Prov 10:15, 22:16, 28:11); it does have the meaning "poor,"
but in light of the narrative background, "weak, lowly" is more accurate.

35. See Carmichael, *Origins of Biblical Law*, 187–89.

report could be regarded as rumormongering.[36] The brothers respond to his report by conspiring to slay him (Gen 37:18).[37] In fact, they too decide to concoct a story: that a wild beast has devoured Joseph (Gen 37:20). In other words, the brothers themselves are guilty of bearing tales, including the false tale that Joseph's blood was shed by the beast. The curious language in the rule about standing against the blood of someone may refer to this aspect of Joseph's alleged fate. His brothers' attitude certainly reveals that they were "standing against the blood" of Joseph.

The lawgiver may also have considered the parallel development that occurs later, when Joseph attempts to get even with his brothers by putting out false stories about them in Egypt, namely, that they are spies and thieves. These alleged offenses could cost their lives (Gen 42:9–22, 44:1–17).

Leviticus 19:17

Thou shalt not hate thy brother in thine heart: thou shalt in any wise reprove thy neighbour, and not carry sin concerning him.

The brothers hate Joseph and "could not speak peaceably unto him" (Gen 37:4). Instead of conspiring against him, however, they should have communicated their complaints to him, as their father did when he was offended by the arrogance of Joseph's dreams (Gen 37:10). Wise counsel calls for the reproof of a companion (Prov 9:8: "Rebuke a wise man, and he will love thee"; cp. Prov 19:25, 25:12, 28:23). The lawgiver judged that if such communication had taken place Joseph's brothers might have avoided their subsequent offenses against him. Likewise, Joseph might not have resorted to falsely accusing them of being spies and thieves (Gen 42:9,

36. Claus Westermann claims that from one angle "Joseph's action in the context of vv. 1–2 together with vv. 3ff. is to be understood as an act of tale-bearing by which he wanted to make himself important"; *Genesis 37—50: A Commentary* (Minneapolis, 1986), 36.

37. The Targum Onkelos on Lev 19:16 reads the sentence in the sense of conspiring against someone: "Do not rise up against the life of your comrade."

44:4–8). The difficult statement "Thou shalt not carry sin concerning him" may well express the problem of consequent wrongdoing, since the original issues that divided the brothers and Joseph are not taken up.[38]

The switch from the term *brother* to the term *neighbor* in the rule represents a common phenomenon in legal drafting, a move from the particular to the more inclusive. The interesting aspect is that the particular focus on the brother in the rule came from the spotlight on Joseph in the story.

Leviticus 19:18

Thou shalt not avenge, nor bear any grudge against the children of thy people, but thou shalt love thy neighbour as thyself: I am Yahweh.

The topic of retribution is central in the Joseph narrative under scrutiny. In this rule the lawgiver turned to Joseph's vengeance against the injustice done to him.[39] Joseph's motives are complex. Although he certainly pursues vengeance against his brothers, visiting upon them precise retribution for their actions, he also shows deep affection for them (Gen 42:24, 43:30–31 [his heart yearning for his brother Benjamin and seeking a place to weep], 45:1–15). Inextricably tied in with Joseph's hounding of his brothers is his kind treatment of them. He is one of their own. In this narrative about

38. In the *Testament of the Twelve Patriarchs* (probably originally from the second century BCE), Joseph's brother Gad explicitly relates the rule found in Lev 19:17 to the relationship between Joseph and his brothers; *Testament of Gad* 6:1–5. For an important discussion, see James L. Kugel, "On Hidden Hatred and Open Reproach: Early Exegesis of Leviticus 19:17," *HTR* 80 (1987), 49–61. At the very least, it is interesting that this early wisdom composition links the law to the Joseph narrative. Whether or not the author of *Testament of Gad* was familiar with the process of legal and ethical formulation that I am describing, and his work consequently represents a continuation of it, is a question that has to remain open.

39. Levine (*Leviticus*, 130), noting the use of the term *naṭar* "to keep, guard, retain" paraphrases: "One ought not to keep alive the memory of another's offence against him." See the Babylonian *Counsels of Wisdom*, *ANET*, 426, "Unto your opponent do no evil; Your evildoer recompense with good; Unto your enemy let justice [be done]."

hatred of a brother, he is portrayed as wanting nothing more than to be part of the family again. Emotions are very much on display. So the narrative is about vengeance and affection—the same odd combination in the law. It is not realistic in most situations to oppose vengeance and love at the same time. More realistic is Prov 27:6: "The kisses of an enemy are perfidious." The situation within Joseph's family, however, presents a coming together of the two emotions of vengeance and affection.

Why does the rule not follow the condemnation of vengeance and grudges with a simple "But thou shalt love thy neighbour"? Why add "as thyself" or, more accurately, "who is like thyself"?[40] The statement is not about self-love. It is about how Joseph as an Egyptian nevertheless treats the Hebrew visitors from the neighboring country of Canaan as kin, because he is indeed one of them. The lawgiver extrapolates from this historical episode the rule about loving one's neighbor who is like oneself: a son of Israel should deal with another son in the wider community of Israel as if he were a brother. In the wider community, one Israelite is a neighbor to the other. The language of the rule first prohibits avenging "the sons of Israel" and then talks of loving "thy neighbor." The exceptional situation of one Israelite's overlaid Egyptian identity brings out the fact that his relationship to these visiting Israelites is that of brother to brother. We have a prime example of how an odd, idiosyncratic development in a story prompts a rule.

*The Sequence of Topics in the Narratives
for the Laws in Leviticus 19:1–18*

The chaotic character of the sequence of laws is especially apparent when we scan those in Lev 18:23—19:11: bestiality, fear of parents, sabbath observance, idol worship, peace offerings, harvest gleanings, and stealing. Their arrangement is dependent on coherent

40. See Takamitsu Muraoka's decisive arguments in favor of the translation of *lere'aka kamoka* as "[thy neighbor] who is like thyself"—that is, "[thy neighbor] who is like thyself, an Israelite"; "A Syntactic Problem in Lev. xix. 18b," *JSS* 23 (1978), 291–97.

moves the lawgiver made in going from one narrative incident to another in (mainly) the book of Genesis.

The incident relevant to the last law in Leviticus 18 about bestiality concerns marriage and trade alliances between the Hivites and the house of Jacob. The negotiations broke down because two of Jacob's sons, rejecting any contact with Canaanites, slaughtered the Hivites. The religious dimension emerges when Jacob commands his household, which has been joined by surviving Hivite women and children, to put away any foreign gods among them (Gen 35:2). The lawgiver turned to the next incident when the issue of unacceptable worship within Jacob's household arises, namely, when Joseph dreams, first, that his brothers' sheaves bow down to his sheaf and, then, that his father, mother, and brothers bow down to him as the sun, moon, and stars bow down to a divine being (Genesis 37). His father's objection prompts the rule about fearing one's mother and father. The lawgiver also sets down the rule about keeping the sabbath day because he opposes the notion that heavenly bodies should worship a mortal like Joseph. On the sabbath an Israelite properly worships God, who created everything, including the heavenly bodies.

From the issue of unacceptable worship which arose within the first family of Jacob/Israel, the lawgiver searched out in later generations other unwelcome, Israelite religious developments. The next occurrence is Aaron and his followers' creation of an object, the golden calf, for the purpose of worshiping it (Exodus 32). In even later generations, certain monarchs also resort to worshiping molten calves (1 Kings 12; 2 Kings 10, 17). In his rule the lawgiver condemns the making of molten idols. Continuing to reflect on Joseph's dreams, the lawgiver follows out the theme of the brothers bowing down to Joseph. This theme reaches its climax when the brothers, in Egypt to obtain food, give Joseph a propitiatory gift, bow down to him, and he, in turn, sets out a meal. In his rule the lawgiver has in mind an Israelite version, the peace offering, of the kind of meal Joseph had with his brothers.

The lawgiver stayed with the meaning of Joseph's dream about the sheaves of grain bowing down to another sheaf, but not as it relates to the topic of worship rather to its pointing forward to the seven years of plentiful harvests in Egypt followed by seven years of failed ones. At the time of the famine, Joseph's role in distributing grain from the stored-up harvests to those in need—including his brothers—prompted the lawgiver to set down a rule about giving a portion of Israel's annual harvests to those in need—including those who, like the brothers in Egypt, might be sojourners in Israel.

Joseph's destiny in Egypt is bound up with his dreams about himself and his family. His brothers resent their implications. They react by stealing him from his father. The topic of stealing received the lawgiver's attention in a number of narrative incidents concerning Jacob. He turned back to the example in the immediately preceding generation when Jacob himself steals from his brother, Esau, the privilege that goes with being the firstborn son. Jacob's act of theft is achieved through false dealing (dressing as someone else), lying (saying he is Esau), and falsely using God's name (claiming that God granted him success in obtaining a meat dish so quickly). The rules that are set down concern stealing, then the three deceptions: dealing falsely, lying, and swearing falsely by God's name.

The topic of stealing still under review, the lawgiver turned to other comparable deceptions in Jacob's dealings with, this time, his father-in-law, Laban. Laban accuses Jacob of stealing his household gods (Genesis 31), and this accusation provokes the trading of other accusations. Each claims that the other attempted to defraud him: that Jacob acquired animals at Laban's expense; that Jacob tried to rob Laban of his daughters; and that Laban constantly tried to change Jacob's wages. Three rules are set down: forbidding fraud, robbery, and untimely payment of wages to a hired servant.

The lawgiver continued to examine the topic of theft in Jacob's dealings. When cheating Esau out of his birthright, Jacob abuses both his father's sense of hearing (he brazenly tells blind Isaac that he is Esau) and sight (dressed as Esau he has Isaac touch him). A rule against treating the deaf with contempt and putting an obstacle in the way of the blind is set down. Jacob's acquisition of the right of the firstborn has a broader context. There is intrigue between himself and his mother. She favors Jacob because she objects to Esau's marriages with women unacceptable to both herself and her husband, but Isaac still favors Esau because he likes his meat dishes. A proper judgment as to who should get the right of the firstborn was likely to get lost in the midst of these parental biases. A rule is set down expressing concern about partiality influencing a judgment.

Jacob's partiality when he becomes a parent next comes under review (Genesis 37). Loving Joseph more than his other sons, Jacob receives from him an ill report about his brothers. The brothers respond by hating Joseph, not speaking a kind word to him, and stealing him. Hatred and revenge dominate the relationship until, now in Egypt, the stolen Joseph himself pursues vengeance against his brothers, but then affectionately reconciles himself with them. The three rules in sequence are: not to bear ill reports, not to nurse hatred against a brother but to speak to him about the issue in contention, and not to seek vengeance for wrongs done but to love one's fellow as someone who is like oneself.

Chapter 4

Forbidden Mixtures: Leviticus 19:19

Pᴿᴼⱽᴱᴿᴮˢ are often condensed stories. The proverbial expression "don't cry wolf" distills the essence of Aesop's tale about the shepherd. Some biblical rules were not only inspired by developments in biblical narratives, they constitute proverb-like encapsulations of the developments themselves. In a sense the injunctions are miniature narratives. I refer in particular to certain rules about forbidden mixtures which have long been a source of puzzlement—and indeed, almost in keeping with their contents, a source of much confusion (on my own part, for example). The rules, appearing in both Deuteronomy and Leviticus, are the following:

Deuteronomy 22:9–11

Thou shalt not sow thy vineyard with two kinds of seed: lest the whole yield be rendered taboo: the seed which thou hast sown and the produce of the vineyard. Thou shalt not plough with an ox and an ass together. Thou shalt not put on *shatnez,* wool and linen together.

Leviticus 19:19

Ye shall keep my statutes. Thy cattle thou shalt not breed with two kinds. Thy field thou shalt not sow with two kinds of seed. And a garment of two kinds, *shatnez* shall not come upon thee.

In an article titled "Forbidden Mixtures," I argue that the Deuteronomic rules about forbidden mixtures (Deut 22:9–11) were not meant to be understood literally but were to be read as commentary, involving figurative language, on sexual matters in the book of Genesis.[1] In that article I claim that the Priestly writer (P) no longer understood the Deuteronomic (D) rules and was the first interpreter in the long history of Jewish law to make literal sense of them. I was mistaken. P understood the Deuteronomic rules very well.

I assumed what critical scholarship in general has assumed, that one should compare the Deuteronomic and Priestly rules as if D came first and P later, or vice-versa, and that P adapted D's rules (or D adapted P's) to meet the changing circumstances of Israelite society.[2] This is too narrow an approach to the relationship between the

1. Calum Carmichael, "Forbidden Mixtures," *VT* 32 (1982), 394–415. Carl Steuernagel in *Deuteronomium und Josua*, HAT 1 (Göttingen, 1900), 81, 82, suggests that the rules in Deut 22:9–11 had to do at some early stage with sexual and religious matters, possibly to do with nature cults. Compare G. J. Botterweck: "These various kinds of hybridization could point back to different spheres of activity and areas of worship of various deities"; entry *"behemah," TDOT* 2:12.

2. The tendency has been to give priority to P, but the arguments are less than convincing. For example, A. D. H. Mayes states on the basis of the use of a single word, the verb meaning "to sow," that Lev 19:19 in relation to Deut 22:9 "is undoubtedly original, as being more suitable to the verb 'to sow'"; *Deuteronomy*, NCBC (Grand Rapids, Mich., 1981), 308. "To sow" is indeed the appropriate term in Deut 22:9 because the vineyard is figurative for human reproduction, and a man sows seed in a woman (e.g. Lev 12:2; Num 5:28; and Sir 26:20; cp. Sir 25:8a with its reference to Deut 22:10 about plowing with an ox and an ass). Michael Fishbane reasons as follows. Originally, the rules in Lev 19:19 had a rhythmical and formulaic character. The word *shatnez* disrupts the rhythm, so it must have been an addition by legal draftsmen whose task it was to qualify and clarify the rule in question for different times in the history of ancient Israel. Solely on his subjective sense of the use of rhythm in a language from a very distant past does he build up a complicated history of development for an original "legal model" that first receives explication in P and, later, further explication in D; see Fishbane, *Biblical Interpretation in Ancient Israel* (Oxford, 1985), 58–62.

two sets of rules. It is an approach, moreover, that is tied to a literal reading of the rules.

The difficulty with giving literal meaning to the rules about mixtures is illustrated by the continuing attempts of modern commentators to do so. They are not bothered by the fact that the ancient Israelites *did* crossbreed their animals, *did* sow mixed seeds in their fields, and *did* wear a mixture of cloths. Jacob's experiment with Laban's cattle presupposes the practice of crossbreeding animals (Gen 30:25–43). Mules existed (2 Sam 13:29, 18:9; 1 Kgs 1:33, 18:5), so even different species were sometimes mated.[3] Different seeds were planted in the same field (Isa 28:25; cp. Cant 1:14).[4] The Israelite priests wore wool and linen together.[5]

Among the views of modern interpreters we find, for example, the claims that the land would have been impoverished more quickly if different kinds of seed were sown in the same piece of ground rather than if the crops were rotated, and that garments made from two different types of material produce static electricity in tropical climates and were consequently uncomfortable to wear,[6] or that the use of different threads in warp and woof would have caused the different parts of the garment to shrink differently.[7] Arie Noordtzij

---

3. C. F. Keil and F. Delitzsch seem to be aware of the problem when they claim that the mules frequently mentioned in the Old Testament were imported from abroad; see *Leviticus* BCOT 2 (Grand Rapids, Mich., 1951), 422. The implication is that the rule in Lev 19:19 was duly observed within Israel.

4. Joachim Jeremias, *The Parables of Jesus* (London, 1963), 170, points out that in the Palestine of the period of the New Testament vineyards and vegetable gardens were also generally planted with fruit trees.

5. "If it [the rule in Lev 19:19] means that two fibers may not be used in a single garment, it goes counter to the specifications for the holy garments, since the girdle calls for wool and linen, and the robe, breastpiece, and ephod call for wool, linen, and gold"; "Cloth," *IDB* 1:654. See also "Dress and Ornamentation," ABD 2:232–38.

6. R. K. Harrison, *Leviticus*, TOTC (Downers Grove, Ill., 1980), 200. Compare Mayes, who states that the rule in Deut 22:9 about the mixed seed in the vineyard "may have a utilitarian reason in the inappropriate and wasteful use of crops and land"; *Deuteronomy*, 308. Fishbane claims that we are dealing not with "theoretical ritual considerations" but with an "entirely practical agronomic concern that overcultivation of a circumscribed area eventually results in the premature exhaustion of arable soil." Different legal draftsmen, modifying the rules to meet changing social-historical circumstances, told the farmers about the modifications, "possibly prior to the planting and breeding season"; *Biblical Interpretation*, 58–62.

7. R. L. Harris, *Leviticus*, EPC 2 (Grand Rapids, Mich., 1990), 606.

states that the prohibition against plowing with the ox and the ass together was meant to prevent excessive strain on the weaker donkey.[8] If any of these factors applied, why would the rules, taken in a literal sense, even have been necessary? Practical experience would have largely taken care of such matters. Moreover, why would the rules be part of the Deuteronomic or Priestly codes, which concern themselves with far weightier matters than agricultural and domestic practicalities?

Another widely accepted view of the rules concerning mixtures is that they offend against the ordering of nature as laid out in the creation story in Genesis 1.[9] "Creatures or things of one nature are not to be mixed with those having another."[10] Thus, wool from an animal should not be mixed with linen from vegetable fiber, and different species of animals should not be mated or used together to perform tasks. There are problems with this view as well. It is not clear, for example, how the sowing of different crops fits into it. Planting different kinds of seeds together on the same plot of land does not usually result in hybrid plants. There is a major problem about mating different species of animals, revealed by Martin Noth's comments. The idea that underlies the rule in Lev 19:19 about cattle (*behemah*) is, he claims, that union between heterogeneous stock is against the divine ordinance. "Concretely, the veto is directed against the pairing of different species of animal."[11] Does he really mean that implausible matings such as that of an ox with an ass or a cow with a sheep were the subject of legislation? The fact that Noth, like other commentators, then brings into his discussion the existence of mules in ancient Israel indicates that he does indeed believe that the lawgiver intends to interdict such bizarre pairings as ox with ass and cow with sheep. Why would the lawgiver have bothered to do so? Fishbane similarly gets caught up in this

---

8. Arie Noordtzij, *Leviticus,* BSC (Grand Rapids, Mich., 1982), 200.

9. See, for example, Gordon J. Wenham, *Leviticus,* NICOT (Grand Rapids, Mich., 1979), 269; see also C. Houtman: "Mixing of kinds has to be prevented, because the order of the world must not be endangered"; "Another Look at Forbidden Mixtures," *VT* 34 (1984), 227.

10. J. R. Porter, *Leviticus,* CBC (Cambridge, Eng., 1976), 157.

11. Martin Noth, *Leviticus,* OTL (Philadelphia, 1977), 142.

kind of confusion. He sees that the mixed plowing in the Deutero-nomic rule may (although he does not spell out the implications) refer to sexual activity and wonders whether the rule confines itself to oxen and asses or whether it includes all mixed plowing.[12]

The sources of the confusion are the wrong assumptions that (1) these rules have to be read literally, (2) the Deuteronomic rules are extensions of the Priestly ones and help to explain them, and (3) the term *kil'ayim* used with regard to animals refers to two animal species rather than two varieties of the same species. If there was such remarkable sensitivity to differences in the natural world, and if combinations of categories were unacceptable, as most commentators imagine, we would then expect that vegetables could not be eaten with meat, and even that two kinds of vegetables could not be eaten together. We would also have to wonder why some combinations are ruled out and others receive no mention.

The true cause for puzzlement here is that commentators have been so ready to interpret these rules literally. If they were to come upon a rule in their own culture that one should not lie on a bed of nails, or a statement that a rolling stone gathers no moss, or, to come closer to the language of the biblical injunctions, that a criminal sentenced to hang must ride a horse foaled by an acorn,[13] would they seek a literal meaning for the rule and accept the statement at face value? Their attempts to give meaning to the biblical material testify to the difficulty of understanding how a different culture chooses to express itself. If he gave up a literal reading of the rules, Gordon Wenham would not need to discuss the view that we go "from the sublime to the ridiculous" in switching from the rule

12. Fishbane, *Biblical Interpretation,* 59, 60. G. J. Botterweck does not interpret in terms of species: "The law against hybridization in Lev 19:19, according to which a cow (*behemah*) was not allowed to copulate with a breed of cattle different from its own"; entry "*behemah,*" *TDOT* 2:12.

13. When the Syrians crucified Rabbi Jose ben Joezer, his nephew Jakum, a Helle-nizer who was rewarded by them with high positions, rode up to him at his cruci-fixion and mocked him: "Look at the horse that my master gives me to ride, and look at the horse that thy Master gives thee to ride"; *Midrash Psalms* 11:7 (cp. *Genesis Rabba* on Gen 27:27; 1 Maccabees 7:9–25, 9:54–56; Josephus, *Jewish Antiquities* 12.385–86, 391–401, 413, 20.235).

about love of neighbor in Lev 19:18 to the rules about mixtures in Lev 19:19.[14]

In rejecting this literal approach, I believe that the rules about forbidden mixtures are like proverbs and represent clever, cryptic judgments on specific aspects of patriarchal history. I have already argued for this view in regard to the Deuteronomic rules. Thus Judah's attempts to increase the vine of (Jacob) Israel by using mixed seed—that is, by uniting his half-Canaanite, half-Israelite sons with the Canaanite Tamar (Genesis 38)—is under review in the Deuteronomic proverb-type rule against sowing two different kinds of seed in a vineyard. Judah's marriage with a Canaanite wife is under review in the Deuteronomic rule against plowing with an ox and an ass. This rule's formulation reflects a typical procedure of the biblical lawgivers. Like the narrators of the traditions, they considered similar developments over succeeding generations, past or future depending on their point of departure. In this instance, D goes back to the first occasion when the issue of a marriage between a Canaanite and a member of Jacob/Israel's family seriously arises, that is, when the Canaanite Shechem seduces Dinah and seeks to marry her (Genesis 34).[15] Shechem is the son of the ass, Hamor, and he seduces (sexually plows, in the colloquial of the time) Dinah, the daughter of the ox, Jacob/Israel (Gen 49:6).[16] The rule against putting on *shatnez*, wool and linen together, is a negative judgment on Judah, who on his way for his yearly supply of wool becomes involved with Tamar, who has disguised herself as a prostitute and

14. Wenham, *Leviticus*, 269.

15. Rebekah and Isaac are concerned about the possibility of Jacob's marriage to a Canaanite woman because his brother, Esau, married Canaanite wives (Gen 27:46—28:1). Isaac takes means to ensure that Jacob will not make such a union. The lawgiver focuses, not on the history of Isaac's family, but on Jacob's, that is, Israel's.

16. The ox in Gen 49:6 is a figure for Jacob/Israel's fighting strength, which is weakened by the vengeful action of Simeon and Levi against the Hivites for Shechem's misconduct with Dinah. See Calum Carmichael, *Law and Narrative in the Bible* (Ithaca, 1985), 195, 196. For the celebrated legal adage about a child's legitimacy, "Whoso bulleth the cow, the calf is yours" (first cited in 1406 as "For who that bulleth my Cow, the calf is mine"), see John Barton, "Nullity of Marriage and Illegitimacy in the England of the Middle Ages," *Legal History Studies*, ed. Dafydd Jenkins (Cardiff, 1975), 40.

wears the typical linen garb of that profession. In sum, the prospect of an Israelite daughter's marrying a Canaanite, Judah's actual marriage to a Canaanite, his attempt to perpetuate his family line by sowing with different seeds and incorporating Canaanite blood, and his intercourse with a Canaanite cult prostitute are all reviewed in Deuteronomy.[17]

What sets the scene for the Priestly rules about prohibited mixtures are issues that arise not in the Judah story but in the Joseph story. The Egyptians had rules against mixing with the Hebrews, and these triggered a comparable Israelite concern on the part of the Priestly writers. Thus both Deuteronomic and Priestly lawgivers give expression in their rules to the direction cited in Lev 18:3: the Israelites are to take stock of Canaanite and Egyptian influences and counter them. Both the Deuteronomic and the Priestly rules about forbidden mixtures serve to remind the Israelites of how their past experiences with Canaanites and Egyptians threatened their national identity. The narrative under review by Deuteronomy was Judah in Canaan (Genesis 38); the Priestly lawgiver was reviewing the narrative about Joseph in Canaan and Egypt (Genesis 37, 39–48)—the narrative into which Judah's history has been incorporated.

Joseph becomes an Egyptian after being forcibly excluded from his own family. At the climax to his story, when he is about to reunite with his family, his Egyptian standing is such that he cannot, as a host normally would, eat with the visiting Hebrews, his brothers, because the Egyptian food laws prohibit it: "The Egyptians might not eat bread with the Hebrews; for that is an abomination unto the Egyptians" (Gen 43:32). The law in Lev 19:18 which precedes the Priestly rules on mixtures is about not avenging or bearing a grudge against the sons of one's people, about loving one's neighbor as (an Israelite like) oneself. The lawgiver has focused on the coming together of Joseph and his brothers in love and harmony after the hostility between them, and on the welcome disappearance of the distinction between the Egyptian Joseph and the Joseph who is the son of Israel.[18]

17. See Carmichael, *Law and Narrative*, 185–203.
18. See Chapter 3 on Lev 19:18.

The Priestly lawgiver had this concern with Joseph's identity in mind when he took up the Deuteronomic rules about contacts with a foreign group (the Canaanites) and forged parallel rules that have similar symbolic force, only this time in relation to Israel's experience in Joseph's Egypt. At the point in the narrative when Joseph and his brothers are sitting down to eat, whatever other factors are at play, Joseph presents the example of a Hebrew who had so lost his identity that he is unable to eat with fellow Hebrews. The scene is one among others that prompted P to compose certain proverb-type injunctions about incompatible mixtures which would bring to the attention of later Israelites the problem of retaining their national identity.

We can observe with some precision how, as regards both their substance and their sequence, the lawgiver worked with the Genesis narrative in setting down his rules. All critics agree that a major Priestly insertion into the Joseph story occurs in Genesis 46.[19] The climax to the Joseph story comes in Genesis 45, when Joseph, reconciled with his brothers, requests that they bring his father down to Egypt. In Genesis 46 a broader perspective shows up. Israel's (Jacob's) role in relation to the larger patriarchal history and future history in Egypt comes into prominence. Jacob's deity, the God of his father, Isaac, communicates with him about the future of his people in Egypt (vv. 1–5). This divine communication may be pertinent to the fact that, unlike the surrounding rules in Leviticus 19, the Priestly lawgiver expressly indicates here that his three rules about mixtures are divine ordinances ("Ye shall keep my statutes"). As we shall shortly see, these rules take up specific issues in the narrative material that immediately follows Gen 46:1–5.

In Gen 46:6–27 comes the Priestly contribution: how the family of Israel take their cattle and the possessions they acquired in Canaan and come to Egypt, "Jacob and all his seed" (vv. 6, 7). The term "seed" (*zera'*), as is common, refers to Jacob's offspring. The Priestly rule employs the verb *zara'*, "to sow seed." The Priestly narrator

---

19. See Artur Weiser, *The Old Testament: Its Formation and Development* (New York, 1961), 136. Gerhard von Rad, in *Genesis*, 3d ed. (London, 1972), 343, refers to "unimportant sections from the Priestly source." One might ask: unimportant from whose point of view?

gives precise details as to who these offspring are, and in verse 26 refers to sixty-six bodily descendants of Jacob ("who came out of his loins") who come down to Egypt. Because Joseph and his sons, Manasseh and Ephraim, by his Egyptian wife Asenath (v. 20) are already in Egypt, P provides a separate notice about them. Including Jacob himself, the total number of the house of Jacob "which came into Egypt were threescore and ten."[20]

After this Priestly insertion in Gen 46:6–27, the narrative resumes the description of the brothers' occupation as cattlemen in Egypt, telling how "every shepherd is an abomination unto the Egyptians" (Gen 46:34). Then, when Jacob and his family eventually meet Pharaoh, the latter requests—curiously because of Egyptians' dislike for shepherds—that some of them oversee his own cattle (Gen 47:6).

P's rule against breeding two different kinds of cattle—it corresponds to the Deuteronomic rule against plowing, in the sexual sense, with an ox and an ass—is in this case not a sexual metaphor at all. It takes up the issue of the Israelite cattlemen in their dealings with the Egyptians. Occupation is a potent indicator of identity, and these sons of Jacob are specifically identified as "men of cattle" (Gen 46:32, 34). Because the Hebrew brothers have cattle of their own, the pharaoh's request that they oversee the Egyptian cattle means that a mixing of breeds is to be expected. The interbreeding of the Israelite and Egyptian cattle represents the merging of the newcomers into the host nation. The example of this potential development in Egypt prompted the Priestly lawgiver to set down an injunction against interbreeding two kinds of cattle.[21] Exactly

20. On the complex nature of the Priestly insertion in Genesis 46, especially the notice about Joseph's sons, see Claus Westermann, *Genesis 37–50* (Minneapolis, Minn., 1986), 160. He states (156) the common view about the Priestly insertion: "The patriarchal stories as a whole and the exodus story as a whole were both at hand to the transmitter." Von Rad states, "Our list has to be thought of as the work of very late and theoretical erudition. It is the product of erudite occupation with ancient traditions and belongs, therefore, to a theological, Priestly literature"; *Genesis*, 398. Von Rad's description of such literary activity well describes, I contend, the work of the compilers of the laws.

21. I presume that Harris (*Leviticus*, 606) has in mind the Egyptian episode regarding the brothers' work with the pharaoh's cattle when he interprets the rule as an attempt to preserve a superior breed of cattle that the Israelites brought from Egypt. In

how the rule was to be understood will be considered shortly. Its aim was to reinforce Israelite resistance to foreign influences. The attitude is doubtless in the spirit of the one expressed in Lev 18:3: "After the doings of the land of Egypt, wherein ye dwelt, shall ye not do; . . . neither shall ye walk in their ordinances."[22]

Many exegetes, as Claus Westermann points out, think that the Egyptians' distaste for shepherds must refer to non-Egyptian nomads.[23] If this is correct, then the pharaoh's invitation to Joseph's brothers to have them settle on the land and supervise his animals is an invitation for them to overcome the stigma and become Egyptian. The Genesis narrative itself would thus indicate an important change of identity undergone by Joseph's brothers.

The Genesis narrative (Gen 47:13–26) next focuses on Joseph's own occupation. In order to feed the Egyptians, he exchanges corn for, first of all, the people's money, then for their animals, and then for themselves and their land. After this, Joseph arranges to give them seed so that in the future they will have food, and the pharaoh will have a portion of what they sow and harvest. P has noted this description of Joseph's occupation and has taken stock of the fact that, just as his brothers face the prospect of merging into Egyptian society, Joseph has already done so. He married an Egyptian woman and produced seed by her in the sense of progeny (Gen 48:4, 19).

Most noteworthy is that the narrative itself goes from the topic of Joseph's dispensing agricultural seed to the topic of his own "seed" by Asenath. Thus Gen 47:27—48:22 describes how Jacob at

---

the Joseph story the term for "cattle" is *miqneh,* probably to indicate that these were the cattle they had acquired (*qanah*) in Canaan (Gen 46:6). Gen 47:18 refers to *miqneh habehemah* "herds of cattle" that the Egyptians give Joseph in exchange for food. In the rule the term is *behemah,* "cattle," and it is commonly used throughout Leviticus. The term is a collective and includes both large and small domestic animals, especially those the brothers possess (Gen 46:32, 34).

22. Several ancient writers (e.g., Juvenal, *Saturnalia* 15; Plutarch, *Isis and Osiris* 379–81; Cicero, *De natura deorum* 3.15.59; Lucian, *The Parliament of the Gods* 10, 11) mention how the Egyptians deified and worshiped all sorts of beasts and consequently bred them with great care. I doubt, however, that these Egyptian practices are relevant to P's stance. For their relevance in the later history of Judaism, see David Daube, "The Finale of Horace's Satire 1.4," *Index* (International Survey of Roman Law) 22 (1994), 375–77.

23. Westermann, *Genesis 37–50,* 168.

the end of his life incorporates Asenath's two children into his own family on an equal standing with his own sons. Their names, Manasseh and Ephraim, actually bring out the concerns that P expresses in his rule. The name Manasseh means "For God hath made me forget all my toil, and all my father's house" (Gen 41:51). This name brings out Joseph's loss of connection with his previous identity as a member of Jacob's family. The name Ephraim means "For God hath caused me to be fruitful in the land of my affliction" (Gen 41:52) and brings out the fact that Joseph has put down roots—sown a field, in the language of the Priestly law—in a new cultural setting.

P sets down his second rule about mixed seed in response to this development in Joseph's family life: among the seventy bodily descendants of Jacob are some of mixed seed. The rule is consequently figurative and very similar to the Deuteronomic rule about the vineyard, which refers to Judah's sons by his Canaanite unions. These sons are actually cited in Gen 46:12 (cp. v. 10). The "field," like the "vineyard," stands for the fruit-bearing capacity of the house of Jacob/Israel.[24] Like the vineyard and the garden, the field is, for example, a figure "for the female reproductive apparatus."[25] From the lawgiver's perspective, Jacob's field consists of Jacob with his wives, and his sons with their wives in their seed-producing capacity. It is noteworthy that P lists the offspring according to the matriarch with whom they are associated in his genealogical list in Gen 46:15, 18, 22, and 25.[26] With Joseph's contribution from

24. The use of the vineyard for Judah's role in adding to the stock of Jacob comes from Jacob's comments in Gen 49:8–12 about Judah's attempts to attend to his family line. Jacob employs a metaphor about tying asses to the vine. The reference is to the fatal outcome that befalls Judah's half-Canaanite, half-Israelite sons because of their unions with Tamar; see Carmichael, "Forbidden Mixtures," 398–403. Judah almost lost all his sons in his dealings with Tamar, and the peculiar sanction in the Deuteronomic rule about how the produce of the vineyard might become forfeit reflects the story. There is no comparable threat of death to Joseph's sons in the story about them, and there is consequently no sanction in the Priestly rule about the field.

25. So M. H. Pope, also: "The plowing and cultivation of a field is a natural figure for sexual intercourse"; *Song of Songs*, AB (New York, 1977), 323. For the biblical and ancient Near Eastern evidence, see 323–28, 644.

26. N. H. Sarna draws attention to this feature in *Genesis*, JPSC (Philadelphia, 1989), 314.

Asenath, foreign seed is mixed in with the other seed. From P's later perspective, some such negative assessment of the Genesis narrative lies behind the formulation of his rule about mixed seed.[27]

The next rule, about the garment of two kinds, takes us to a facet of Joseph's integration into Egyptian society which is bound up with his marriage to Asenath. The result is that P presents a rule parallel to D's rule about *shatnez*. D's rule pinpoints how Judah, on his way to collect his yearly supply of wool, lay with Tamar, who has disguised her identity by changing out of her widow's clothes into those of a prostitute—indeed, those of a Canaanite cult prostitute. Prostitutes typically attracted their clients by donning a linen costume. The proverb-type rule expresses Judah's encounter with Tamar. He puts her on sexually, as one puts on a garment.[28] It is a mixing of wool and linen. P in turn looks at Joseph's sexual life—he has just done so in formulating his rule about mixed seed—and how it brings out the issue of his, and hence Israelite, identity. Remarkably, in the Joseph story wool and linen again prove to be key elements in the issue of identity.

The lawgiver worked with the Genesis narrative in the following way. Joseph's stewardship of the Egyptian agricultural resources concludes with his decree that the Egyptians have to give the pharaoh a

27. The intent of the rule about mixed seed has echoes in later literature. In Sir 26:20 the young man who is the recipient of Ben Sira's counsel is urged to "single out from all the land [among the Jews] a goodly field [literally, a portion of good soil, that is, a good wife] and . . . sow the seed [beget a family]." See P. W. Skehan and A. A. Di Lella, *The Wisdom of Ben Sira*, AB (New York, 1987), 351. Somewhat similar to the sentiment expressed by Ben Sira is Tob 4:12, 13: "Choose your wife from the seed [race] of your ancestors. Do not take a foreign wife who is not of your father's tribe. . . . Remember, my son, that Noah, Abraham, Isaac and Jacob, our ancestors, back to the earliest days, all chose wives from their kindred" (NEB). Note that Joseph is not cited. Interestingly, some texts in Tobit are related both to the legal material in Leviticus 19 and to the Joseph story (e.g., Tob 4:14 to Lev 19:13; and Tob 3:10 and 6:15 to Gen 42:38 and 44:29, 31). The concern about mixed seed in Tob 4:12, 13 may reveal an awareness of Lev 19:19. The Apocryphal Josephus and Aseneth shows how sensitive later interpreters were to Joseph's marriage to an Egyptian woman. See D. Cook's introduction to his translation in *The Apocryphal Old Testament*, ed. H. F. D. Sparks (Oxford, 1984), 468–70.

28. On this sexual sense of *labaš*, "to put on a garment," see Carmichael, *Law and Narrative*, 198–201; cp. G. A. Hugenberger, *Marriage as a Covenant*, SVT 52 (1994), 74–76. There are many interesting texts about linen and the prostitute's trade: see Josh 2:6; Isa 1:18; Jer 4:30; Hos 2:7 (5); Prov 7:16; Jdt 16:8; Rev 18:16.

fifth part of the produce of the seed that Joseph has given to them (Gen 47:26). The narrative then describes how Joseph's sons are incorporated into the family of Israel, which brings the lawgiver to set down his prohibition of mixed seed. Joseph's decree about the tax on the land has its precedent in the tax that he established to cope with the earlier problem of the famine (Gen 41:34). The lawgiver typically returned to such precedents and noted that it is because the pharaoh approves of Joseph's initial tax policy that Joseph is received into Egyptian high society. Because this reception involves the pharaoh's giving Joseph a wife, and because the lawgiver has just been concerned with Joseph's children by her, he turned back from the issue of the incorporation of Joseph's mixed seed into the family of Israel to the issue of the incorporation of Joseph into Egyptian society.

Joseph's wife, Asenath, is the daughter of an Egyptian priest. Her link to a foreign temple recalls the text in Gen 38:21, 22, which describes Tamar as a cult prostitute. Joseph's union with Asenath is an important part of his Egyptian identity. The text relates how the pharaoh first changes Joseph's name to an Egyptian one and then gives him a wife (Gen 41:45).[29] Immediately before this development the pharaoh "arrayed him in fine linen" (Gen 41:42). Joseph's coat played a major role in the acquisition and loss of an elevated status within his family. His new linen garb betokens that his status is again an elevated one, but this time as an Egyptian.[30]

The Priestly equivalent of the Deuteronomic rule again drops the sexual metaphor, as did P's rule about cattle in relation to D's rule about the ox and the ass. The Joseph narrative determines P's formulation. A key element is a tantalizing notice in Gen 46:34. That text raises the possibility that, just as in the Deuteronomic law, so

29. Von Rad comments, in regard to Joseph's getting an Egyptian name, "By it [the name] Joseph was drawn completely into the Egyptian court circle, and this did not happen, furthermore, without Joseph's being placed within the protective sphere of an Egyptian deity." He expresses surprise at the development and contrasts Daniel's situation (Dan 1:7, 8); *Genesis*, 378.

30. According to Herodotus (*Histories* 2.37), the Egyptian priests wore such linen garb. For an illuminating discussion of the role of clothes in the Joseph story, see V. H. Matthews, "The Anthropology of Clothing in the Joseph Narrative," *JSOT* 65 (1995), 25–36.

in the Priestly law, not just foreign linen (in the form of Joseph's attire as the pharaoh's top official) but wool too played a role in P's thinking. Commentators puzzle over the reference that "every shepherd is an abomination unto the Egyptians" (Gen 46:34). It is Joseph who communicates this information to his father's household, and he is referring to his brother Israelites' trade. Note how, as in the rule about crossbreeding cattle, the focus is on the occupation of the brothers, just as Joseph's linen garment indicates his official occupation.

The Egyptian abhorrence of shepherds would not have extended to the products of sheep—for example, wool—because the Egyptians had their own flocks and herds (Gen 47:17; Exod 9:3). Their abhorrence, it appears, extended only to non-Egyptian nomadic shepherds. It follows that the opposition in the Joseph story is between linen as an indicator of Egyptian societal status and wool as an indicator of Israelite societal status. This contrast brings out the clash between Joseph's Egyptian identity, symbolized by his linen dress, and the brothers' Hebrew one, symbolized by their dealing in wool. What is also brought out—in fact, it will be the primary contrast— is the clash between Joseph's previous identity as a member of Jacob's shepherding family, when he was favored with a special garment, and his new identity as a member of the Egyptian ruling class in his distinctive linen garment.

P's alertness to such a conflict of identity is what underlies his injunction about a garment of two kinds. For P, the type of clothing an Israelite wears proclaims his identity, and with Joseph's Egyptian garb particularly in mind, he prohibits the mixing of foreign attire with native in order symbolically to maintain Israelite identity uncompromized.[31] The prophet Zephaniah predicts dire punishment for those in Judah of high status who dress in foreign attire (Zeph 1: 8): "The garments they [the upper class] wear reveal the nature of

31. In the summary of his overview of Israelite dress, Douglas R. Edwards states, "What you wore conveyed who you were and the nature of your relationship to those around you. The biblical writers adeptly tapped the symbolic power of ancient dress to convey social, theological, or political messages"; "Dress and Ornamentation," *ABD* 2:238. D. K. Edelman describes how the narrator of the story of King Saul uses clothing as a marker of ethnic or national identity in *King Saul in the Historiography of Judah*, *JSOT* suppl. 121 (Sheffield, 1991), 297.

their ideal. They do not hesitate to surrender their distinctive national characteristics in their desire to make themselves and the nation one with the neighbouring peoples."[32]

The foreign term *shatnez* in the Deuteronomic law probably designates a prostitute, because the linen clothing she uses to attract clients identifies her ("A sweet disorder in the dress/ Kindles in clothes a wantonness").[33] It is common for a distinctive item of clothing to convey a person's identity, for example, *sans-culotte*, Brown Shirt, high hat, hard hat. Even a general term such as "skirt" can designate a woman (Deut 22:30; Ruth 3:9; Ezek 16:8).[34] In the Deuteronomic law we should read: "Thou [the Israelite] shalt not put on [sexually] *shatnez* [the linen-bedecked prostitute], wool [emblematic of the Israelite] and linen [emblematic of the prostitute] together." In the Priestly law the term *shatnez* refers to the foreign linen garment that is put on Joseph and conveys the notion of undesirable foreignness. We should read the second half of the Priestly law as unfolding the meaning of the first half: "A garment of two kinds—*shatnez* [foreign linen dress] shall not come upon thee [whatever the Israelite is wearing]."[35] The *shatnez* worn by an Israelite like Joseph betokens an unacceptable dual identity.[36] By

32. G. G. V. Stonehouse, *Zephaniah and Nahum*, WC (London, 1929), 36. "Double allegiance is the root evil here"; so C. L. Taylor, noting particularly Zeph 1:5, in *Zephaniah*, IB 6 (Nashville, 1956), 1015, 1016. On the tragedy of Esther: "delivering her nation at the price of her place in it," see David Daube, *Esther* (Oxford Centre for Postgraduate Hebrew Studies, 1995), 57.

33. From Robert Herrick's "Delight in Disorder." Like *shatnez*, the term "clothes" is personified.

34. Compare the Koranic statement that wives are "raiment for you and ye are raiment for them" (Q.2:187).

35. Fishbane wrongly claims that "the now obscure term *shatnez* was introduced" to indicate the precise constitution of a mixed garment; *Biblical Interpretation*, 58. It has to be stressed that the Hebrew formulation of the sentence with its use of the term *shatnez* is crucial in imparting the meaning intended. The *shatnez* in conjunction with the Israelite dress *is* the garment of two kinds.

36. Milgrom's conventional understanding of *shatnez* produces confusing results. He takes for granted that the term refers to a mixture of wool—not mentioned in Lev 19:19—and linen, and interprets Lev 19:19 to mean that an ordinary Israelite must not wear such a mixture. An Israelite priest, on the other hand, must wear a garment that combines wool and linen (a combination that Milgrom, with no textual base, designates *shatnez*). A few lines later he interprets the rule (Num 15:37–41) requiring an ordinary Israelite to attach fringes (*tsitsit*) to his garment as a requirement

relating the Deuteronomic and Priestly rules about *shatnez* to re-
spective issues in the narratives, we can do what no interpreter has
accomplished before, namely, we can account for the significant
differences in the formulation of each rule.

It is important to stress the proverbial nature of the rule. Like
many a proverb, its abbreviated language is designed to put the
hearer into a reflective mode, and the second half of the sentence is
intended to illumine the first half. The rule's odd content is also an
integral feature of its makeup. Presumably, in ordinary life there
was nothing untoward about mixing materials in clothing. The idea
that there was something wrong about it would have occasioned
surprise. Hence, a prohibition on mixing two materials is intended
to puzzle. What enlightens the hearer is the use of the foreign word
shatnez. In the Deuteronomic law the word conveys the use of linen
to elevate a foreign woman to the peak of sexual attraction for an Israelite, while in the Priestly law the word conveys the use of linen
to elevate an Israelite to high standing in a foreign land. The lawgiver uses the foreign word to indicate that he is raising the issue of
national identity. Had a standard Hebrew word been used instead,
the meaning would not have been conveyed and the result would
have been puzzlement.[37]

How are we to understand the rules about prohibited mixtures?
All three prohibitions are, in fact, arresting in nature. Not to appreciate this feature is to lose the significance of what they communicate. If the rules had prohibited animals (of the same species) from

---

to wear wool and linen. In his commentary, *Leviticus 1–16*, AB 3 (New York, 1991),
548, 549, there is no awareness of the contradiction. In his "Of Hems and Tassels,"
BAR 9 (1983), 65, Milgrom argues that "in a small way" an ordinary Israelite wears
a priestly garment: "Every Israelite wears his priestly clothing, the *tsitsit*." The Israelite, then, is both a priest and a nonpriest. Even if there was some merit in this position, the clash with the prohibition of *shatnez*, as understood by Milgrom, remains.
Actually, his reading of the tassels rule in Num 15:37–41 would support my contention that there was nothing untoward about an Israelite's wearing a combination
of wool and linen so long as it did not denote a dual identity. Moreover, if Milgrom
gave up his reading of the *shatnez* rule, his position would be more intelligible.

37. The term *šeš*, "fine linen," used of Joseph's Egyptian garb is an Egyptian loan-
word, but its frequency in the Old Testament suggests that it had become part of standard Hebrew vocabulary.

crossbreeding, a field from being sown with different seeds, and clothing from comprising different materials, they would have prohibited ordinary, sensible usage. The appearance of denying standard practice is what makes them arresting. The rules' intended meaning lies in the language used. Thus the term *kil'ayim*—only two, not three or more—plus the foreign word *shatnez* would make the hearer realize that the lawgiver is evoking a particular set of circumstances, in this instance the experience of an Israelite in Egypt.[38] In light of that past situation, the hearer would see that involvement in foreign ways could compromise his cultural and ethnic identity.

How are we to understand the reception of these rules about prohibited mixtures? Critical scholarship rightly distinguishes between the two audiences who might read the texts in question. First there is the fictional Israelite audience about to enter the new land of Canaan, to which Moses addresses these rules. This audience was close in time to the previous situation in Egypt and probably still remembered what had happened there. Consequently, these people should have been able to understand the rules in the soon-to-be-acquired land of Canaan.

These rules, however, are not in fact from Moses, but from some later lawgiver, and they are addressed to an audience unknown to us. This lawgiver's Israelite (or Judean) audience was centuries removed from the first-time entry into Canaan, and the rules would consequently strike the hearers as odd. But it is precisely the effect of startling the hearer that the lawgiver aims for. This actual audience had to identify itself with the fictional audience addressed by Moses and consequently become familiar with its situation and history. The rules elicited reflection and made the hearer perceive that they encode historical messages, in this instance, about problems of Israelite identity in the past. The Israelites who were now long settled in the former land of Canaan were therefore to pay regard to threats to their national identity in their current lives. Or alternatively, and more likely, if the historical setting of this audience was in fact the

38. The proverb "Don't look a gift-horse in the mouth" is an example of a prohibition that seemingly goes against sensible procedure; in fact, one should always look at the horse's mouth to judge its health. The introduction of the word *gift* indicates that in this particular situation one should not do what one ordinarily does.

Judean one in exile in Babylon, then all the more appropriate to remind it of past problems of Israelite identity in a host foreign nation.

The Sequence of Topics in the Narratives
for the Laws in Leviticus 19:19

First is the pharaoh's invitation to Joseph's brothers to become
supervisors of his cattle; then Jacob's reception of Joseph's children
into the house of Israel; and, finally, the account of Joseph's second
tax on the Egyptians, which caused the lawgiver to turn back to his
first tax when the pharaoh, making Joseph his top official, attired
him in an Egyptian garment. The rules set down are: an Israelite is
not to breed two kinds of cattle, or to sow his "field" with two different seeds, or to wear mixed attire.

CHAPTER 5

A Strange Sequence of Rules:
Leviticus 19:20–26

LIKE the history of any national group, the history of ancient Israel as found in the Bible is an attempt to invent a past.[1] A feature of the narratives in the book of Genesis, for example, is that they anticipate issues in the life of later Israel—which means that the narratives have been written up at a much later date than the events described in them. One such issue that emerges is a concern with Israelite identity in the face of foreign cultural influences. S. R. Driver wonders whether the narrative in Genesis 34 about Jacob's encounter with the Canaanite group, the Shechemites, is one in which individual persons stand for tribes and whether the focus is really on the larger issue of national identity. He points out that, after the conquest of Canaan, Israelites and Canaanites dwelt in Shechem side by side (Judges 9). In that there is such similar language in Gen 33:19 and Judg 9:28, the name Shechem that signifies a place in Judges may in the person Shechem in Genesis 34 really be

1. On the invention or reinvention of a nation's legal system in particular, see, for seventeenth-century England, J. G. A. Pocock, *The Ancient Constitution and the Feudal Law* (Cambridge, Eng., 1957); for Scotland, Hector L. MacQueen, *"Regiam Majestatem*, Scots Law, and National Identity," *Scottish Historical Review* 74 (1995), 1–20; for ancient Athens, David Cohen, "Greek Law: Problems and Methods," *ZSS* 106 (1989), 101; also, on more general aspects, *The Invention of Tradition*, ed. Eric Hobsbawm and Terence Ranger (Cambridge, Eng., 1983).

a personification of the inhabitants of the place. Consequently, we may not be dealing with the sexual seduction of Dinah by Shechem, but with the later religious seduction of Israel by a Canaanite group.[2] A standard view of the Judah and Tamar story in Genesis 38 is that Judah's marriage to a Canaanite woman reflects later territorial expansion of the tribe of Judah and consequent intermarriage with Canaanites.[3] D. J. Redford states that the Joseph story "blandly ignores the difficulties inherent in the encounter of Hebrews and pagans."[4] He may be right, but plainly the story does reveal such an encounter.

Like the rules about forbidden mixtures in Lev 19:19, the tradition about Abimelech and his brothers in Judges 6—9 also suggests that the Joseph story was viewed as raising issues of national identity. In the Judges tradition motifs similar to those in the Joseph story appear. An Israelite, Gideon, unlike the bondman Joseph when confronting Potiphar's wife, has a sexual relationship with a Canaanite bondwoman in the Canaanite city of Shechem. Abimelech is the product of that union (Judg 8:31). Like Joseph's dual Hebrew-Egyptian identity, Abimelech's dual identity, half-Israelite, half-Canaanite, dominates the tradition about him. Like Joseph, Abimelech shows overweening ambition and makes himself king. In doing so, unlike Joseph's brothers, he succeeds in slaughtering his many brothers with the exception of one of them, Jotham. Fratricide surfaces in each generation, Joseph's and then Abimelech's, because the same issue of dominance in a family arises. Abimelech reigns for three years but vengeance is visited upon him because of his treatment of his brothers,[5] just as Joseph's brothers experienced retribution for their treatment of him.

The story of Abimelech illustrates how, when the biblical narrators recorded history, they sought out patterns of similar conduct and development in succeeding generations of the nation Israel and

2. S. R. Driver, *Genesis*, WC, 9th ed. (London, 1913), 307–8.

3. See E. A. Speiser, *Genesis*, AB (New York, 1964), 300.

4. D. J. Redford, *A Study of the Biblical Story of Joseph*, SVT (Leiden, 1970), 22 n. 3.

5. Although his fellow Shechemites turn against him, the text is explicit about the fact that the vengeance is retribution for his murder of his brothers (Judg 9:23, 24).

molded their history accordingly.[6] This method of writing history
by harking back to what happened in a previous generation applies
to the write-up of Abimelech's history in relation to Joseph's in at
least four ways. First, the congruence of subject matter—rivalry for
dominance among brothers, fratricide, and the dual national identity of the main character—is such that coincidence alone cannot
account for it. Second, the tradition in Judges explicitly draws a link
between Gideon's era and Joseph's. Thus the Israelites, confronting
oppression at the hands of the Midianites, are reminded about how
God delivered them from their troubles in Egypt (Judg 6:8, 9, 13).
Included in these troubles were those of both Joseph and his brothers in Egypt. Third, Gideon and Abimelech are descendants not just
of the patriarchs Abraham, Isaac, and Jacob but specifically of Manasseh, one of the sons born to Joseph by an Egyptian woman. Fourth,
Shechem, the city central to Abimelech's life story and where he
is made king (Judg 9:6), is the place where his ancestor Joseph is
buried (Josh 24:32).[7] Other parallels are observable. To cite but one:
a dream employing agricultural imagery about sheaves of grain
bowing down to another sheaf describes Joseph's rulership over his
brothers (Gen 37:7, 8). Similar agricultural imagery, this time in a
fable about trees that single out one of them to reign over the others,
describes Abimelech's rulership over his brothers (Judg 9:7–21).

In looking at this example of how biblical narrators recorded history, I aim to explain why the four rules in Lev 19:20–26 occur in
the seemingly haphazard sequence they do. These rules have proved
very difficult to interpret, and by addressing the problem of their

6. The biblical procedure is but a reflection of a universal one. See David Daube:
"All history-writing transfers features of one event or one great personage to another,
and, indeed, much history-acting is in imitation of previous occurrences. Whoever
nowadays writes about Napoleon is likely to lend him some traits of Caesar, and
Napoleon himself—not to mention de Gaulle—would on occasion look to that example"; *He That Cometh* (London: Council of Christians and Jews, 1966), 1.

7. It is also the place where Joseph's other direct descendants, the Ephraimites, as-
semble and with the other tribes of Israel confer kingship on Jeroboam (1 Kgs 12:20).
Joseph's brothers pasture their father's cattle in the fields of Shechem (Gen 37:12–14).
On the influence of Abimelech's kingship on the write-up of another fratricide, Absa-
lom, who became king, see Calum Carmichael, *The Spirit of Biblical Law* (Athens,
Ga., 1996), 159.

sequence I hope to solve many of the puzzles about them. The rules prohibit sex with a betrothed bondwoman, eating certain fruit that is regarded as uncircumcised, eating when it involves an association with blood, and divination and soothsaying. It is clear from a cursory reading of them that they are narrow in scope and this feature alone suggests that special factors may have been at work in their presentation. The key to their comprehension is, I contend, that the lawgiver engaged in the same process of historical reflection as the narrators. He went back and forth between issues and problems thrown up by the two related traditions about Joseph and Abimelech.[8]

Leviticus 19:20–22

And whosoever lieth carnally with a woman, that is a bondmaid, betrothed to an husband, and not at all redeemed, nor freedom given her; there shall be an enquiry; they shall not be put to death, because she was not free. And he shall bring his trespass offering unto Yahweh, unto the door of the tabernacle of the congregation, even a ram for a trespass offering. And the priest shall make an atonement for him with the ram of the trespass offering before Yahweh for his sin which he hath done; and the sin which he hath done shall be forgiven him.

About this sexual rule one wants to ask: why is it so narrow in scope and why does it follow the prohibition about a garment of two kinds, which was a judgment on Joseph's incorporation into Egyptian society? The rule takes up an infringement by a freeman of another freeman's arrangement to marry a bondwoman who has not yet been given her freedom. Jacob Milgrom thinks that the case is a marginal one.[9] Raymond Westbrook refers to it as "the curious

8. Commentators see the hand of the P redactor both in the narrative about Abimelech and the narrative about Joseph's family in Egypt. Judg 8:30–32 and Gen 46:26 contain the same phrase about those "issuing from his loins." On P's redactive activity in adding the Abimelech story to the book of Judges, see G. F. Moore, *Judges*, ICC (Edinburgh, 1895), 234–35. I am going further and claiming that the P lawgiver set down rules inspired by both narratives.

9. Jacob Milgrom, in his comments to the *HarperCollins Study Bible* (New York, 1993), 183; see also his "The Betrothed Slave-Girl, Lev 19,20–22," *ZAW* 89 (1977), 43–50.

case of Lev 19:20–22."[10] I wish to argue that, despite the manifest differences between the situation in the Joseph story and the situation in the rule, it is in fact Potiphar's wife's sexual encounter with the bondman Joseph which inspired the rule.

The lawgiver has continued his interest in Joseph's sexual history. Before his marriage to an Egyptian woman, at the time he received his special linen garment (the matter pertinent to the preceding rule about the garment of two kinds), Joseph has a sexual encounter with the Egyptian wife of Potiphar. Before we turn to it for its relevance to the rule about illicit sex with a bondwoman, it is worth noting how the Deuteronomic lawgiver proceeded at the comparable point in the presentation of his rules. His rule about a garment, *shatnez*, has as its focus Judah's sexual transaction with the prostitute Tamar. In D the rule that follows his *shatnez* rule concerns the tassels on the edges of an Israelite garment (Deut 22:12). These tassels serve a symbolic function in that they are intended to proclaim that an Israelite like Joseph is not given to illicit sex. The Deuteronomic rule takes up the false conviction that arises from Joseph's problem with his garment. Because Joseph expresses to Potiphar's wife his opposition to illicit sex with her, to spite him she pulls off his garment and uses it to have him falsely convicted of attempting to have sex with her.[11]

Although Joseph is innocent in the matter, the case against him is a strong one (she has his cloak in her hands) and he is, however wrongly, convicted. Such an unjust conviction will arouse interest among legal and ethical thinkers at any time. One aspect of Joseph's situation which engaged the biblical lawgiver's interest is in line with his intent in many of his other rules, namely, to forge an Israelite national identity.[12] As expressed in Lev 18:3: "After the doings of the land of Egypt, wherein ye dwelt, shall ye not do," the lawgiver's aim is to prevent the occurrence of comparable deeds among

10. See Raymond Westbrook, "Slave and Master in Ancient Near Eastern Law," *Chicago-Kent Law Review* 70 (1995), 1669; *Studies in Biblical and Cuneiform Law*, Cahiers de la revue biblique 26 (1988), 101–9; also "Adultery in Ancient Near Eastern Law," *RB* 97 (1990), 564–69.

11. See Calum Carmichael, *Law and Narrative in the Bible* (Ithaca, 1985), 206–10.

12. On identity, especially Joseph's, as the paramount feature of the preceding rules in Lev 19:19, see Chapter 4.

his own people. In this light, it is understandable that he might have chosen to examine an actual example of an Israelite's exposure to bad conduct on the part of an Egyptian.

In working out the relationship between a law and a narrative there is not, nor should we expect, an exact one-to-one correspondence between them. The lawgiver exploited the narrative to make his own legal and ethical points. As in all his rules, so in this one the Levitical lawgiver addresses males. Primarily taken up with their offenses, he came up with, I submit, a comparable male offense to that of Potiphar's wife. An additional factor would have encouraged a switch from a female to a male offense. In the biblical world in matters sexual the man does the pursuing and not the woman as in Gen 39:7. Her initiative with Joseph, when she says to him, "Lie with me," is, like Lot's daughters' initiative with their father (Gen 19:32), unique in biblical material.[13] "To lie" in the sense of "to have sexual intercourse" is generally the man's bidding. In this light it is understandable that a lawgiver might have looked at a male offense that approximates Potiphar's wife's offense.

The rule applies to an Israelite situation that mirrors the Egyptian one. In an Israelite, or in any household for that matter, domestic servants are more likely to be bondwomen than bondmen. The same lawgiver later sets down a rule that an Israelite should not enslave a fellow Israelite (Lev 25:39–46).[14] To him, then, an Israelite woman cannot be enslaved. It is therefore likely that the bondwoman in the rule about illicit sex is not an Israelite. Like Joseph in Egypt, she is probably a captive from abroad. The triangular set-up in the story—Potiphar, his wife, and their foreign bondman—has its counterpart in the rule, namely, the foreign bondwoman, her future husband, and the offending male.

The switch from a sexual violation involving a woman with a bondman in the story to a sexual violation involving a man with a bondwoman in the law required that the lawgiver imagine the cu-

13. On the outrageous way in which the slave Aesop came to be released, because of the demand of his master's wife that he pleasure her ten times in succession, see David Daube, "Counting," *Mnémosyné* 30 (1977), 176–78.

14. The position was similar in ancient Rome, although there were exceptions. See W. W. Buckland, *The Roman Law of Slavery: The Condition of the Slave in Private Law from Augustus to Justinian* (Cambridge, Eng., 1908), 397–436.

riously complex set-up that we meet with in the law. The male-female relationship in it equivalent to Potiphar's wife's entanglement with Joseph has to involve males from outside the household. There would have been no problem for the lawgiver to exercise his judgment on if the head of household had sex with his own bondwoman: he is her owner and entitled to her services. Thus the lawgiver lays out the case depicted in the rule: a freeman is the future husband of the bondwoman and another freeman gets involved sexually with her before she is given her freedom, before she becomes the other man's wife. A violation of this legal tie is the offense the rule focuses on. Because she is still a bondwoman, not yet freed from her servitude, the offenders are not given a death sentence.[15] The Deuteronomic rule that intercourse with a betrothed woman is a capital offense appears to be recognized (Deut 22:23, 24) because of the statement that had the bondwoman been free the violation of her betrothed status would have incurred capital punishment: "they shall not be put to death because she was not free."

In the Levitical rule there is no penalty for the offending male—other than his conscience compelling him to make acknowledgment before Yahweh, the Israelite God, that he is guilty of misconduct. Interpreters are puzzled by the limited concern with punishment in the rule. They wonder why there is no reference to the punishment of the bondwoman—there are unsatisfactory attempts to introduce it[16]—and why there is no concern with compensation for her owner and/or future husband.[17] Again the Joseph story proves illuminating.

A reader might think that the story concentrates solely on the

15. In classical Roman law a female slave was not harshly punished for irregular sex, but once freed, she was. See Theodor Mommsen, *Römisches Strafrecht* (Leipzig, 1899), 691.

16. For example, instead of the reading "There shall be an enquiry," the Authorized Version of 1611, following the Vulgate, reads "She shall be scourged."

17. So Nathaniel Micklem, *Leviticus*, IB (Nashville, Tenn., 1953), 2:98. For the attempts to understand the unique term *biqqoret* as "indemnity," not "inquiry," see Westbrook's discussion, *Studies*, 102–4. Westbrook's own solution is that the slave is a man's wife pledged to a creditor to pay off a debt, and it is the creditor, not some outside party, who has intercourse with her. The woman's husband can then claim his wife back from the creditor. His analysis depends on dubious philological considerations that radically alter the usual reading of the text, getting rid of one of the parties, and interpreting the law within the context of other Near Eastern legal material that suits his position.

punishment of the innocent Joseph. But that is to miss a most interesting aspect of the story, especially when we keep in view the
lawgiver's sole interest in the offending male's conscience. Receiving no penalty for her offense against her husband, Potiphar's wife
has, nonetheless, to reckon with her conscience. During her sexual
advances to Joseph, he reminds her that sexual activity between
them is "wickedness, and [a] sin against God" (Gen 39:9). In both
story and rule, then, there is in regard to the offending seducer solely
a focus on an offense against God, sin, and not on a deed that has
earthly repercussions. In the Joseph story there is no focus on the
real-life consequences of the seducer's, Potiphar's wife's, offense because she avoids discovery.

The Joseph story may also throw light on three other matters that
interpreters regularly draw attention to in the rule: the issue of the
bondwoman's punishment, the issue of compensation for her owner
and her future husband, and the rule's puzzling reference to an inquiry. First, absent from the law is any focus on the bondwoman's
wrongdoing (other than to say that as a bondwoman she is not to
be put to death). Features of the story are again to be reckoned with.
If the bondwoman were to be punished (short of execution), her
owner would do so as he saw fit—just as Potiphar punished Joseph.
Her punishment is not for the lawgiver but for her owner to decide.
Joseph may have been cast into the palace prison with a view to his
eventual execution—recall the fate of the baker (Gen 40:22)—but,
if so, it is puzzling that Potiphar did not have him executed immediately. D. B. Redford views Joseph's sentence as unsatisfactory but
does not explain why this might have been so. He thinks that ordinarily someone in his situation would have been summarily executed.[18] The point is, I think, that the matter was for Potiphar himself to decide.

Second, the absence from the rule of any reference to compensation for the bondwoman's owner and for her future husband may be
attributable to the fact that this issue is not one that arises in the
Joseph story. I noted that the lawgiver brought in the outside males
because without them he could not set out a rule that has a male offense comparable to Potiphar's wife's. So focused was the lawgiver

18. Redford, *Story of Joseph*, 92.

on the features of the story that he left aside such issues as interpreters raise about compensating the bondwoman's owner and future husband.

Third, a major puzzle in the rule is its call for an inquiry. Interpreters rightly ask exactly what is to be inquired into, and does not every legal matter bring with it an inquiry? If the law were lawyers' law I would agree that it is unsatisfactory in failing to address all the issues that arise from the offense. If, however, the incident with Potiphar's wife was the dominant influence on the construction of the rule, then the failure to inquire into the truth of her accusations against Joseph stands out. I suggest that the lawgiver, aware of this major fault in the story, demanded an inquiry into the alleged sexual offense hypothesized in the law.

Leviticus 19:23–25

And when ye shall come into the land, and shall have planted all manner of trees for food, then ye shall count the fruit thereof as uncircumcised; three years shall it be as uncircumcised unto you: it shall not be eaten of. But in the fourth year all the fruit thereof shall be holy to praise Yahweh withal. And in the fifth year shall ye eat of the fruit thereof, that it may yield unto you the increase thereof: I am Yahweh your God.

How do we account for the bewildering switch from the topic of wrongful sexual congress between an Israelite and a foreign bondwoman to the topic of trees and their uncircumcised fruit? The explanation is that the lawgiver turned from the story of Joseph in Egypt to a related tradition in the book of Judges about Israel in Canaan, specifically to the tradition that begins with the sexual union between the Israelite Gideon and a Canaanite bondwoman (Judg 8:31).[19] This lawgiver lumps together Egyptian and Canaanite influences and warns the Israelites about them (Lev 18:3).

19. In Judg 9:18 the woman is referred to as an 'amah, a term that is synonymous with šiphah, the term for bondmaid in the rule in Lev 19:20. B. J. Schwartz suggests that in Lev 19:20a the unexpected selection of the term šiphah and not 'amah for a "slave girl" is a word-play due to the fact that she is not ḥpš, "free"; "The Slave-Girl

I have already indicated why the lawgiver might have switched from the story of Joseph's presence in an Egyptian household to the story of his descendant Gideon's involvement in a Canaanite household. The lawgiver came upon similar issues that arise in the two traditions. Gideon's sexual relationship with a bondwoman in a Shechemite household begins the saga of the son, Abimelech, who is born to them and whose story recalls Joseph's. Abimelech's reign lasts but three years. It comes to an end when his fellow Shechemites become instruments of vengeance against him, when "God sent an evil spirit between Abimelech and the men of Shechem . . . that the cruelty done to the threescore and ten sons of Jerubbaal [Gideon] might come and their blood be laid upon Abimelech their brother" (Judg 9:23, 24). An incident that occurs at the beginning of this process of retribution explains the rule about uncircumcised fruit and why it takes the form it does. In this incident the men of Shechem bring in the grape harvest and hold a festival in the house of their god. While eating and drinking during the course of the festival the celebrants seek to influence Abimelech's fate by cursing him (Judg 9:27).

Why, however, did the lawgiver focus on this particular aspect of the tradition about Abimelech? The key lies in a particular development that the lawgiver had been contemplating in the Joseph story. After Joseph is cast into prison for his supposed sexual offense against Potiphar's wife, the very next incident is his interpretation of the dream of his fellow-prisoner, the pharaoh's butler. The butler dreams of a vine with three branches that blossom and produce clusters of grapes ready to harvest. He takes these new grapes and squeezes their juice into the pharaoh's cup, which he then places in the pharaoh's hand. Joseph informs the butler that the pressing of the grapes into the cup signifies that he can look forward to taking

Pericope," *Scripta Hierosolymitana* 31 (1986), 244. Note that the Joseph story has a bondman but the story of Gideon has a bondwoman. In his preceding rule against illicit sex the lawgiver made a switch from the bondman in the story to the bondwoman in his rule. Note also that one story has an attempted seduction but the other an actual sexual relationship—similar again to the lawgiver's switch from the unsuccessful seduction in the Joseph story to actual sexual activity in his rule about the seduction of a bondwoman.

up his job again as the pharaoh's butler (Gen 40:9–13) (unlike the baker, whose dream Joseph next interprets as foreshadowing his execution). It is the link between fruit trees and the fate of a person (when the butler's dream about vines foreshadowed his fate) which prompted the lawgiver to turn to the similar incident in the Judges tradition about the fate of Abimelech.[20]

In the Judges tradition the men of Shechem celebrate their grape harvest: "They went out into the field, and gathered [the grapes from] their vineyards and trod [them], and gave praise, and went into the house of their god, and did eat and drink, and cursed Abimelech" (Judg 9:27). The lawgiver, Moses, anticipating Israel's entry into the land of Canaan, calls for an Israelite harvest festival to be held in honor of the Israelite god. The rule is an ideal construction of what should take place when the Israelites first experience the new land—it is introduced by the phrase "And when ye shall come into the land."[21] Three aspects of the rule call for comment: why such a festival exists; why there is a period of time between entering the new land, planting trees, and celebrating the festival; and why the fruit is regarded as uncircumcised.

First, the rule was intended to recall the history of Israel's mixing with the Canaanites in Gideon's time, which was when Israel acquired the land. Once in Canaan, the Israelites are to celebrate their own harvest festival and not the one celebrated by the Canaanites. The requirement of an Israelite festival has been prompted, then, by the lawgiver's scrutiny of the Canaanite festival in Judg 9:27. The term *hillulim*, about giving praise at the festival, occurs in the Bible only in the rule about uncircumcised fruit which requires that Yahweh be praised, and in the narrative about Abimelech in which the Canaanite god receives acclamation.

---

20. The same link also plays a crucial role in the puzzling rule that comes after the fruit-trees rule, namely, not "to eat upon the blood."

21. Those commentators, ancient and modern, who think that the rule was geared to the actual life of the ancient Israelites miss the influence of the narrative. They try to give the rule a practical basis by suggesting that it requires that the fruit of all newly planted trees be removed for the first three years because it is not especially good fruit. See Josephus, *Jewish Antiquities* 4.226; Philo, *De plant.* 95–100; *De virt.* 156. N. H. Snaith refers to the rule's "sound agricultural principle"; *Leviticus and Numbers*, CB (London, 1967), 133.

Second, the Israelites' festival is to be delayed until their fourth year in the land. The fruit from their newly planted trees is to be regarded as uncircumcised and therefore taboo. The stricture thus puts a period of time between their entry into the land of Canaan and the harvesting of their trees. The reason for the hiatus is probably that the Canaanites subjected their harvests to their own religious rites, and it was deemed important that the Israelite festival should have no association with such rites. In the story God is said to have caused the Shechemites to pursue vengeance against Abimelech, and they proceeded to do so in the context of their festival. It might have been important for the lawgiver to indicate to the recipients of his laws that the fact that God directed events even among the Shechemites did not mean that God approved of such Canaanite festivities. The statement in the rule "I am Yahweh" makes clear that an allegiance to Yahweh is being called for, not one to a Canaanite deity in the house of the god where the Shechemite festival was held.

Third, why does the rule attribute to the fruit of trees the negative feature of lack of circumcision? The Canaanite context that prompted the rule would appear to explain this attribution. The Canaanites were uncircumcised, and the lawgiver's aim was to remove any association with them in Israelite life. Why, however, did the human practice of circumcision come to be relevant to the product of a fruit tree? Again the Abimelech story may prove illuminating. Before Abimelech's downfall his one surviving brother, Jotham, communicates his opposition to Abimelech's rule by means of a fable in which trees appoint a bramble as king over them (Judg 9: 7–21).

In the fable Abimelech is the bramble that is appointed to rule over the other trees.[22] Unlike the fruit of the olive tree, fig tree, and vines in the fable, over whom the bramble comes to rule, Abimelech represents a tree whose fruit is worthless, and whose potential for fire and hence for destruction is very real. After three years his reign does indeed come to a fiery end (Judg 9:52–57). The particular association between the Canaanite background of Abimelech and

---

22. Joseph too is compared to a tree in Gen 49:22.

the description of him as a worthless tree might, then, account for the odd link between the idea of circumcision and a fruit tree.

As a Shechemite, Abimelech would have been uncircumcised (like the Shechemites in the story of Dinah's seduction by one of them in Genesis 34). If the half-Canaanite, half-Israelite Abimelech had succeeded in becoming ruler of all Israel the threat to Israel's national identity would have been enormous. Although interpreters dispute the significance of the statement, the text in Judg 9:22 actually states that "Abimelech ruled over Israel three years."[23] The Deuteronomic law about the institution of kingship warns about the possibility that someone like Abimelech might become king over Israel. By typically picking up from a tradition, namely, the one about Abimelech, it sets down the odd requirement that the Israelites should not appoint a foreigner over them who "is not thy brother" (Deut 17:15). It is warning against appointing someone like Abimelech, a foreigner and not a true brother, as king.[24]

The reason that the fruit for the first three years after Israel's entry into the land cannot be touched is, I am suggesting, to recall directly the actual threat posed by Abimelech's kingship over all Israel. His father had declined kingship for himself and his offspring and had affirmed Yahweh's rule (Judg 8:22). Contrary to his father's wishes, Abimelech reigned for three years, and his reign is characterized as the barren rule of one useless tree over other fruitful ones. The law, in effect, says that the trees newly planted in the acquired land of Canaan are to be treated as if they are barren. Their fruit cannot be touched. Eventually, in the harvest of the fourth year, the Israelites are to celebrate Yahweh, that is, affirm his providence on their behalf. Only after such affirmation can the Israelites consume the fruit. We might compare how the avoidance of leavened bread during the Passover festival is intended to recall a historical event—

---

23. The tendency is to explain it away by claiming that he is but a local military overlord. See, for example, R. G. Boling, *Judges*, AB (New York, 1975), 175. But the text does not say this, and the issue of the Israelites' wish for a king to reign over them, specifically, a member of Gideon's family, is a major feature of the traditions in Judges (Judg 8:22, 23; 9:2, 8–15). The fable's reference to olives, figs, and vines, that is, to landed estates, also suggests that the whole of Israel is meant.

24. See Carmichael, *Law and Narrative*, 100.

namely, the haste with which the Israelites had to leave Egypt (Deut 16:3)—or, how the rule about the forgotten harvest sheaf in Deut 24:19–22 is intended to recall the first time the Israelites were delivered from famine because of Joseph's policy on behalf of the hungry in Egypt.[25]

The rule about the uncircumcised fruit raises the interesting issue of the "deep" meaning that I attribute to it. I claim that it makes no sense to give the rule the practical meaning—as has been the standard way of reading it—that sound agricultural practice requires a farmer to discard the fruit of new trees for a period of three years. For one thing, farmers know what to do with the fruit of new trees without needing to be told in a directive. What the standard reading of the rule fails to do is give proper significance to the weighty language used by the lawgiver when he speaks of the Israelites entering the land and when he describes the fruit of the first three years' crop as uncircumcised. My solution addresses the significance of the rule's language. The rule, I claim, directs historical memory to the time of Israel's entry into the land, in particular, to the involvement of Gideon with the Canaanites. The rule serves as a warning to Israelites to avoid loss of their identity, for example, by giving themselves over to someone like Abimelech who is as much Canaanite as Israelite. Its curious formulation is one indication of the richness of its background. In real life the lawgiver may well have been familiar with a customary practice whereby farmers discarded the fruit of newly planted trees or treated it differently from the fruit of maturer ones.[26] This awareness, however, would have been but a stimulus to his imagining Moses' concern with the occasion of Israel's taking up residence in Canaan—when it was not just a matter of new fruit but new fruit that had negative connotations because of Canaanite influences at the time.

25. See Carmichael, *Law and Narrative*, 282–88.

26. This awareness seems to underlie the rule in CH 60: "If, when a seignior gave a field to a gardener to set out an orchard, the gardener set out the orchard, he shall develop the orchard for four years; in the fifth year the owner of the orchard and the gardener shall divide equally, with the owner of the orchard receiving his preferential share."

Leviticus 19:26a

Ye shall not eat upon the blood.

The rule's language is cryptic. The standard translation—"You shall not eat any flesh with the blood in it"—is, I think, wrong. The rule's literal meaning militates against such a meaning. There is no reference to the animal's flesh, and the preposition ʿal, "upon," and not ʿim, "with," is used. The reference to eating but not to what is eaten, and the reference to blood but not to its source should caution against our making a direct link between the eating and the blood, as if both are thought of as being consumed together. The rule's curious formulation requires a full explanation, not a rationalization, which in effect is what the standard translations and commentaries give.

This rule about eating follows the food rule prohibiting eating uncircumcised fruit, so that there is a tantalizing connection of some kind between the two rules. One is even tempted, but I think the temptation should be resisted, to see a link between the blood in the second rule and the notion of circumcision in the first. The way to comprehend these rules is not to use the immediate context for illumination. Rather we have to scrutinize the narrative context that prompted the rule.

The same incident that accounts for the rule about the fruit trees also raises the issue that prompts the rule forbidding eating "upon the blood." During the vintage festival the Shechemites celebrate, they eat and drink and revile Abimelech in the house of their god (Judg 9:27). Wine or the juice of grapes is a well-established metaphor for blood. Gideon's history provides a good illustration. When he successfully routs the Midianites, the Ephraimites—who, like Gideon, are direct descendants of Joseph—are furious that they are not asked to be involved. Gideon had, however, given them the opportunity to slay the two Midianite princes, Oreb and Zeeb. In response to their outburst, Gideon asks them rhetorically, "Is not the gleaning of the grapes of Ephraim [the two princes killed by the Ephraimites] better than the vintage of Abiezer [Gideon's rout of the Midianites]?" (Judg 8:2). This language well conveys the link between the juice of grapes and the blood of one's enemies. Other biblical authors depict Yahweh's wrath as a wine press (Isa 63:3; Lam 1:15; and Rev 14:10); that is, his wrath brings destruction on his enemies.[27]

In his rule the lawgiver had the eating and drinking of the She-chemites in focus, and what he prohibits is any Israelite activity that reflects a comparable link between eating and the slaughter of an enemy. In the story God uses these Shechemites "to lay the blood of" Abimelech's brothers upon ('al) Abimelech (Judg 9:24). The lawgiver would have approved of this activity, but he did not accept in an Israelite context what the Shechemites do at their wine festival, namely, eating with a view to preparing to kill an enemy.

I still have to explain, however, the rule's curious formulation and how exactly its language is to be understood. The crucial observation is that the lawgiver also kept in focus the story of Joseph and his brothers. After all, it was his scrutiny of the Joseph story, specifically, the link between pressed grapes and the butler's fate, that got him in the first instance onto the incident about the grapes and Abimelech's fate in Judges 9. The lawgiver looked at a comparable, prior incident in Joseph's life.

The juxtaposition of eating and shedding someone's blood shows up in the Joseph story for the first time in Israelite history, and it was characteristic of biblical lawgivers always to turn to the first indication of an unacceptable practice.[28] The brothers seek to kill

27. In Gen 49:11 the blood of grapes refers to the death of Judah's sons. See Calum Carmichael, *Women, Law, and the Genesis Traditions* (Edinburgh, 1979), 63, 64. The battle against the Midianites also provides an example of a symbolic action in which drinking water, in this instance, is associated with defeating an enemy. In a test to determine which men should proceed to battle, those who drink water after the fashion of dogs are selected. Biblical dogs are ferocious.

28. Compare how Jezebel tells her husband King Ahab that he should go and eat while she arranges the murder of Naboth, who had refused to sell Ahab his vineyard (1 Kgs 21:1–7). The later episode in which King Jehu sits down to a meal after he has her slain for her role in the murder of Naboth, but before arranging for her burial (2 Kgs 9:30–34), recalls Jezebel's order to Ahab which began the events that led to the murder of Naboth. In this light Jehu's eating is a scornful reminder of Jezebel's command to her husband to eat and, by implication, await the death of Naboth. See Carmichael, *Spirit of Biblical Law*, 116.

Joseph and then to cover up the killing by claiming that a wild beast has devoured him. The oldest brother, Reuben, opposes their plan and appeals to them not to shed Joseph's blood (Gen 37:22). They, however, proceed to assault Joseph, strip him of his coat, and cast him into a pit. They then sit down to eat (Gen 37:25), still intending to kill him despite Reuben's opposition. Judah then comes up with an equally outrageous scheme: they should not in fact shed their brother's blood because there is no profit in doing so; rather, they should sell him to an approaching caravan of Ishmaelites. Presumably, if this caravan had not appeared they might well have proceeded to slay Joseph.

The Joseph story thus sets out a situation that anticipates what the Shechemites do: over a meal a group of men plan bloodshed. It is this scene in the Joseph story which prompted the rule's formulation—no eating upon the blood, that is, where the focus is the slaughter of a person. The preposition ʿal, "upon," frequently bears a hostile sense: for example, in Judg 16:12, "the Philistines are upon thee Samson" and, in Judg 9:31, when the Shechemites try to kill Abimelech they "fortify [or stir up] the city upon him." As for the term *dam*, "blood," in a Deuteronomic rule (Deut 17:8) there is a provision about offenses "between blood and blood" (*ben dam le-dam*). The reference is to persons who have been slain. The term *dam* by itself can therefore refer to the blood of a human victim, and that is how it is to be understood in this rule: "You shall not eat upon the blood [of a person]." The verb "to eat" (ʾakal), by the way, frequently has the hostile sense of devouring an enemy (for example, Deut 32:42; 2 Sam 2:26).[29]

Contrary to the standard view, I do not think that this particular Levitical rule is yet another prohibition against eating meat that still contains blood. The lawgiver thought of the occasion when the brothers of Joseph sit down to eat and plot his fate. Why did he pay particular attention to this incident? These brothers are sons of Israel and, apart from the fundamental wrongness of their action, what they do too closely foreshadows the more fully developed Canaanite

---

29. For ʿal in a hostile sense, and examples of ʾkal in the sense of "to devour" an enemy, see BDB, 757–58 and 37 respectively. In English we sometimes refer to a man as a "young blood."

practice he found in the tradition about the Shechemites. The law-giver prohibits Canaanite practices not because anything they do was automatically to be opposed but because anything he found among his own Israelite group that smacks of Canaanite ways invited condemnation. The rule therefore condemns eating after the fashion of the Shechemites while focusing on the blood of an actual or potential victim of slaughter. Like many proverbs, the rule picks up on a pattern of conduct that recurs throughout the generations. A Priestly lawgiver with his special interest in blood would understandably have condemned the practice. Food rules in the Bible are intended to contribute a measure of ethical, religious, and ritual distinctiveness to an Israelite's way of life.

Once the rule is understood in the way I have described, an incident in the time of King Saul takes on more significance than has been hitherto realized. In a battle against the Philistines, Saul lays an oath on his people not to eat food before he has been avenged on his enemies. After the successful rout of the Philistines the Israelites are faint from hunger, take the animals they capture as spoil, and "slaughtered them on the ground; and . . . ate upon the blood" (1 Sam 14:32). Again the translations and commentaries understand the offense to be the same as those prohibited in Gen 9:4 and Deut 12:23, eating the animals with their blood. But the text does not say this. They ate upon ('*al*) the blood—after they had slaughtered the animals, not when they were slaughtering them. The implication is, I suggest, that the eating upon the blood, as in the rule in Lev 19:26, refers not to the Israelites' eating blood on the occasion but to their celebrating the slaughter of their enemies by observing the blood that flows to the ground from the slaughtered animals.

One should not lose sight of the cryptic nature of the rule. It distorts the sense and devalues the sophistication of the lawgiver to give it the meaning "You shall not eat anything with its blood." The sense is, "You shall not celebrate killing, however justified, as in war, by festive eating." The cryptic language serves to warn against taking the rule out of its context. It is thus crucial to underline the assumption that originally the lawgiver's scrutiny of the narrative histories produced the rules.

Leviticus 19:26b

Neither shall ye practise divination or soothsaying.

In his move from the rule about blood to the next rule about divination we can follow exactly how the lawgiver has proceeded. The topic at issue is again vengeance, and the focus is the Joseph story, in particular, on Joseph's retribution against his brothers, who, in getting rid of him, do in fact go on to use the blood of an animal to make it appear that he has died.

Recall that Joseph's dreams drive his brothers to conspire to kill him: "And we shall see," they exclaim as he approaches them, "what will become of his dreams" (Gen 37:20). Dreams belong to the world of the occult and the mysterious. The brothers devise an effect, blood on Joseph's garment, to counter another effect, Joseph's dreams. Thus they use the blood of a slaughtered animal on Joseph's special garment to trick their father into believing that a wild beast has killed Joseph: "Torn, torn is Joseph," laments Jacob (Gen 37:17). By interpreting the cloth as containing the sign of a wild beast's activity, Jacob concludes that Joseph has died. The brothers' ruse is such that they successfully rid themselves of their enemy without suggesting that they were in any way involved. Joseph matches this make-believe when he later tricks the brothers by falsely suggesting that an external agency, a divining cup, is responsible for their fate.

In formulating his rule against divination, then, the lawgiver noted Joseph's act of retaliation against his brothers which mirrors their specific act against him.[30] To avenge what had been done to him when they used his special clothing to deceive their father, the disguised Joseph tricks his brothers. He does so, significantly, by means of cloth sacks when they leave Egypt with the food for their family back in Canaan. Joseph, unknown to the brothers, has his silver divining cup placed in Benjamin's sack of grain.[31] It is a deliberate

---

30. Other interpreters comment on the mirroring character of Joseph's act, for example, David Daube, "Rechtsgedanken in den Erzählungen des Pentateuchs," in *Von Ugarit nach Qumran: Festschrift für Otto Eissfeldt*, ed. J. Hempel and L. Rost (Berlin, 1958), 38. Redford states, "By thus falsifying evidence Joseph has committed the same violation as that perpetrated by his brothers with his coat!"; *Story of Joseph*, 74.

31. So cloth again plays a role in a deception.

move by Joseph to accuse them of stealing not just a cup but one that has magical properties enabling him to divine (Gen 44:1–5).

The same term *nahaš* (*Piel*), "to divine, observe signs," is found in both the law and the story. Although Joseph's claim to divine with the cup is a false one, what is true at another and more decisive level is the unfolding reality of his dreams. Because of the deception with the sack, the brothers believe in Joseph's magical powers, and they tear their garments and fall before Joseph on the ground (Gen 44:13, 14)—just as Joseph's dreams had predicted in Gen 37:7–10. Moreover, as part of their response to this trickery, Judah tells Joseph about the fate of their brother, that is, about Joseph himself (Gen 44:18–28). In other words, at this point in the narrative we return to the issue of blood on Joseph's garment, precisely the issue that belongs to the context out of which the preceding rule against eating "upon the blood" was forged. The blood the brothers placed on Joseph's garment successfully deceives Jacob into believing what they claim it signified, just as Joseph's placement of the divining cup successfully deceives the brothers into believing what Joseph claims it signifies, that he has rare powers at his disposal. The lawgiver, opposed to the brothers' use of the animal's blood, is equally opposed to Joseph's use of the divining cup to suggest that he, an Israelite, is given to divination.

I conclude by turning to a crucial aspect of my approach, that is, how to explain the arrangement of the material that is set out in the texts. Why did the lawgiver add "soothsaying" (*'anan* [*polel*]) to divination in his prohibition? He could have cited a number of other practices, for a variety of magical individuals are listed in a rule in Deut 18:10, 11: one who passes children through fire, augur, diviner, sorcerer, one who casts spells, medium, familiar spirit, and necromancer. In the narrative Joseph's divining cup is *not* available to him because of its supposed theft by his brothers. Yet from the viewpoint of the deceived brothers Joseph "knows" that they stole it and exactly where it is to be found. So from their stance they presumably recognize that Joseph has some means of prediction at his disposal other than the divining cup to ascertain its whereabouts. The lawgiver, setting aside the fraudulent story told to the brothers, thinks of the form of prognostication that is associated with soothsaying. This feature of the story, then, about another form of fore-telling the future, explains why he added soothsaying to divination.

Always abreast of the history of the generations, the lawgiver would have been alert to future instances of the practices sooth-saying and divination. That is why he took seriously the incident in the Joseph narrative despite its fraudulent aspect. In the historical narratives there are two references to soothsaying. One is in the story about Abimelech, in which there is a reference to the Diviner's oak, Elon-meonenim (Judg 9:37),[32] and the other is from the time of the kings when King Manasseh resorts to soothsaying (2 Kgs 21:6). Instances of the practice of divination in the time of the kings are 2 Kgs 17:17; 21:6 (cp. 1 Kgs 20:33). Just as the brothers are taken in by this Egyptian's (Joseph's) deceptions, so later Israelites are to be on guard against the deceptive practices of foreigners.

In regard to divination and soothsaying the lawgiver would have found it particularly important to underscore the falsity of Joseph's machinations. The idea that he predicted events by means of his cup or by some other comparable means could not be encouraged be-cause a fundamental feature of the Joseph story is that he indeed pre-dicted events by means of his dreams, which are inspired by God. The lawgiver had to be of two minds about Joseph's dreams. On the one hand, they represent divine providence, with Joseph as the agent for the rescue of his family and his people. On the other hand, they represent, on the face of it, mysteries that could be aligned with the forbidden foreign practices of divination, soothsaying, and the like against which his rules take a firm stand.

It is taken for granted that priests are interested in mysteries, but what form these mysteries take is often far from clear. Some in-sight into the interests of biblical priests comes from the above rules and the traditions that prompted their formulation. It is surely no accident that what captured the attention of the Priestly lawgiver is that the rules and their influencing traditions are about particular ways of interpreting certain phenomena. Potiphar's wife uses Joseph's garment so that her husband will interpret it as signifying Joseph's

---

32. On the extent of divinatory practices in the Gideon-Abimelech narrative, see Boling, *Judges*, 160, 161.

attempt to rape her. Joseph's brothers soak his garment in blood so that their father will interpret it as signifying Joseph's death. The use to which wine or the juice of grapes is put determines a man's fate (the butler's and Abimelech's). Joseph's divining cup is intended to convey that he can predict events. Another form of prediction, soothsaying, suggests that such a practice can locate a stolen object. Joseph's dreams and Jotham's fable are endowed with special significance such that the future can be interpreted from them. The Priestly lawgiver, then, was alert to those who, illegitimately to his mind in most instances, devise phenomena that require a particular interpretation or claim to possess special powers in interpreting other phenomena. For him, presumably, such powers were primarily the province of his priestly class.

The Sequence of Topics in the Narratives for the Laws in Leviticus 19:20–26

Like the preceding rules on mixtures (Lev 19:19), the rule about illicit sex with a bondwoman has the topic of Egyptian influence on the Israelites, Joseph in particular, under consideration. The Egyptian, Potiphar's wife, attempts to seduce him when he is a bondman in her household. The lawgiver lays out circumstances in which, contrastingly, a male is the offending party who has sex with a bondwoman contracted to marry another Israelite.

A Canaanite threat to Israel's identity followed the Egyptian threat. The book of Judges recounts the mixing of Joseph's direct descendants with the Canaanites. The union between Gideon (of the tribe of Manasseh, Joseph's son) and a Canaanite bondwoman produces Abimelech, who grows up to become a Canaanite ruler claiming rulership over the Israelites themselves. In the struggle to put an end to Abimelech's ambitions, a Canaanite harvest festival becomes a rallying point against him. During its celebration the worshipers eat and drink and curse Abimelech. Two features of the episode engaged the lawgiver. First, in his rule about uncircumcised fruit he institutionalizes an Israelite harvest festival that requires the fruit of the first three years after the Israelites' entry into the land of

Canaan to remain uneaten so that there is no association with previous Canaanite festivals. Food becomes a marker of cultural identity. Second, opposing the way in which the Canaanites link festive
eating to the slaughter of Abimelech, the lawgiver turned back to
an earlier, analogous example when Joseph's brothers seek the life
of Joseph. Over a meal they conspire to be rid of him and go on to
use the blood of an animal to trick Jacob into thinking that Joseph
is dead. The lawgiver sets down the rule not "to eat upon [against]
the blood [of a person]," that is, there should be no association between an Israelite's consumption of food and the slaughter of an enemy. The hocus-pocus involved in such an association prompted
the lawgiver to turn to Joseph's own magical practices in Egypt
when, pursuing vengeance against his enemies, he claims that he
has powers to divine by means of a drinking cup. Not only does he
claim supernatural insight into the future by using his divining cup
but, in its absence, he indicates his use of other magical agents to
foretell an outcome. The lawgiver set down the two rules prohibiting divination and soothsaying.

CHAPTER 6

Netherworlds: Leviticus 19:27–37

THE rules of the Pentateuch constitute commentary on the biblical narratives. No obvious change of focus in that commentary is discernible such that I might claim that the lawgiver's agenda was to work his way through one distinct topic after another. Although such clear-cut divisions by legal topic are not detectable, it is nonetheless decidedly the case that topics are pursued and different facets of them taken up in the rules. In those that I discussed in the previous chapter about eating "upon the blood" and divinatory practices, one such topic was the relationship between the living and the dead. The major motif in the Joseph story is that, from Jacob's perspective, Joseph is dead, whereas in fact he is not. Time and again incidents occur because Joseph conceals the fact that he is indeed very much alive. This motif, both in the Joseph story and in related narratives, proves relevant to the rules I analyze in this chapter.

Leviticus 19:27, 28

Ye shall not round the corners of your heads, neither shalt thou mar the corners of thy beard. Ye shall not make any cuttings in your flesh for the dead, nor print any marks upon you: I am Yahweh.

To account for these rules about mourning we stay with the Joseph story. There are consequences to Joseph's planting his divining cup in Benjamin's cloth sack, the incident responsible for the lawgiver's setting down the preceding rule about divinatory practices. After the brothers are caught with Joseph's cup, Judah tells (the disguised) Joseph about the reaction their father is likely to have should Joseph compel Benjamin to remain behind in Egypt rather than return with his other brothers. For that is what Joseph has decreed for Benjamin.

Judah recalls how Jacob reacted to the news of their other brother's (Joseph's) death; how Jacob recognized that Joseph's blood-soaked garment signified that his son's body had been "torn, torn" (Gen 44: 28); and how, if Benjamin is taken from him, "ye [the brothers] shall bring down my [Jacob's] gray hairs with sorrow to the grave" (vs. 29, 31). On the actual occasion of Joseph's presumed death Jacob rent his clothes and put sackcloth on his loins (Gen 37:34).[1] It is conceivable that the narrator intended that Joseph's use of the sacks to deceive his brothers is to remind them of their father's use of sack when mourning Joseph's death. However that may be, the role of garments in mourning connects with the role of cloth or clothing in the parts of the narratives which inspired the preceding rules about blood and divination, namely, the brothers' deceptive use of Joseph's blood-soaked garment and Joseph's deceptive planting of his divining cup in Benjamin's sack.

There are two links between the rules about mourning and the narrative about Jacob's reaction to his loss of Joseph. There is first an association between the hair of the mourning Jacob and the grave, where the idea that his hair will end up in the grave is explicitly mentioned. Other biblical contexts indicate that certain mourning customs involved cutting the hair of the head or the beard as a sign of mourning (Isa 3:24; 22:12; Jer 16:6; Ezek 7:18; Amos 8:10: "I [God] will turn your [Israel's] feasts into mourning . . . and I will bring . . . baldness upon every head").

The Priestly lawgiver sat in judgment on the entire range of

---

1. The author of Jubilees sees the sons' deed against their father as the worst aspect of their offense (Jub 34:12–19). See R. H. Charles, *The Old Testament Pseudepigrapha* (New York, 1985), 2:65.

Israelite history up to and including the end of the monarchy. Jacob's situation is the first in that history to raise a problem about mourning, and it drew the lawgiver's attention to Israelite customs after Jacob's time. Like the Deuteronomic lawgiver (Deut 14:1), the Priestly lawgiver also prohibits them. Both do so despite the fact that these mourning customs were observed among the Israelites down to at least the time of Jeremiah. Why should they do so?

The practices were, to be sure, also those of the surrounding cultures, for example, Moabite and Philistine (Isa 15:2; Jer 47:5). Both lawgivers may then have opposed them on account of such association with foreign cultures. There is, however, a more fundamental reason why the two lawgivers opposed the practices. I have argued elsewhere that the main reason for the Deuteronomic prohibition is the requirement that the mourner keep life and death apart by not imprinting upon his live person "the visible tokens of death,"[2] that is, the removal of his hair and the marks on his body.[3] When Jacob mourns Joseph, he mourns, albeit unwittingly, not a dead Joseph but a Joseph who is still alive. To mourn a living person is to confuse life and death.[4] The Priestly lawgiver shared this concern to keep them apart. By noting the odd confusion over Jacob's mourning someone, Joseph, who is in fact still alive, he was doubly alert to the entanglement of life and death inherent in these conventional mourning customs.

Alternatively, the rule may be like so many other biblical rules in that it was intended to recall a significant event in Israel's history, especially its beginnings. If we assume that the standard custom among the Israelites was to tear their hair and cut their bodies when mourning the dead, the rule in question would have been arresting

2. S. R. Driver's way of expressing it; *Deuteronomy*, ICC, 3d ed. (Edinburgh, 1902), 156.

3. On the reasons for opposing the customary practices, see Calum Carmichael, "On Separating Life and Death: An Explanation of Some Biblical Laws," *HTR* 69 (1976), 4; also Calum Carmichael, *The Spirit of Biblical Law* (Athens, Ga., 1996), 129–30.

4. On this feature as a key to understanding the rule in Deut 21:10–14 about the captive woman who has to mourn parents who may not be dead, see Carmichael, *Spirit of Biblical Law*, 134–37.

in character because it prohibits the normal practice. The point of doing so would have been to remind the rule's audience of the first time when the nation's eponymous ancestor (Jacob/Israel) mourns a son. Instead of mourning a son who is dead, he in effect mourns a live person. To deny the Israelites the customary practice of imprinting on their person marks associated with the dead is to focus attention on the custom's jarring juxtaposition of life and death—and recall that the first Israelite (Jacob) is forced into a similar confusion about life and death.[5]

I turn to the second link between the rule about mourning and the narrative about Jacob's reaction to his loss of Joseph. Although in the story there is no mention of Jacob's cutting his body, he mourns a son whose dead body has been badly torn. The fact that Jacob tears his clothes suggests that when a man grieves he may at the same time proceed to tear or make marks on his body. Whether Jacob grieved in this way or not, we do know that it was often customary for mourners to cut their own bodies to mourn the dead, especially those torn at death. Four texts in Jeremiah refer to such practice, for example, Jer 16:6: "Neither shall men lament for them, nor cut themselves, nor make themselves bald for them"; compare 41:5; 47:5; 48:37.[6] In these texts the mutilation of the mourner's body is in response to people who have been mutilated at death, by the sword, for example. Jacob's situation has again drawn the lawgiver's attention to those practices by which a mourner does proceed to imprint marks on his own body in order to be in sympathetic contact with the torn person. Like D (Deut 14:1), P prohibits mourning rites that require bodily mutilation.

Another factor in P's setting down certain prohibitions about mourning may well have been his negative response to the fact that both Jacob and Joseph are buried according to Egyptian custom

---

5. Compare the punishment in England in which a person has his effigy burned and the funeral service read over him. See E. P. Thompson, *Customs in Common: Studies in Traditional Popular Culture* (New York, 1993), 480. King David mourned his child by Bathsheba before it died and behaved in a contrary manner after it died. See Carmichael, *Spirit of Biblical Law*, 154–55.

6. For Canaanite examples, see Michael Coogan, *Stories from Ancient Canaan* (Philadelphia, 1978), 109.

(Gen 50:1–14, 26).[7] Such foreign practice would have elicited comparison with later, unacceptable foreign practices.[8] The statement in the rule "I am Yahweh" may point to a requirement that the Israelites drop foreign ways and customs from their mourning rites.

Leviticus 19:29, 30

Do not prostitute thy daughter, to cause her to be a whore; lest the land fall to whoredom, and the land become full of wickedness. Ye shall keep my sabbaths, and reverence my sanctuary: I am Yahweh.

It is again difficult to see why a lawgiver switched from a concern with mourning practices to a rule against prostituting one's daughter. There is an explanation. The rule about the mourning rites has in focus the deception by Joseph's brothers when they use his garment to cause their father to lament Joseph's death. The rule about prostitution concerns a father and his daughter, and it has in focus a similar deception because it too involves both a garment and a man's dead son. The deception is recounted in the story of Judah and Tamar (Genesis 38), which follows on from and interrupts the sequel to Jacob's mourning Joseph (Genesis 37).

Before turning to the precise nature of the deception in Genesis 38, I wish to point out that the two deceptions are also related in that Judah has a central role in each: in the first deception involving Joseph's garment in Genesis 37, Judah convinces his brothers to rid themselves of Joseph not by killing him but by another means. In Genesis 44 Judah is the spokesman for the brothers in the presence of the disguised Joseph. Just before Joseph reveals himself to his brothers, he hears Judah's account of the family history. Judah re-

7. See August Dillmann's comments, *Genesis, Critically and Exegetically Expounded* (Edinburgh, 1897), 483–88, 491–92; and D. J. Redford, *A Study of the Biblical Story of Joseph, SVT* (Leiden, 1970), 22. Redford states that the Joseph story "blandly ignores the difficulties inherent in the encounter of Hebrews and pagans" (22 n. 3). He may well be right, but the biblical lawgivers take up the issues.

8. See S. R. Driver, *Deuteronomy,* 156–57, on the extent of such practices. On early Roman provisions that reflected hostility to Etruscan ritual, see David Daube, *Roman Law: Linguistic, Social, and Philosophical Aspects* (Edinburgh, 1969), 124.

counts what allegedly happened to Joseph: how he had died and how his father had mourned him. The story that Judah tells in Genesis 44 after Joseph plants his divining cup in Benjamin's sack is the context out of which the lawgiver fashioned his preceding rule about mourning rites.

In the second deception in Genesis 38 Tamar deceives Judah by removing her widow's garments and disguising herself in the clothes of a prostitute to seduce Judah. It is a deception involving a garment. Judah, in fact, is responsible for his daughter-in-law's resort to prostitution. By not sending his youngest son Shelah into Tamar to conceive a child for her dead husband, he fails to have the levirate custom fulfilled. She consequently takes the matter into her own hands, to act on behalf of the dead, namely, her dead husband. So it is for a dead person that she engages in the deceptive action.

Tamar's move is thus comparable to the brothers' action in communicating that Joseph is dead because each time a garment is used to perpetuate a deception concerning the dead. Tamar becomes a prostitute to make herself pregnant by Judah. The lawgiver took up the topic from this incident. In circumstances less extraordinary than Tamar's, a daughter more than a daughter-in-law was likely to have been pushed into the trade of prostitution by a father. In typical fashion the lawgiver looked at the idiosyncratic development in the story and set down a comparable development in less dramatic circumstances.

There is another dimension to the rule that directly brings up the issue of Israelite daughters' becoming prostitutes. The lawgiver was fearful that the land would become full of wickedness should the Israelites resort to prostitution. Such a concern came from his thinking of the example of Judah: how by taking up with a Canaanite cult prostitute—that is how Tamar is depicted (Gen 38:21, 22)—he produces descendants through children born to her; and how cultic prostitution became a feature of later Israelite life. The daughters of Israelites became prostitutes (Deut 23: 17, 18; Hos 4:12–14; Amos 2:7).[9]

---

9. Driver (*Deuteronomy*, 264) rightly speculates that although the rule in Lev 19: 29 about prostituting a daughter is general in wording, it was aimed primarily at the practice of cultic prostitution. In Gen 38:15, 21, 22, 24 Tamar is described as both a *zonah*, "prostitute," and a *qedešah*, "cult prostitute."

The term for "wickedness" in the rule is *zimmah*. It is used one other time in the Holiness Code for a man's union with certain in-laws (Lev 18:17). Judah's intercourse with Tamar is not just that of a man with a prostitute but also of a father with a daughter-in-law. Hence the lawgiver uses the term *zimmah* in these two rules (sex with a woman, her daughter, and her granddaughter—the rule derived from Tamar's relationships with Judah's family[10]—and prostituting a daughter).

Following a rule about prostitution there is a rule calling for the Israelites to observe the sabbath. Why should there be such an apparently unrelated move? The explanation is that the lawgiver continued to focus on Judah and Tamar.

Judah and Tamar share the same problem. There is no offspring, in Tamar's case, to provide security for her future, and in Judah's case to continue his line, that is, an Israelite line. But prostitution—especially with its Canaanite cultic overtones in Tamar's initiative—for the purpose of procreation is contrary to the original order of creation as set out for the Israelites in the Priestly view of it in Genesis 1. The sabbath is a reminder of that order, part of which is the blessing on human beings to produce children (Gen 1:28).

A major feature of the sabbath in Genesis 1 is that God rests after six days of sustained creativity. When human beings seek to be fertile they are participating in the original order of creation. As the English word well brings out, procreation is thus bound up with creation. That is why in the decalogue the honor that is owing to parents as one's progenitors is juxtaposed with the requirement to observe the sabbath.[11] An improper way of accomplishing procreation is the example of the Canaanite cult prostitute Tamar when she seeks to perpetuate an Israelite line. The means she employs to become pregnant offends against the created order. Elsewhere P expresses the view that the institution of the sabbath serves to remind the Israelites that they must show proper regard for that order (Exod 20:8–11; 31:12–17). The issues of prostitution and procrea-

10. See Chapter 1 on Lev 18:17.

11. See my discussion in Chapter 3 of the jointly presented rules in Lev 19:3 about fear of a mother and a father and the observance of the sabbath.

tion which arise from the Judah and Tamar story account for the lawgiver's placement of the sabbath rule just after the rule about prostituting a daughter.

A rule about reverencing the Israelite sanctuary (*miqdaš*) follows the sabbath command. Why? The explanation is that Tamar's role as a cult prostitute made the lawgiver aware of the subsequent role of cult prostitutes in the life of his nation. In later history such prostitutes, especially the male variety—for example, 1 Kgs 14:24; 15:12 about sodomites—are indeed attached to the Israelite sanctuary, the temple (Deut 23:17, 18; 2 Kgs 23:7, cp. Hos 4:14). Because Tamar furnishes the first example of wrongful cultic influence on the Israelites, her example brings into review the desecration of the later Israelite sanctuary by cult prostitutes. This is the background against which the lawgiver calls for a reverencing of the Israelite sanctuary.

In the rule the term for the sanctuary is *miqdaš*, "sacred place." Tamar is a *qedešah*, "sacred woman." The terms *zonah*, "prostitute," and *zanah*, "to be a prostitute," are also used of her (Gen 38: 15, 24). In the preceding rule aimed at preventing prostitution by forbidding a father to encourage his daughter to become a prostitute, *zanah*, "to be a prostitute" is the term used. The terms *zanah* and *miqdaš* in the two rules about prostituting a daughter and reverencing the sanctuary therefore reflect the language of the story, Tamar as both a *zonah* and a *qedešah*. A feature of the story is how a friend of Judah's unsuccessfully traverses the land in search of Judah's prostitute (Gen 38:20–23). Although at this time the Canaanites inhabit the land, Judah's presence in it foreshadows its later Israelite takeover and consequent exposure to Canaanite ways. In his rules Moses anticipates later developments. That is why he thinks ahead to the land "falling into harlotry."

Leviticus 19:31

Regard not them that have familiar spirits, neither seek after mediums, to be defiled by them: I am Yahweh your God.

Biblical authors characterized cultic prostitution as a foreign phenomenon. The traditions underlying the previous rule (a daughter's
prostitution) about Judah and Tamar and the history of the kings
bring out this view. The example of Tamar's resort to acting the part
of a cult prostitute prompted, I submit, the lawgiver to turn to
other foreign religious influences on the Israelites. The two cited—
'*oboth* and *yed'onim*—are about those who traffic in ghosts and
spirits of the dead, mentioned in Isa 8:19 (consulting the dead on
behalf of the living); 29:4; and 1 Sam 28:3, 7.[12] Why, out of many
such unacceptable foreign activities—there is a long list in Deut 18:
10, 11—did the lawgiver single out these two practices that are associated with the dead?

Tamar, almost certainly a Canaanite, acts not only the part of a
cult prostitute, but she also acts on behalf of her dead husband, Er,
half-Israelite, half-Canaanite himself. To raise a child for a dead husband by the levirate custom may or may not have been acceptable
to the P lawgiver,[13] but any other action, either on behalf of the
dead or on behalf of someone seeking contact with the dead, is certainly unacceptable to him. As his preceding rule brings out, Tamar's
playing the role of a cult prostitute in order to conceive a child for
her dead husband is not acceptable. Indeed, it would have been
doubly unacceptable if, as Karl Elliger and Walther Zimmerli argue,
children by cult prostitutes such as Tamar were sacrificed to Molech, the god of the netherworld.[14]

The lawgiver made, I suggest, a typical move at this point in the
presentation of his rules. He found in the history of the traditions
available to him another example of a woman who involves herself
with the dead in a generation after Tamar's, namely, the woman of
Endor who possesses "a familiar spirit" and whom King Saul uses

12. A familiar spirit, either in the sense of a spirit of a deceased relative or close ac-
quaintance, or the necromancer himself or herself, is meant. J. Lust argues that '*oboth*
and *yed'onim* are types of spirits and not those who deal in them; "On Wizards
and Prophets," in *Studies in Prophecy*, ed. G. W. Anderson, *SVT* 26 (Leiden, 1974),
133–42.

13. See my doubts about P's position, Chapter 1 on Lev 18:16.

14. See Karl Elliger, "Das Gesetz Leviticus 18," *ZAW* 67 (1955), 17; Walther Zimmerli, *Ezekiel* (Philadelphia, 1979), 1:344.

to bring up the dead Samuel (1 Sam 28:7). The two terms in the rule, 'oboth and yed'onim, appear in the narrative (1 Sam 28:3, 7). So from the first incident in Israelite history which raises the topic of reaching out to the dead, the one in which Tamar is the key player, the lawgiver targeted a quite specific incident when the two practices in his rule find expression. Time and again we have found this procedure to have been at work.

There are indeed links between the story of King Saul's use of the woman of Endor and the story of Tamar. First, a woman is a prominent actor in each story, each acting as a medium for another person, a dead husband in Tamar's situation and the doomed King Saul in the unnamed woman's. Second, Tamar disguises herself in order to use Judah to do something for her dead husband. Saul disguises himself in order to use the woman to get in touch with the dead Samuel. Third, Tamar's life is in danger because of her action. She is given a sentence of death by burning for harlotry. So too is the woman of Endor's life in danger, for necromancy has become a capital offense (1 Sam 28:9). Fourth, each incident has to do with the loss of sons. Judah almost loses the two sons he has given conception to in Tamar's womb, and Saul learns of the deaths of his sons (and of his own forthcoming death). Fifth, in each story the aims of both Tamar and Saul in their dealings with the dead are to attend to the future, to provide a son for the dead Er and to influence the outcome of a forthcoming battle.

The rule warns that a person could become defiled by associating with the agents of magic. The term used for "to be defiled" is *ṭame'*. It often has a sexual connotation. Its use in the rule may be owing to the lawgiver's initial focus on the story in Genesis 38, when Judah is beguiled by the charms of the prostitute Tamar as she seeks to provide a son for her deceased husband.

Leviticus 19:32

Thou shalt rise up before the grey hairs, and honour the face of the old man, and fear thy God: I am Yahweh.

On a first reading this rule seems a rather tame ethical injunction, especially in light of the preceding rules that deal with weighty customs and practices: prostitution, sanctuaries, magic, and the occult. The rule has a puzzling formulation. It requires that respect be shown to an old man—not to an aged parent, that is, to both a man and a woman. It also brings in the need to fear God, and it goes on to state, "I am Yahweh." Why is there, moreover, specific reference to the old man's appearance, to his grey hairs and his face? Its curious content, I submit, points to a profound matter that arises in a certain historical incident, again the story of Saul and the dead Samuel.

Unacceptable dealings with the dead have been the hallmarks of the contexts out of which so many of the preceding rules have been formulated. The rule about the old man is no exception. When setting out his preceding law forbidding dealings with familiar spirits and mediums, the lawgiver went from the story of Tamar to the story of Saul and the woman of Endor. This latter story also prompted the law about honoring an old man. In focus was the dead Samuel, whom the woman brings up from the netherworld. Saul asks her what she saw, and she replies, "I saw a god ascending out of the earth." When asked about his appearance, she replies, "An old man [*zaqen,* as in the rule] cometh up" (1 Sam 28:13, 14). Saul reacts by bowing with his face to the ground—not by rising before the old man as the rule requires when greeting such a person.

The lawgiver, I suggest, opposed Saul's attitude to the dead, but in some sense living, old man Samuel, precisely because Saul treats him with the respect due to a god. He bows down in an attitude of worshipful reverence to Samuel.[15] If we assume a negative response by the lawgiver, every aspect of the rule can be explained.

The rule calls for rising up before—not bowing down with one's face to the ground—and honoring the face of an old man (*zaqen*). The rule does not call for honoring an old woman also, nor is it

---

15. Contrast how, for Josephus, Mordechai refused to bow down to Haman (Esth 3:2) because the act would not be consistent with the exclusive worship of God; *Jewish Antiquities* 11.6.5.210. Herodotus tells of two Spartan envoys who when told to bow down before Xerxes refused. They declared that they would die rather than prostrate themselves before any mortal being; Herodotus 7.136.

specifically about parents. In the decalogue and Lev 19:3, for example, both sexes—parents in these two instances—are cited. The fact that in the story the focus is the old man Samuel explains the rule's bias.[16] Also explained, because of the story's explicit interest in the appearance of the figure emerging from the earth is the rule's focus on the old man's appearance. Saul says to the woman, "What form is he of?" and she responds, "An old man cometh up; and he is covered with a mantle" (1 Sam 28:14). The lawgiver, turning from the strange episode of the dead, of old man Samuel, mentions in his rule the more conventional aspect of an aged male, namely, his grey hair (*śebah*) and face.

The lawgiver also calls for fear of God and introduces the words "I am Yahweh." The issue of fearing a god is prominent in the story. Thus Saul exhorts the woman not to show fear at the sight of the god rising up from the earth (1 Sam 28:12, 13). Moreover, the "god" (Samuel) who arises from the earth speaks on behalf of Yahweh. Samuel, in turn, who is identified with this god, responds to Saul's complaint that God has departed from him. Samuel tells Saul that because he failed to obey Yahweh, Yahweh has indeed departed from him and become his enemy (1 Sam 28:15–19). An implication is that if Saul had shown fear of Yahweh he would not be compounding his offenses by bowing down to the divine being that is the "dead" old man Samuel. The rule states that an Israelite is to "fear thy God," not, it might be implied, some other god such as a figure from the netherworld.

There were other instances of disrespect for the old in the traditions available to the lawgiver. One might well then argue that any one of these could have been used to formulate the rule about honor to an old man. Here are three such instances: (1) Tamar prostitutes herself with her aged father-in-law to get a child for Er, and the lawgiver focuses on her intent. Despite Tamar's motivation her

16. Moshe Weinfeld argues that the rule in the decalogue about honoring parents inspired the construction of this rule; *Deuteronomy 1–11*, AB5 (New York, 1991), 251. To support his argument he translates the object of the rule as "the elderly," suggesting that all old people, including parents, are included. He makes no argument to account for the quite different language of the two rules in the decalogue and Leviticus.

action dishonors the aged Judah. (2) In the preceding generation Jacob's wife Rachel also provides an instance of how a daughter is unable to do her customary duty of honoring an elder by rising up—*qum* as in the rule—on her father's entrance (Gen 31:35), claiming she could not do so because of her menstrual period. Like Tamar, she too is engaged in a deception and consequently dishonors her father, Laban. (3) In the rule we have the infrequently used term *śebah*, "grey hair." The term is used in descriptions of Jacob when he mourns Joseph and Benjamin (Gen 42:38; 44: 29, 31). Jacob's grief prompted the formulation of the rules in Lev 19:27, 28 (about mourning practices), and his mourning is brought about by his sons' outrageous treatment of him when he is well on in years. The other term in the rule for an old man, *zaqen*, is not only used of Samuel but also of Jacob (Gen 43:27).

Each of these examples does not satisfy the rule on two counts. First, each involves a father (or a father-in-law in Tamar's situation), not an old man. If either of these examples had determined the rule's formulation the rule would have been about respect to a parent. Second, and most important, what counts in the evaluation of how a rule came to be set down is the context in which it had been fashioned. In the rule about the old man, the fundamental consideration was the lawgiver's continuing focus on the topic of wrongful dealings in regard to the dead. Because of this focus, he moved from Tamar's situation to the woman of Endor's. My thesis stands or falls on the recognition that such precise moves determined the lawgiver's procedure. To be sure, he may well have incorporated some of the language of these other examples, but that is because he was familiar with them.

Leviticus 19:33–36

And if a sojourner sojourn with thee in your land, ye shall not vex him. But the sojourner that dwelleth with you shall be unto you as one born among you, and thou shalt love him as thyself: for ye were sojourners in the land of Egypt: I am Yahweh your God.

Here again is the obvious problem that the lawgiver moves from the topic of honoring an old man to the topic of not oppressing a sojourner. The explanation is the lawgiver's typical shift back to a tradition that furnishes the first example of the issue he had under consideration. From the topic of Saul's bowing down to honor the divine being Samuel, he turned back to the Joseph story because it brings up for the first time in the history of the Israelite nation the issue of treating a mortal as a divine being.

Why, first of all, did the lawgiver for the purpose of focusing on the topic of oppressing a sojourner switch back from the story of Saul's communication with the dead but "living" Samuel to the Joseph story? Just as Saul bows down with his face to the ground before the living/dead Samuel at Endor—a town that belongs to the tribe of Joseph's son Manasseh (Josh 17:11)—so do Joseph's brothers bow down with their faces to the ground before the supposedly dead but very much alive Joseph in Egypt (Gen 42:6). The situation, moreover, is one in which Joseph is about to oppress these sojourners in a foreign land. The reason that the lawgiver would have found their stances objectionable is that, as was noted in the discussion of the rule about fearing one's father and mother and keeping the sabbath in Lev 19:3,[17] Joseph, like the dead Samuel, is treated like a divine being. Joseph's dreams so portray him, and it is at this point in the story, when the brothers first visit him in Egypt, that the dreams begin to come true: "And Joseph remembered the dreams which he dreamed of them" (Gen 42:9). When the brothers again come to Egypt to obtain food they again bow down to him to the ground. In response Joseph asks them, "Is your father well, the old man [*zaqen*] of whom ye spake?" (Gen 43:26, 27). This old man is the one they had dishonored in making him believe that his son had died.

A further, possible parallel between Saul's and Joseph's situations is that dreams play a role. In each instance, moreover, the dreams revolve around the issue of rulership. When Saul tries to find out how things will fare with his enemies, the Philistines (1 Sam 28:6), his dreams yield nothing because he has lost his rulership over his

17. See Chapter 3 on Lev 19:3.

people. That failure leads him to get in touch with the dead Samuel. Joseph's dreams, on the other hand, yield the secrets of his future rulership. The consequence is that he makes enemies of his brothers. The success portrayed in his dreams leads to his role as both a dead and a living being from his family's viewpoint.

There is yet another reason why the lawgiver switched back from Saul's problem to the brothers' problem when they come to Egypt for the first time to obtain food. Saul is a Benjaminite (1 Sam 9:1), and the original Benjamin comes very much into focus at this point in the Joseph story. Jacob refuses to let Benjamin accompany his brothers because Jacob fears for his life (Gen 42:4). Benjamin is now Jacob's youngest son, because Joseph is supposedly dead, and his role duplicates that of Joseph before him. Moreover, it is Joseph himself, unbeknown to his family, who in oppressing his brothers attempts to duplicate a fate for Benjamin similar to his own. Immediately after the brothers bow down to him, Joseph insists that they return to their father and bring Benjamin back with them to Egypt (Gen 42: 15, 20).

Just as the lawgiver moved back and forth between Joseph and his direct descendants, Gideon and his son Abimelech, when laying down his rules about illicit sex with a bondwoman and prohibiting the consumption of uncircumcised fruit,[18] so the lawgiver similarly worked with Benjamin and his direct descendant, Saul, when laying down his rules about honor to an old man and this rule about treating sojourners well.

The brothers come to Egypt to obtain food, and Joseph pursues a policy of precise retribution against them because of what they did to him. He immediately and falsely accuses them of being spies and casts them in prison (Gen 42:9, 17). It is a prime example of the oppression of sojourners in a foreign land. It is also the topic of the Levitical rule. When we read the rule stating that the Israelites should treat a sojourner as one who is born among them, we might recall how in fact Joseph and his brothers were born into the same family. When protesting Joseph's false accusation that they have come into the land as spies, the brothers tell him twice that they are the "sons of one man," that is, they have been born to the same

---

18. See Chapter 5 on Lev 19:23–25.

father (Gen 42:11, 13). Little do they know that the Egyptian Joseph is included also. The law's commendation that the sojourner "shall be unto you as one born among you" picks up from the language the sojourning brothers use in their appeal to the Egyptian Joseph.

The further language of the rule also becomes wholly intelligible once we relate it to the Joseph story. Switching from the topic of vexing the sojourner to the topic of loving him, the lawgiver uses the same language ("Thou [an Israelite] shalt love him [the sojourner] as thyself") as in his rule in Lev 19:18 ("Thou [an Israelite] shalt love thy neighbour as [an Israelite] like thyself"). The latter rule about not avenging the son of one's people, but loving him as someone who is like oneself, also had under review Joseph's initially hostile actions against his brothers which are followed by his kindly treatment of them.[19] Soon after the point in the narrative when the brothers come to obtain food and Joseph oppresses them by insisting on having Benjamin brought to him, Joseph does indeed give them all the food they need. His motive for doing so is very much a double one. He is intent on making sure that as a family they are well looked after. But he will also use the food to oppress them yet again. It is this development that takes us to the topic of the next rule, concerning cheating in a transaction.

Leviticus 19:35–37

Ye shall do no unrighteousness in judgment, in meteyard, in weight, or in measure. Just balances, just weights, a just ephah, and a just hin, shall ye have: I am Yahweh your God, which brought you out of the land of Egypt. Therefore shall ye observe all my statutes, and all my judgments, and do them: I am Yahweh.

When Joseph sends his brothers back to their father in Canaan to fetch Benjamin, he surreptitiously slips into their sacks the money they gave for the grain they received from him (Gen 42:25, 35). By doing so Joseph frightens them in order to further his vengeance against them. Returning money in the sacks is in fact cheating in

---

19. See Chapter 3 on Lev 19:18.

the matter of giving true weights and measures, although the law-giver's rule applies to the more usual situation in which the recipient in a transaction receives less than he pays for. The verb used in the rule, *yanah*, "to oppress," usually connotes, as here, economic exploitation. In its other use, in a rule in Lev 25:14, we have the kind of transaction the brothers are involved in with Joseph: "And if thou sell anything unto thy neighbour, or buyest anything of thy neighbour's hand, ye shall not oppress [*yanah*] one another."

I can therefore explain why a general rule about oppressing a sojourner is followed by a quite specific rule about cheating in weights and measures. The experience of the brothers in Egypt is the law-giver's focus. No doubt that is why he appends to the two rules: "I am Yahweh your God, which brought you out of the land of Egypt. Therefore shall ye observe all my statutes, and all my judgments, and do them: I am Yahweh." Why, however, did the lawgiver single out the topic of cheating in weights and measures from the many examples of oppression that Joseph is guilty of? After all, he falsely accuses the brothers of being spies. He wrongly imprisons one of them. He places the money in their sacks on two occasions, and he plants the divining cup in Benjamin's sack. These are all very serious examples of oppressing visitors to a foreign land. Yet he singled out the incident involving grain.

The explanation is that, after Simeon is chosen to stay behind in Egypt as a surety that Benjamin will be brought to Egypt, Joseph tells the brothers: "Bring your youngest brother unto me: then shall I know that you are no spies, but that ye are honest men; so will I deliver you your brother, and ye shall trade in the land" (Gen 42:34). In inviting the brothers to become sojourners in his country and not just visitors for the purpose of buying food, Joseph specifically asks them to be traders in it. But in so inviting them, it is Joseph who is dishonest at this point in time. The very next verses in Gen 42: 35–38 describe the problem the brothers face when they discover the money deceitfully placed in their sacks of grain. The combination in the narrative of honesty and sojourners' trading in a foreign land prompted the lawgiver to set down his rule about honesty in trading by the use of correct weights and measures immediately after a rule about treating a sojourner well.

The topic of a sojourner's lot in life came not from the lawgiver's observing a conventional situation of a sojourner's plight in a foreign land, but from his observing an Israelite in the odd position of oppressing his fellow Israelites when all of them are sojourners in it. It speaks volumes about how biblical rules have come to be formulated that this is how this particular rule came to be set down.

The formulation of the rule about weights and measures likewise provides a good illustration of how the social reality in the lawgiver's time which is suggested by the rule's substance was in fact not primary in prompting its presentation. The preceding rule about the requirement to honor an old man also illustrates how an odd development in a narrative, Saul's bowing down before the risen Samuel, motivated the lawgiver to set down what on the surface appears to be a rather obvious, if curiously expressed rule. The procedure was the same for the rule against prostituting a daughter, because that rule came from reflection on the unusual incident of Tamar's act of prostituting herself on behalf of her dead husband.

The Sequence of Topics in the Narratives for the Laws in Leviticus 19:27–37

The engagement between Joseph and his brothers at the time he trips them up with his divinatory practices—prohibited in the preceding rule (Lev 19:26)—turns on the pretence that he, Joseph, no longer exists. The lawgiver moved from Joseph's pretence back to the pretence in the account of the brothers' exploitation of Jacob, which had led to their predicament with the disguised Joseph in Egypt. They deceived Jacob into believing that Joseph was dead by presenting the false evidence of his blood-soaked coat. The result was that they manipulated Jacob into mourning someone who in fact was not dead. The lawgiver set down a law that is about an unwanted entanglement of life and death: an Israelite like Jacob who mourns the dead must not imprint on his living person marks that signify death.

The next incident in which a person engages in a deceptive action involving the dead involves Tamar, who disguises herself as a cult prostitute to conceive a child for her dead husband. She takes this step because she feels that her father-in-law Judah has left her no alternative—he has refused to have his youngest son, Shelah, impregnate her. A rule concerned with Israelites' prostituting their daughters is set down because Israelite daughters in later times became cult prostitutes like Tamar (see, for example, Hos 4:14). The lawgiver also reacted negatively to Tamar's attempt to conceive a child through prostitution. To procreate in this way is to offend against the order of creation, in particular, against the institution of marriage and its function of producing children. The sabbath is the occasion on which one recalls that order, and the lawgiver sets down a rule affirming its importance. Cultic prostitution at the Israelite sanctuary in monarchical times came under review in the next rule about reverencing the sanctuary.

Tamar's deception in disguising herself as a cult prostitute on behalf of the dead has a parallel in a later deception in which King Saul disguises himself so that the woman of Endor will raise the dead Samuel on his behalf. The woman is a medium, and the lawgiver prohibits such agents because they engage with the dead. He stayed with the incident concerning the dead Samuel and Saul because it presents a further example of an Israelite's wrongly relating to a dead person. Saul reverentially bows down to the aged man who appears before him from the underworld and accords him the respect due to a god. The rule requires an Israelite to rise respectfully before an aged man and to fear God, that is, the Israelite god Yahweh.

Typically, the lawgiver turned back to a comparable incident: Joseph's brothers reverentially bow down to a "dead" being, Joseph himself, whose identity, like Tamar's and Saul's, is disguised. On this occasion the brothers are seeking food for their family back in Canaan, and Joseph takes advantage of his "dead" state to oppress them. He slips money into their sacks of grain because his aim is to have them learn that he is alive and not dead. He also invites them to become sojourners in Egypt and to trade there. When doing so he explicitly appeals to their honesty, precisely when he is himself not acting honestly in slipping the money into their sacks. The rules set down are: an Israelite is not to oppress a sojourner but is to treat him as a fellow Israelite, and an Israelite when trading has to act honestly by using correct weights and measures.

CHAPTER 7

The Incest and Other Laws
of Leviticus 20

A major problem in the study of biblical law is how to account
for rules that, if not identical to ones already set down, are very similar to them. A casual glance at the laws in Leviticus 20 shows that
many of them—for example, some of the incest rules—duplicate
either identical or similar laws in Leviticus 18 and 19. Why should
there be such repetition? The existence of rules that are repeated in
close proximity militates against the notion that the biblical codes
of law represent sources of reference for use in a court of law. The du-
plication of rules for such a practical purpose would confuse rather
than guide. On the other hand, the comparable, widely accepted view
that the duplicate rules represent judgments on similar cases that
arose at different times and places in ancient Israel has more of a
ring of plausibility to it. If there is merit in this view, however, it remains puzzling that similar cases are not set down together, for example, the two judgments about the worship of Molech in Lev 18:21
and Lev 20:2–5.

I account for the duplications by assuming that they constitute
judgments on similar incidents and developments in the history of
the nation which lie before the fictional all-seeing figure of Moses.
Characteristic of those who present the history is that they recorded
matters that recur from generation to generation. Characteristic of

the lawgivers is that they in turn went through this history and incorporated in their rules similar issues that arise in it. The lawgivers formulated a rule in relation to a narrative incident, then at some point returned to the incident by a different route and made the same judgment again or took up a different facet of the incident and made the same judgment on it. If a lawgiver made the same judgment it is not because he failed to realize that the issue had just come up but because his approach to the issue was different from the one he made on the previous occasion.

The reason for the different approach is the nature of the topics the lawgiver had under consideration at the time. These he derived from his reading of the history of his people. Some of these topics are, to illustrate from the preceding rules in Lev 19:20–37: particular kinds of deception (for example, those involving garments); monetary transactions; the living and the dead; and differences in status (for example, freeborn versus slaves). A different topic in the narratives could take him to the same issue in the history. If it did, he formulated the rule again.

Duplicate topics in the narratives account for duplicate topics in the laws. The lawgiver's procedure mirrors the one adopted by the narrators of the histories. Each time they recorded a similar, recurring incident they explored its different legal and ethical aspects. The two narratives in Genesis 12 and 20, for example, about Sarah's compromising her virtue with a foreign potentate express from different perspectives the deity's negative attitude toward her behavior in each episode. The lawgiver in turn recorded similar rules, but each time he did so he was responding from a different perspective to issues in the incidents he had under scrutiny.

Leviticus 20:2–5

Whosoever he be of the sons of Israel, or of the strangers that sojourn in Israel, that giveth any of his seed unto Molech; he shall surely be put to death: the people of the land shall stone him with stones. And I will set my face against that man, and will cut him off from among his people; because he hath given of his seed unto Molech, to defile my sanctuary, and to profane my holy name. And if the people of the land do any ways hide their eyes from the man, when he giveth of his seed unto Molech, and kill him not: Then I will set my face against that man, and against his family, and will cut him off, and all that go a whoring after him, to commit whoredom with Molech, from among their people.

The rule in Lev 20:2–5 forbidding giving seed to Molech illustrates the phenomenon of duplicate rules because there is a similar rule in Lev 18:21. The patriarchal incident that prompted the latter's formulation is Abraham's near sacrifice of his son Isaac to Yahweh as a burnt offering (Genesis 22).[1] The rule about Molech worship in Lev 20:2–5, on the other hand, came from the lawgiver's reflection on Judah's involvement with the Canaanite cult prostitute Tamar. The implications of Judah's intercourse with her prompted a series of the preceding rules in Lev 19:29–31 (prostitution, familiar spirits and mediums, for example). A consequence of Judah's involvement with Tamar is that, as with Abraham's son Isaac, it almost led to the burning of his own offspring because he had sentenced her to be burned when she was pregnant. To be sure, Judah is unaware that the twins in her womb are his; however, the near burning of the pregnant Tamar, plus other about-to-be-noted aspects, raised for the lawgiver the topic of Molech worship which involved the sacrifice of children by fire. These children were typically those born to cult prostitutes. Both Isaac's god Yahweh (if we go by God's initial intent in Genesis 22) and Molech the Canaanite god required children to be sacrificed by fire.

A more immediate problem is to explain how the lawgiver moved from a rule (weights and measures) about cheating in a transaction to one about giving seed to Molech. The answer is that both rules are based on incidents in which there is cheating in a transaction involving seed. The disguised Joseph deceives his brothers when he returns their money in the sacks of grain. This deception prompted the formulation of the preceding rule in Lev 19:35, 36 about cheating in matters of weights and measures. The incident inspiring the next rule about giving seed to Molech is the disguised Tamar's

---

1. See Chapter 3 on Lev 18:21.

deception in Genesis 38. She deceives Judah into thinking that he is paying a harlot for her sexual services. She is in fact his disguised daughter-in-law seeking to obtain his seed to make herself pregnant.

The significance of Tamar's deception led the lawgiver to the topic of an Israelite or a sojourner who gives his seed to Molech. Judah is an Israelite, but he is a sojourner in Canaan when he and his family become involved with Tamar. The lawgiver and seer Moses thought ahead to parallel developments among later Israelites after they acquire the land of Canaan and live in it. A standard view of the Judah and Tamar story is that Judah's marriage to a Canaanite woman reflects the later territorial expansion of the tribe of Judah and the consequent intermarriage with Canaanites.[2] What Judah does by giving his seed to a Canaanite cult prostitute—he refers to her as such (Gen 38:21, 22)—brings to the lawgiver's mind the later problem of Israelite involvement in the Canaanite cult, that is, in the language of the rule, giving one's seed to Molech (2 Kgs 16:3; 17:17, 21:6; 23:10). Cult prostitutes served the god Molech. In his rule the lawgiver anticipates that in the later period of settlement in Canaan such involvement in the Canaanite cult would desecrate the sanctuary (*miqdaš*) and profane God's holy (*qdš*) name. The lawgiver linked the issue of holiness (*qdš*) at that later period of time to the ancestor Judah's earlier relationship with the cult prostitute (*qedešah*) Tamar.

The penalty in the rule is that the person so compromising the deity's holiness will be stoned to death and cut off from his people. These are two separate penalties. Moreover, if the offender is stoned to death he is also cut off from his people. The penalties represent the lawgiver's response to the development in the story. Judah is not stoned to death for giving his seed to a cult prostitute, but he is cut off from his people: separated from the rest of his family and losing sons in Canaan at an alarming rate, he is threatened with loss of any son to succeed him. The lawgiver judged that when the Israelites settle in the land of Canaan a person found guilty of giving his seed to Molech is to be stoned to death. If his crime goes undetected God will still punish him by bringing about the loss of his family.

2. See E. A. Speiser, *Genesis*, AB 1 (New York, 1964), 300.

The second part of the rule is about those people who hide their eyes from a fellow Israelite or from a sojourner who offends by giving his seed to Molech. Again the narrative proves illuminating. Judah is a sojourner in Canaan when he gives his seed to the cult prostitute. He tries to find her again by sending his friend Hirah the Adullamite to pay her—in a way, sacred dues—for her services. Despite inquiries about her whereabouts she cannot be found. The men of the locality are thus aware that someone has had a relationship with a cult prostitute: Hirah specifically asks the townspeople of Enaim, "Where is the cult prostitute who was at Enaim by the wayside?" (Gen 38:21). The lawgiver, anticipating the situation during the later settlement in the land, condemns those who would not report such involvement in Canaanite cultic activity.

The Levitical lawgiver's association of Molech worship with the events of the Judah story strengthens the arguments of Karl Elliger and Walther Zimmerli that Molech worship involved sacrificing to Molech the children who were newly born to cult prostitutes.[3] Zimmerli emphasizes the text in Ezek 16:20, 21: Jerusalem's children are sacrificed by fire to Canaanite gods as part of the practice of cultic prostitution. Ezekiel depicts Jerusalem—a city belonging to the tribe that is called after the ancestor Judah—as a harlot in this context and refers to how her garments—we might recall Tamar's—are used to indulge her promiscuity (Ezek 16:16).[4]

In sum, Judah lives among the Canaanites and marries a Canaanite woman. After she dies he has intercourse with a cult prostitute, and his offspring by her are almost burned by fire. What happens to this son of Israel has raised for the lawgiver the wider issue of Israelite involvement in that particular form of Canaanite religion,

---

3. See Karl Elliger, "Das Gesetz Leviticus 18," *ZAW* 67 (1955), 17; Walther Zimmerli, *Ezekiel* (Philadelphia, 1979), 1:344.

4. N. H. Snaith thinks that the Talmud's view of Molech worship (*babylonian Sanhedrin* 64a)—that parents handed children over to the priests, who lit two large fires and passed the children between the fires—is correct. These children were given over to priests and trained as temple prostitutes. See "The Cult of Molech," *VT* 16 (1966), 124. Cp. John Day, who refers to the rabbinic view that the rule about Molech worship forbids sexual relations with a pagan woman; *A God of Human Sacrifice* (Cambridge, Eng., 1989), 21, 22. Judah's situation again comes to mind. Although probably inaccurate, both rabbinic views bring out features that are pertinent to the rule's original meaning.

namely, giving seed to Molech. The issue would be of special concern because of the influence of Molech worship on later generations of Israelites (2 Kgs 23:10; Jer 32:35, cp. Zeph 1:5). Judah's extensive involvement with Canaanites foreshadows these later developments. That is why his story in Genesis 38 plays an enormous role in the construction of so many laws.

Leviticus 20:6

And the soul that turneth after such as have familiar spirits, and after mediums, to go a whoring after them, I will even set my face against that soul, and will cut him off from among his people.

Familiar spirits and mediums are typically women who are involved with the dead. Tamar seeks to be impregnated by Judah to appease her dead husband, Er, by giving him an heir. The god Molech, who comes into the preceding rule, is associated with the cult of the dead. He is the god of the netherworld associated with the shades of the dead ancestors. (In biblical material they are the *Rephaim* [for example, Ps 88:10].)[5] The Bible repeatedly attributes the cult of the dead to the Canaanites. From a Canaanite perspective Tamar's children, born to a Canaanite cult prostitute, could consequently be sacrificed to Molech.

The story in Genesis 38 brings out not just a link between Tamar and her dead husband but also a link between a sinister Tamar and her dealing in death. Judah's reason for not wishing his last remaining son, Shelah, to give seed to Tamar is that his two other sons perished in their involvement with her.

For his rule, then, about those who deal with the dead the lawgiver is again thinking of Judah's involvement with Tamar. Her situation and her role in the life of an Israelite (Judah) brings up the problem of comparable Canaanite influences on later Israelites, namely, those persons who possess familiar spirits or are mediums (1 Sam 28:3, 9; Isa 8:19; 19:3; 29:4; 2 Kgs 21:6; 23:24; 1 Chr 10:13).

5. See *ABD* 4:895, also Day, *A God of Human Sacrifice*, 46–55, 84, 85, who cites Isa 57:9 as evidence that Molech was an underworld deity.

The lawgiver looked at a specific aspect of Tamar's role in the story, her prostituting herself on behalf of the dead Er. Judah becomes involved with her in her role as a prostitute. In his rule the lawgiver concentrates on the person who seeks out a practioner of occult arts. Judah is the example the lawgiver thought of because even though Judah at the time is unaware of Tamar's real aim, what the rule anticipates is the future involvement of Israelites with Canaanite mantic arts. The language in the rule forbidding an Israelite to prostitute himself with familiar spirits and the like is not just the transference of the notion of sexual attraction to idolatrous agents,[6] but came from Judah's solicitation of an actual prostitute. The penalty in the rule refers to the loss of offspring to carry on a man's name as a member of the Israelite nation. The threat that hangs over Judah in the story would have inspired it. He is faced with the extinction of his family line.

As I noted for the rule in Lev 19:31, familiar spirits and mediums are those who traffic in ghosts and spirits of the dead. The two rules differ in that the focus in Lev 19:31 is on the example of King Saul when he seeks out the woman medium of Endor, while in Lev 20:6 it is on the example of Judah when he becomes involved with Tamar. The duplicate rules can be explained by the lawgiver's characteristic procedure of sifting through similar developments in succeeding generations of his ancestors.

Leviticus 20:7–9

Sanctify yourselves therefore, and be ye holy: for I am Yahweh your God. And ye shall keep my statutes, and do them: I am Yahweh which sanctify you. For everyone that treateth his father or his mother with contempt shall be surely put to death: he hath treated his father or his mother with contempt; his blood shall be upon him.

To understand how the lawgiver got from the topic of an Israelite's prostituting himself with familiar spirits and mediums to the

---

6. As Day thinks; *A God of Human Sacrifice*, 23, 24.

topic of his treating his parents with contempt, we stay initially with the Judah-Tamar story in Genesis 38. Tamar treats her father-in-law with contempt by approaching him disguised in a harlot's garment (Gen 38:14, 15). To be sure, she feels driven to do so because he has denied her the means of obtaining offspring. There is in Genesis 37 a prior example of such contempt—and again it involves the use of a garment *and* denying a man offspring.

When Judah and his brothers make light of Jacob—*qalal,* "to render contemptible," in the rule and in the very similar rule in Exod 21:17—the contempt in this instance is aimed at a biological parent. They produce "evidence" that Jacob's offspring, Joseph, is dead. Their presentation of the blood-stained garment to their father is tantamount to a magical trick to deceive someone about the dead. It is this association between a deceptive practice and the dead which accounts for the seemingly awkward setting down of the rule about contempt for parents after the rule about familiar spirits and mediums. There is an interesting contrast. Just as familiar spirits and mediums manipulate people to think that the dead still live, so, contrastingly, the brothers trick their father into concluding that Joseph is dead.

The penalty for the one who treats his parent in a contemptible way is death: "his blood shall be upon him." The use of blood by the sons when deceiving their father into thinking that his son is dead—in a way he is because he has been sold abroad[7]—probably accounts for the lawgiver's choosing to formulate the death penalty in this way for this law. The harshness of the penalty is in line with the gravity of their offense. To be sure, the lawgiver continues the formulation in some of the succeeding laws.

Just before the rule about parents come statements about the sanctification (*qadaš*) of the Israelites (Lev 20:7, 8).[8] The rules in Lev 20:2-6 that precede the rule about parents concern Tamar who was a

7. In antiquity, for example, the Roman *poena capitalis,* death sentences often actually took the form of exile or selling a person abroad. Later in the Joseph story Benjamin comes under a sentence of death for allegedly stealing Joseph's divining cup, but the form it takes is spelled out as enslavement (Gen 44:9, 10, 16, 17).

8. In the rule of Exod 22:31 the brothers' act of killing a beast and using its blood similarly raised the issue of holiness: "Holy men you shall be to me. You shall not eat any flesh that is torn by beasts in the field; you shall cast it to the dogs." See Calum Carmichael, *The Origins of Biblical Law* (Ithaca, 1992), 182–84.

qedešah, "a sacred prostitute." Consequently, Judah's involvement with a Canaanite sacred prostitute brings up the issue of Israel's sanctity. The statements about this sanctity readily bridge the issue of holiness in Judah's involvement with the Canaanite cult prostitute Tamar and the deception of Judah and his brothers with the blood-soaked garment. A Priestly lawgiver would have been particularly concerned about an Israelite involved in foreign cultic activity and the misuse of blood.

Leviticus 20:10

And the man that committeth adultery with another man's wife, that committeth adultery with his neighbour's wife, the adulterer and adulteress shall surely be put to death.

In focus is Joseph's alleged attempted adultery with Potiphar's wife, in which a garment is again used to deceive. The "dead" Joseph was central to the lawgiver's concern in his preceding rule about the contemptible treatment of a parent, and Judah's sexual encounter with Tamar has been the primary focus in so many of the preceding rules. Not surprisingly, Joseph's sexual encounter with Potiphar's wife presented the lawgiver with the opportunity to bring in adultery. In that Israelite involvement with Canaanite religion was typically thought of as adultery or harlotry, it might also be understandable why he would have turned to Joseph's involvement with a foreign Egyptian woman in this instance. The rule refers repetitiously to a neighbor's wife as well as to another man's wife. Fishbane thinks that the reason for such redundancy is that the term "neighbor" limits the penalty to Israelites. If so, that is because the lawgiver switched from Joseph's relationship with a foreign woman to a comparable relationship between two Israelites.[9]

9. Michael Fishbane, *Biblical Interpretation in Ancient Israel* (Oxford, 1985), 169: "The initial formulation of the law has thus been restricted to manageable ethnic proportions." Fishbane does not ask about the implications of his view. It seems obvious to him that the rules are so constructed as to apply to Israelite society. In what circumstances, then, in any society would it be necessary to restrict adultery to "manageable ethnic proportions"?

Marked features of the Joseph episode are that the woman is the guilty party and the man is the innocent one and, further, that he, the innocent party, is punished and she, the guilty party, escapes punishment. In his rule the lawgiver spells out in seemingly unnecessary detail the offense of adultery and how both parties are to be punished. The narrative in Genesis 39 might explain why there is this redundancy in the rule's formulation.

The rule spells out the actual offense of adultery in response to the complicated situation in the narrative. The relationship in the rule is between a freeborn man and woman unlike the unequal status of one party (the slave Joseph) in relation to Potiphar's wife in Genesis 39. Recall how the rule in Lev 19:20–22 (illicit sex with a bondwoman) formulates a situation contrasting to Joseph's (a freeborn married woman and a bondman) in Genesis 39. The earlier rule about the bondwoman spells out that, because of the unequal standing of the two parties, a capital offense has not been committed.[10] The adultery rule, in turn, spells out the offense of adultery where the two parties are free, unlike the unequal situation in Genesis 39.

There is a further equally telling link with the preceding rule about treating a parent in a contemptible way and its background tradition about Joseph's brothers' treatment of their father. They deceive their father with a made-up story about Joseph's garment. In the tradition underlying the rule about adultery, Potiphar's wife deceives her husband with Joseph's garment by her made-up story of how she comes to have it in her possession. This link is probably the primary one in the lawgiver's move from the topic of treating a parent with respect to the topic of adultery.

Deception by means of a garment is a feature common to the three incidents: Tamar's disguise as a prostitute, the garment soaked in animal blood, and Joseph's garment. The three incidents have prompted the three rules: an Israelite's prostituting himself with those who act on behalf of the dead, the contemptible treatment of a parent, and adultery. The Levitical lawgiver had a special interest in garments. They have power to convey uncleanness (Lev 13: 47–59). They indicate status (the priestly garments, for example [Exod 28:1–43]). They communicate integrity (Num 15:37–41).

---

10. See Chapter 5 on Lev 19:20–22.

The death penalty in the rule for the adulterers is in line with God's pronouncement to Abimelech in a previous incident involving Sarah (Gen 20:37). The lawgiver may have taken it over from this tradition because he was abreast of similar developments in different generations. In Genesis 20, moreover, there is the problem similar to Joseph's with Potiphar's wife: the innocent party (Abimelech) is branded as guilty and the woman (Sarah) is the guilty party but goes unpunished.

A series of rules involving sexual offenses follows. Just as no two events are the same, so also are no two laws the same. The incest laws in Lev 20:11, 12, 14, 17, 19–21 might, nonetheless, come very close to illustrating the contrary because they are so similar to those in Lev 18:6–18. The explanation is not, as is usually claimed,[11] that those in Leviticus 20 lay down the penalties that are somehow left out in those in Leviticus 18 (the latter in fact do contain general statements about sanctions). There is much more to be said when we ponder this issue of duplicate rules. The following rules again illustrate the process by which the lawgiver set down rules similar or identical to those he had already set down but for different reasons.

Leviticus 20:11

And the man that lieth with his father's wife hath uncovered his father's nakedness: both of them shall surely be put to death; their blood shall be upon them.

In Lev 18:8 the lawgiver takes up the issue of sex with a father's wife just after scrutinizing the incidents in which a son and daughters (Ham and the daughters of Lot respectively) sexually abuse a father. Reuben's sexual intercourse with his father's wife (Bilhah) provided him with a further example of the abuse of a father's sexuality. A son who lies with his father's wife "uncovers his father's nakedness." In the same rule in Lev 20:11 the lawgiver has come to

---

11. See J. E. Hartley, *Leviticus,* WBC (Dallas, Tex., 1992), 332; Gordon J. Wenham, *Leviticus,* NICOT (Grand Rapids, Mich., 1979), 277; R. K. Harrison, *Leviticus,* TOTC (Downer's Grove, Ill., 1980), 203.

Reuben's offense again but by a quite different route. Here is how he proceeded.

The preceding rule but one (treating a parent with contempt) has in focus Jacob's sons' offense against him. That offense, involving Joseph's life, takes Joseph away from his father, and, as a bondman in an Egyptian household, he has to confront Potiphar's wife's seductiveness. The preceding rule about adultery in Lev 20:10 took up that particular problem. The rule about wrongful intercourse with a father's wife has again an offense against Jacob in focus, an offense, moreover, that concerns a wife (Bilhah) whose status is that of a bondwoman (*šiphah*) in a household (Gen 29:29). The issue of status is probably the decisive reason that the lawgiver moved from the bondman Joseph's sexual encounter with a freewoman married to an Egyptian to a free Israelite's (Reuben's) intercourse with a woman who is a bondwoman married to the Israelite's own father. The rule, then, has in focus Joseph's brother Reuben, who lies with his father's wife Bilhah (Gen 35:22). Bilhah is the maidservant and surrogate mother standing in for Rachel (Gen 30:1–8), Joseph's own mother.

Reuben's conduct stands in contrast to Joseph's. As a full member of his father's household, Reuben lies with his wife, who is of a lower station than Reuben. As an inferior but intimate member of Potiphar's household because of Potiphar's trust in him, Joseph resists lying with his wife, who is above Joseph's station.

The preceding rule about adultery spells out in seemingly unnecessary detail the nature of the offense because the tradition about the bondman Joseph and Potiphar's wife brings up only indirectly the issue of adultery between two persons of equal standing. There was a need to spell out what the offense consisted of between two people of similar status who engage in sex.

The rule about intercourse with a father's wife spells out that both parties are to be put to death. In the tradition about Reuben and Bilhah nothing is done to either party at the time of the offense. All that the tradition records is "Israel heard of it" (Gen 35:22). To be sure, later Reuben is to lose the privilege that went with being the firstborn son (Gen 49:4). This is no mean penalty but still not an immediate response to the sexual offense. The death penalty in the rule is in line with the preceding rule about adultery because the offense is akin to adultery.[12] It is also in line with it on another ground. Just as in the adultery rule the two parties are of equal standing, unlike Joseph in relation to Potiphar's wife in the tradition, so in this rule about the father's wife there is equality of status, unlike the bondwoman Bilhah in relation to Reuben in the tradition. Recall that the law in Lev 19:20–22 (illicit sex with a bondwoman) explicitly rules out a capital sentence for a sexual relationship between a freeman and a bondwoman (*šiphah*) for whom a marriage has been arranged with another freeman.

In the Deuteronomic rule about Reuben's offense the lawgiver uses the metaphor of a garment as a wife: "A man shall not take his father's wife, nor shall he uncover his father's skirt" (Deut 22:30).[13] A garment played a significant role in the presentation of the three preceding rules. The language of the Levitical rule about uncovering nakedness implies the removal of a garment. The view expressed in both the Deuteronomic and Priestly rules that intercourse with a father's wife is tantamount to uncovering the father's nakedness is in line with Jacob's own depiction of Reuben's offense against him in Gen 49:4: "Thou wentest up to thy father's bed; then defiledst thou it: he went up to my couch."

Leviticus 20:12

And if a man lie with his daughter-in-law, both of them shall surely be put to death: they have wrought confusion; their blood shall be upon them.

From an example of a son who lies with his father's wife, the lawgiver turned to an example, Judah with Tamar, of a father who lies with a son's wife (Genesis 38). The lawgiver apparently pursued contrasting examples: Reuben's conduct with Bilhah contrasts with

---

12. Compare Gaius 1.63: "I may not marry one who once was my stepmother. We say, who once was, since if the marriage producing that alliance were still continuing, I should be precluded from marrying her on another ground."

13. See Calum Carmichael, *Law and Narrative in the Bible* (Ithaca, 1985), 221–23.

Joseph's conduct with Potiphar's wife; and a father's conduct with a son's wife is looked at after an example of a son's conduct with his father's wife.[14] The way in which the lawgiver arrived at the topic of intercourse between a man and his son's wife is different from the way in which (in Lev 18:15) he set down the same rule after a rule prohibiting sex with an uncle's wife (Lev 18:14)—not as here (Lev 20:12) after a rule prohibiting sex with a father's wife (Lev 20:11). Isaac's odd relationship to his mother, Sarah, as being also that of nephew to his uncle's wife is the tradition that led to the formulation of the rule in Lev 18:14.

Although Reuben's intercourse with his father's wife is wrong, there is a sense in which Judah's intercourse with his daughter-in-law may not seem wrong because of the levirate custom. There are, however, negative aspects to Judah's sexual activity: he is involved with a harlot and she conceals that she is his daughter-in-law. The negative aspect would have provided the lawgiver with the general rule against intercourse with a son's wife. Although it is far from certain, if the lawgiver acknowledged the validity of the levirate custom he might have admitted an exception in the circumscribed instance in which only the father-in-law was available to provide a son by that custom.

There are features of the story which point to an implicit norm against a man's union with a daughter-in-law. Tamar's approach to her widowed father-in-law in such a devious way indicates that a sexual relationship with a father-in-law may have been regarded as fundamentally out of order, a judgment probably confirmed by the notice in Gen 38:26 that Judah never lay with Tamar again. The use of the term *tebel*, "confusion," in the rule to describe such a union brings out the implications of Tamar's devious approach to Judah and Judah's shocked reaction to his discovery that he has slept with his daughter-in-law.[15] The use of *šakab*, "to lie with," in both this

14. On the role of contrast in the presentation of biblical laws and proverbs, see Carmichael, *Law and Narrative*, 301, also 213, 297, 298.

15. I am aware of the fact that "to sleep with" in the extraordinary sense of intercourse is not found in the Bible (or Talmud). On its Egyptian origins, its use in Homer, its appearance in the Septuagint and Vulgate, and then in the European languages, see David Daube, "Perchance to Dream" (unpublished paper).

rule and the preceding one about intercourse with a father's wife reflects the fact that Reuben (probably, *šakab,* Gen 35:22) and Judah (certainly) lie with the women in question on one occasion only. The penalty of death is again in line with the two preceding rules, the first of which is about adultery. The offense of the father-in-law and the daughter-in-law is akin to adultery.

The three brothers Joseph, Reuben, and Judah have been the focus of the preceding three laws (Lev 20:10–12): adultery (from Genesis 39), intercourse with a father's wife (from Genesis 35), and intercourse with a son's wife (from Genesis 38).

Leviticus 20:13

If a man also lie with mankind, as he lieth with a woman, both of them have committed an abomination: they shall surely be put to death; their blood shall be upon them.

Tamar presents the first example of the problem of cultic prostitution, which becomes acute in later generations during the history of the kings. Most relevant, what receives prime attention by the Deuteronomic redactors of that history is the problem of male homosexuality. From one Israelite, Judah, who lies with a female cult prostitute in his time, the lawgiver turned to those Israelites of a later generation who lie with male cult prostitutes. This later history of cultic prostitution involves heterosexual as well as homosexual activity: Deut 23:17, 18 (both); 1 Kgs 14:24 (male); 15:12 (male); 2 Kgs 23:7 (male); for example, 1 Kgs 14:24 refers to how "There were also male cult prostitutes in the land."

It would again appear that, as for the preceding rules, the lawgiver worked with contrasting examples: from an instance of intercourse with a female cult prostitute to an instance of intercourse with a male cult prostitute. From the latter example he proceeded from the particular to the general, to the setting down of a general prohibition against male homosexual intercourse. The death penalty in the rule may reflect the fact that Tamar received a capital sentence (that was not carried out) for her harlotry.

There is also a prohibition against homosexuality in Lev 18:22, but a different tradition underlies its formulation, namely, the attempted rape of the male visitors to Sodom by its male inhabitants. Moreover, the rule in Lev 18:22 comes after a rule about the worship of Molech (Lev 18:21), not as in Lev 20:13 after a rule about intercourse with a son's wife. In Lev 18:21 and 22 the background focus is God's use of fire in his dealings with human beings: God requires Isaac to be offered up by fire to him, and God removes the Sodomites with fire from heaven (Gen 19:24 and 22:2–9). In Lev 20: 12 (intercourse with a son's wife) and 13 (homosexuality), on the other hand, the background interest is the person of Tamar as a son's wife and as a cult prostitute, respectively.

Leviticus 20:14

And if a man take a wife and her mother, it is wickedness: they shall be burnt with fire, both he and they; that there be no wickedness among you.

The rule speaks of taking a woman and her mother in marriage, not simply lying with them sexually. Tamar is first married to one man (Er) and then to Onan. When he dies she remains tied in a marital bond to Shelah, but she decides to seek out his father instead. Strictly speaking, in terms of levirate marriage Tamar is taken by and has not just lain with both a son (Er or Onan) and his father. The idiosyncratic circumstances described in the tradition prompted the lawgiver to come up with a contrasting male situation in different circumstances: a man who marries a woman and her mother. The rules are addressed to males, and a feature of a succession of laws to this point is the lawgiver's interest in contrasting situations.

The penalty in the rule is death by burning for all three parties. Why did the lawgiver not adhere to his previous formulation about "their blood being upon them" (Lev 20:9, 11, 12, 13)? Tamar's penalty as decreed by Judah is that she be burned to death. Her penalty is for her act of harlotry, but when she points out to Judah that he is the father of the children in her womb he recognizes his own wrongdoing in not marrying her to Shelah. Judah has, in effect, forced her to resort to harlotry—with him as the other partner—to remedy her childless situation. Judah's recognition of his culpability carries with it a condemnation: a son and a father should not be involved with the same woman. The lawgiver judged that all three parties deserve punishment in the reverse situation involving a man with a daughter and her mother and in which there is none of the peculiarities of the story in Genesis 38.

In the tradition, burning is the penalty because of the notion that it is the appropriate penalty for someone who burns with sexual passion. Prov 6:27, 28, for example, expresses the notion "Can a man [indulging his sexual appetite] take fire in his bosom, and his clothes not be burned? Can one go upon hot coals, and his feet not be burned?" Judah is Tamar's partner in passion, and hence the lawgiver might have judged that both deserve to burn for their act. A further possible consideration is that because Tamar's unions with a son and his father are on behalf of the dead (her husband Er) and therefore for a sacred cause, the lawgiver viewed burning as the appropriate penalty for a trespass in connection with the sacred.[16] In any event, it is the development in the Judah story that the lawgiver brought to bear when he came up with the male equivalent to Tamar's union with a son and a father and with the use of fire as a penalty.

The lawgiver may have been opposed to the levirate custom because, being fundamentally opposed to certain incestuous relationships, he was not prepared to admit exceptions. So much in the story of Judah and Tamar came under his negative scrutiny because of its Canaanite character. Opposition to the levirate custom might have constituted but one more aspect of that scrutiny.

The rule about marriage to a woman and her mother in Lev 20:14 differs from the one in Lev 18:17 in that this one deals with two generations of women (as in HL 191) and not with three, mother, daughter, and granddaughter (a son's daughter and a daughter's daughter) as in Lev 18:17. The difference between the two rules may indicate

---

16. Note, however, that stoning and not burning is the penalty for the man who involves himself in the worship of Molech (Lev 20:2).

that these legal constructions are academic exercises. There was a willingness to look repeatedly at the same case in the narrative with a view to formulating differently and paying attention to an aspect of it (the question of an appropriate sanction, for example) not dealt with in the previous formulation.

The lawgiver uses the term *zimmah*, "plan," "device," "wickedness," in Lev 18:17 (a man's sexual relations with three generations of women in a family); 19:29 (a man's making his daughter a prostitute); and here in Lev 20:14 (a man's sexual relations with two generations of women in a family). In each instance the background story is Tamar's scheming to obtain seed by her father-in-law. The lawgiver was not impressed with her mode of operation. His use of the term may reflect his negative judgment on Tamar's deviousness.

Leviticus 20:15, 16

And if a man lie with a beast, he shall surely be put to death: and ye shall slay the beast. And if a woman approach unto any beast, and lie down thereto, thou shalt kill the woman, and the beast: they shall surely be put to death; their blood shall be upon them.

The Canaanite character of much that takes place in the Judah-Tamar story was a major factor in the presentation of a number of the preceding rules. The narrator describes Tamar at one point as a (Canaanite) cult prostitute (Gen 38:21, 22). A son of Israel's (Judah's) involvement with the Canaanites presaged much more widespread involvement with them by later generations of Israelites. In coming up with a rule about bestiality the lawgiver stayed with the same issue of harlotry in a Canaanite context, in the same generation as Judah's. The offense that concerned him is that the Canaanite Shechem had sex with Dinah without the approval of her family.

Just as Judah takes himself off to live and marry among the Canaanites and subsequently engages with the harlot Tamar, so Dinah, Judah's full sister, takes it upon herself to visit the women members of the Canaanite group, the Hivites. While there, one of the male members, Shechem, the prince of the Hivites, treats her as a harlot (Gen 34:2, 31). As the Deuteronomic law (Deut 22:10) expresses what took place, Shechem the son of the Ass (Hamor, the head of the Hivites) plowed (sexually) Dinah the daughter of the Ox (the house of Jacob).

The Priestly lawgiver took over the animal imagery from the story—the sexual offender Shechem ("shoulder [of an ass]") is the son of the Ass Hamor—and from Jacob's comment on the incident at the end of his life (Gen 49:5–7)—the house of the Ox, Jacob/Israel, has been put under threat by the other Canaanites. The lawgiver translated the metaphorical language of the tradition—humans engaging with humans is described in terms of beasts engaging with beasts—into a rule about sexual relations between humans and beasts.[17] Moreover, he took up the issue of both a male and a female offender because it was not just Shechem who was culpable; Dinah was much too brazen in going off alone to make a call on the daughters of the house of the Ass Hamor.[18]

The lawgiver presented his rule about bestiality in Lev 18:23 because he moved from the homosexuality of the story of Sodom and Gomorrah to the story about Dinah. In particular, his focus shifted from the attempted homosexual rape of the two men who visit Sodom to the actual violation of Dinah when she visits the Hivites. In each development the consequence is the near destruction of all the inhabitants of the two places. In the bestiality rule in Lev 20:15, 16 the lawgiver made a different move. He came to the subject of bestiality not after a rule about homosexuality but after a rule prohibiting a man to marry a woman and her mother. He made this move because Tamar's harlotry in Genesis 38 (that meant she had sexual relations with a son and his father)[19] took him to Dinah's loose behavior that invites Shechem to treat her as a harlot (Gen 34:2, 31).[20]

---

17. At all times language employs animal images to speak of human sexuality, for example, in contemporary slang: a cathouse (brothel), bitch, chick, bird, cow, fox, stud, stallion. An example in a biblical law is Deut 23:18: a male prostitute is a dog. On the prohibition against plowing with an ox and an ass (Deut 22:10), see Carmichael, *Law and Narrative*, 193–97.

18. On the looseness of Dinah's conduct, see the discussion in Chapter 2 of Lev 18:23 (bestiality).

19. Note how Hamor is drawn into Shechem's offense so that the traditions in Genesis 38 and Genesis 34 both revolve around the actions of a father and his son.

20. Both Dinah in Genesis 34 and Shelah in Genesis 38 disappear from the historical record—no union is cited for either—possibly because a Canaanite violated Dinah and because Shelah is (partly) Canaanite.

The bestiality rule in Lev 18:23 has no penalty. The comparable rule in Lev 20:15, 16 has the death penalty, and it is in line with what happens to Shechem (Genesis 34) because he is slain with the sword: in the language of the rule, his blood is upon him. The woman and the beast also receive the death penalty. Unlike the description of the man's intercourse with the beast, it is said of the woman that she approaches it to lie with it. This difference reflects what happens in the narrative, namely, Dinah's initiative in visiting the Hivites. The penalty in the preceding rule in Lev 20:14 (marriage to a mother and her daughter) is death by burning, reflecting Tamar's near fate for her act of harlotry. The narratives can thus explain why the penalties in the rules vary.

Leviticus 20:17

And if a man shall take his sister, his father's daughter, or his mother's daughter, and see her nakedness, and she see his nakedness; it is a shameful thing; and they shall be cut off in the sight of their people: he hath uncovered his sister's nakedness; he shall bear his iniquity.

As he characteristically did, the lawgiver turned back to an earlier generation and located an example parallel to Dinah's sexual relationship with a foreign prince (the story in Genesis 34 that prompted the preceding rule about bestiality). It cannot be emphasized enough that both the narrators of the traditions and the presenters of the laws sought out parallel developments from generation to generation. The example that mirrors Dinah's is Sarah's relationships with two foreign kings, the pharaoh and Abimelech (Gen 12:10–20; 20).

Like Dinah, Sarah is in foreign parts and becomes a participant in sexual wrongdoing. She claims to be Abraham's sister and therefore available to the foreign men. In fact, according to Gen 20:12, she is both half-sister and wife to Abraham. Dinah unwisely takes it upon herself to go into the midst of a foreign culture unaccompanied by any of her brothers and ends up by being treated like a harlot, in a way because she is not accompanied by a brother. Accompanied by her husband-brother Abraham, Sarah pretends at his request that he is only her brother, the aim being to encourage a foreigner to relate to her sexually. Exploiting her brotherly relationship to Abraham, Sarah plays the harlot. The lawgiver looked at the complicated relationship between Abraham and Sarah, noted how its exploitation led to the sexual offense, and set down the prohibition against a marriage between a brother and a sister. In the rule the man takes (in marriage) his sister.

Deut 22:22 sets down a rule about adultery because the focus is on Sarah as Abraham's wife in the narratives about her with the pharaoh and Abimelech.[21] In Lev 20:17 the lawgiver chose to focus on Sarah's relationship to Abraham as a sister because he saw in their exploitation of it the source of the wrongdoing in the two incidents.

The term *ḥesed* in the sense of "a shameful thing, reproach," is found only in the rule and in Prov 14:34: "Sin is a reproach to peoples." As expressed in this proverb,[22] the issue of the universal character of sin is the one with which the king of Gerar, Abimelech, confronts Abraham and Sarah. Their tawdry action brings sin on him and his people too: "What hast thou [Abraham] done unto us? And how have I [Abimelech] offended thee, that thou hast brought on me and on my kingdom a great sin? Thou hast done deeds unto me that ought not to be done" (Gen 20:9). Equally noteworthy is that Abimelech anticipates that a reproach will befall Sarah among her people unless he makes an attempt to deflect it from her: "Behold I [Abimelech] have given thy brother a thousand pieces of silver; it is thy vindication in the eyes [literally, "a covering of the eyes"] of all who are with thee; and before every one thou are righted" (Gen 20:16).

The lawgiver's procedure when presenting the rule in Lev 20:17 against marriage with a half-sister is different from the move he made to present the same rule in Lev 18:9. In Lev 20:17 he turned to Abraham's relationship to Sarah because Sarah's loose sexual conduct with foreign royalty provides an earlier parallel to Dinah's loose behavior with a foreign noble. In Lev 18:9, on the other hand,

21. See Carmichael, *Law and Narrative*, 214–16.
22. "Theodicy operates in respect of nations as well as individuals"; William McKane, *Proverbs*, OTL (London, 1970), 475.

the lawgiver moved from the example of Reuben's lying with his father's wife, Bilhah, to Abraham's marriage to Sarah, the daughter of
Terah, his father's wife.[23]

The penalty for the offenders in Lev 20:17 is that God will cut
them off in the sight of their people, that is, as Milgrom points out,
that God will terminate the person's line.[24] In the tradition, Sarah is
barren until very late in her life, and God visits a plague of sterility
upon Abimelech's house (Gen 20:17, 18). The penalty again reflects
an aspect of the narrative.

Leviticus 20:18

And if a man shall lie with a woman having her sickness, and shall uncover her nakedness; he hath discovered her fountain, and she hath uncovered the fountain of her blood: and both of them shall be cut off
from among their people.

Sarah is again the focus of the rule, and again the focus is on her
sexuality. Between her sexual adventures with the pharaoh and
Abimelech she behaves in a frivolous way—probably from the lawgiver's moralistic perspective it is more the response of a harlot—
when she laughs in hearing that in their old age she will bear a child,
her first, to Abraham. Later she denies that she laughed, that is, she
sees that she should not have responded the way she did (Gen 18:
15). She is postmenopausal when she learns of her forthcoming
pregnancy: "It ceased to be with Sarah after the manner of women"
(Gen 18:11). She not only laughs but raises the question whether
she will have sexual pleasure at her age. She is to have sexual pleasure. In fact, the issue comes up twice after God's announcement:
with Abimelech to whom Abraham will pass Sarah off as his sister
(the incident in focus in the preceding rule) and with Abraham with
whom she will eventually conceive Isaac.

23. See Chapter 1 on Lev 18:9.
24. Jacob Milgrom, *Leviticus 1–16*, AB 3 (New York, 1991), 424, 457–60. In his
tabulation of *karet* (458) Milgrom omits the text in Lev 20:17.

Thinking of the ordinary situation of conjugal relations within an Israelite marriage and alert to the direct link that is made in the narrative between sexual activity and menstruation in Sarah's history, the lawgiver turned to the ordinary situation when the issue of sexual pleasure during a woman's period of menstruation arises. He used the opportunity to prohibit intercourse with a menstruant woman (cp. Lev 15:24). Unusual for the Bible, the story focuses on the woman's interest in sexual activity. The lawgiver, in turn, explicitly commented on the woman's role: she uncovers the fountain of her blood. The rule illustrates how an extraordinary development prompted the lawgiver to formulate a rule for a normal situation.

The lawgiver was not influenced, as we might be, by the problem posed by the chronology of the Genesis events. As we read them, Sarah is an old woman when Abimelech takes Sarah, but it is not likely that the narrator saw her as so. As is the case with Cain's marriage (Gen 4:17) or with Tamar's pregnancy by her single encounter with Judah (Gen 38:18), the narrators themselves knew perfectly well that they were not recounting documentary history.[25] Their interest was in what happens in a generation and how its significance is important for all generations.

The penalty in the rule is extirpation from one's people. The notion can include childlessness. The term used is not *niph. karat*, "to be cut off," as in other rules but *'ariri*, "stripped, cut off," in the sense of childlessness. Why did the lawgiver choose to vary his language in this particular rule? The word *'ariri* is used in one other passage in the Pentateuch and, most significantly, it is when Abraham informs God that he has no child by Sarah (Gen 15:2). This conversation between God and Abraham is the prelude to Sarah's eventually hearing that they will have a child, that is, that she will begin to menstruate and can anticipate sexual pleasure. The language of a tradition pertinent to the rule was taken over into the rule.[26]

25. For Cain's marriage, see Calum Carmichael, *The Spirit of Biblical Law* (Athens, Ga., 1996), 96.

26. On the association between childlessness and extirpation (*niph. karat*), see Baruch A. Levine, *Leviticus*, JPSC (Philadelphia, 1989), 241, 242. The one other use of *'ariri* in the Bible is in Jer 22:30.

Leviticus 20:19

And thou shalt not uncover the nakedness of thy mother's sister, nor of thy father's sister: for he uncovereth his near kin: they shall bear their iniquity.

The result of Abraham's sexual intercourse with his half-sister Sarah in old age is the birth of Isaac—not the termination of a line as the lawgiver threatens in his rules about such incestuous unions (Lev 20:17). Childlessness was the focus both of the traditions that the lawgiver had under scrutiny (the sterility afflicting Abimelech's house and Sarah's barrenness) and the rules he set down (intercourse with a half-sister and menstruation). Because the patriarch's incestuous union produces a child, Isaac, the lawgiver followed through on Isaac's complicated relationships with his parents. It is understandable that the lawgiver should have done so. In that he found that the tradition about Abraham's union with Sarah records a development that is contrary to what he judged should happen to those who engage in incestuous conduct, he would have been especially interested in its implications. Thus the relationships between Isaac and Abraham and Isaac and Sarah are not just the obvious ones of son to father and son to mother. They are also those of a nephew to his aunt—Sarah is his father's half-sister—and of a nephew to his uncle—Abraham is his mother's half-brother. Just as he prohibits the union that Abraham had with Sarah, brother and half-sister (Lev 20:17), so he prohibits (in Lev 20:19 and 20) unions between nephews and aunts.

The lawgiver proceeded as follows. Turning from the topic of menstruation back to the topic of unacceptable marital unions, he first noted Isaac's odd relationship to his parents as a nephew to them. He then scanned the generations that come after and found an actual example of a marriage involving a nephew to an aunt: in the generation before Moses his father Amram marries his aunt Jochebed. Like Sarah to Isaac, Jochebed is Amram's father's sister (according to Exod 6:16 *taken together* with Num 26:59)—the very union prohibited in the rule. The mother's sister is brought into the rule too, and the reason is that the notice in Exod 6:20 (without the one in Num 26:59) cites a marriage between Amram and his aunt (*dodah*). On the basis of this notice alone she could be either a father's or a mother's sister.

It is puzzling that the rule formulates first for the mother's sister because the example of an actual union between a nephew and an aunt in the traditions is Amram's with his *father's* sister. Conceivably, the reason is the primary focus on Sarah in the preceding rules. If so, the lawgiver thought of the fact that Isaac has a relationship to his mother's brother (his own father, Abraham). Because his rules focus on male unions with female relatives, the lawgiver came up with the equivalent to a mother's brother, namely, a mother's sister. We have noted before how the lawgiver works with the traditions in this way, for example, Lot's daughters' lying with their father prompted the equivalent relationship of a son with a mother in the rule in Lev 18:7, and Tamar's intercourse with a son and a father prompted the equivalent relationship of a man's intercourse with a woman and her mother in the rule in Lev 20:14.

In accounting for the lawgiver's switching to Moses's parents because of Isaac's relationship to his, it was important to recall that he had in Lev 20:17 prohibited the union between a brother and his sister that Abraham and Sarah contracted. In other words, it is understandable that, having dealt in his preceding rule with an issue (sexuality and menstruation) to do with their union, the lawgiver should have turned again to the topic of prohibited unions which arises from it. It is otherwise difficult to determine why the topic of intercourse during menstruation should interrupt the sequence of rules about prohibited unions.

Moses, like Isaac, is the offspring of a union that the lawgiver prohibits. Both almost lost their lives at a young age (Genesis 22, Exodus 2). Presumably the "bearing of iniquity" that the couple in the rule in Lev 20:19 is to experience includes problems with their offspring of the kind that both Isaac and Moses experience, namely, the threat of death. In the rule in Lev 20:17 prohibiting marriage with a half-sister (Abraham and Sarah), the threats that the culprit will be cut off in the sight of his people and will bear his iniquity appear to be synonymous. The cutting off refers to the termination of a line of descent.

Amram's union with his aunt comes in a context in which the history of Abraham is recounted (Exod 6:1–9). Like the lawgiver's procedure in formulating his rules, the narrative illustrates how the history of the generations (Abraham's and Moses') is a major feature of the presentation of biblical traditions.

Leviticus 20:20

And if a man shall lie with his uncle's wife, he hath uncovered his uncle's nakedness: they shall bear their sin; they shall die childless.

Continuing his focus on the consequences of Abraham's incestuous union with Sarah, the lawgiver noted that Sarah is the wife of Isaac's uncle Abraham. This odd relationship between Isaac and Abraham again prompted the lawgiver to scan the generations. He was again led to the notice in Exodus 6:20 about Amram's marriage because the term *dodah* can refer to a father's sister, a mother's sister, or, as in the rule under discussion, an uncle's wife.

The formulation of this rule in Lev 20:20 does not spell out as the equivalent rule in Lev 18:14 does—it specifies solely a father's brother—whether the uncle is the father's or mother's brother. The rule in Lev 20:20 keeps the indeterminacy of the notice in Exod 6:20.

The rule threatens childlessness to those who contract the union in question. The issue at the forefront of the narrative about Abraham, Sarah, and Isaac is childlessness.

Leviticus 20:21

And if a man shall take his brother's wife, it is impurity: he hath uncovered his brother's nakedness; they shall be childless.

The topic of Sarah's menstrual uncleanness led to the lawgiver's focus on Isaac's curious relationships to his parents because her resumption of menstruation led to his birth. There follow the two prohibitions against a man's relationship with his aunts where they were his father's or mother's sister or his uncle's wife. The topic of uncleanness again surfaces in the rule about intercourse with a brother's wife: a man taking her constitutes uncleanness, *niddah*, the term typically used of menstrual impurity.

The lawgiver turned from the tradition about Sarah's childless situation, and the unexpected sexual activity to which it gives rise, to Tamar's childless situation in a later generation, and the unexpected sexual activity to which it gives rise. In particular, he found occasion to focus on the male equivalent to female impurity, namely, Onan's spilling his seed on the ground when he unites with his brother's wife, Tamar.[27]

As usual in these narratives, the circumstances surrounding this particular union are exceptional. From Judah's perspective, Onan, in fulfilling the levirate custom, has legitimate intercourse with Tamar. In doing so, however, his act of spilling his semen on the ground renders the union void. Moreover, by having intercourse and taking deliberate action not to give conception Onan ends up simply having sex with his brother's wife—the specific issue in the rule. Onan's wrongdoing, then, has brought up the issue of prohibited unions in nonexceptional circumstances between a man and his brother's wife. Or, alternatively, the Levitical lawgiver opposed levirate marriage also.

In the rule the term *niddah*, "impurity," commonly used of menstrual blood in Leviticus, is surprisingly used of the union between a man and his brother's wife. The sobriquet is used of no other comparable union. Why? I suggest that the extension of the term to depict this particular union is owing to the exceptional feature of Onan's intercourse with Tamar, namely, his ejaculation of semen outside her. The Priestly lawgiver would have viewed the expulsion and destruction of Onan's life-giving fluid as similar to a woman's loss of menstrual blood. Leviticus 15 sets down together impurity that is

27. The contrasting aspect of narrative elements is characteristic of a number of his rules and their background: for example, Reuben's conduct with Bilhah contrasts with Joseph's conduct with Potiphar's wife (Lev 20:10, 11); and a father's conduct with a son's wife is looked at after an example of a son's conduct with his father's wife (Lev 20:11, 12).

caused by male and female discharges. The loss of semen and vaginal blood was similarly regarded, each embodying the polarity of life and death.[28]

The apparently general terms, *niddah*, "impurity," in Lev 20: 21; *zimmah*, "device, wickedness," in Lev 18:17, Lev 19:29, and Lev 20:14; and *tame'*, "defiled," in Lev 19:31 occur in rules where the lawgiver had specific, negative developments in focus: respectively, Onan's use of his seed with Tamar (Gen 38:9); Tamar's intercourse with her father-in-law (Gen 38:18); and her seduction of Judah (Gen 38:14). Milgrom's argument that *niddah* has the limited, concrete sense of menstrual discharge in Leviticus 1–16 but is a metaphor for impurity in H (Leviticus 17–26) is not convincing as a linguistic criterion for separating H as a different document from Leviticus 1–16.[29] Onan's specific action is behind the extended sense of *niddah* in Lev 20:21.

The lawgiver uses the verb *laqah*, "to take in marriage," not *šakab*, "to lie with," in his rule (Lev 20:21). Onan's union with Tamar is a form of marriage. The penalty of childlessness in the rule reflects the problem of childlessness which Judah's family experiences. The rule in Lev 20:21 states, "They [the man and his brother's wife] shall be childless," whereas the preceding rule (Lev 20:20) states, "They [a man and his uncle's wife"] shall die childless." The reference to dying in the latter statement *may* reflect the context out of which the rule in Lev 20:20 issued, namely, the great age of Abraham and Sarah and hence their proximity to death.

In Lev 18:16 the differently expressed but same rule about a brother's wife ("Thou shalt not uncover the nakedness of thy brother's wife: it is thy brother's nakedness") comes after a rule about intercourse with a daughter-in-law (Lev 18:15), not as in Lev 20:21 after a rule about an uncle's wife (Lev 20:20). I argued that the lawgiver's focus in Leviticus 18 was also the tradition about Tamar, in particular, Judah's intercourse with his daughter-in-law.[30] The dif-

---

28. See Milgrom, *Leviticus 1–16*, 767, 768, 934: "Vaginal blood and semen represent the forces of life; their loss—death," 1002. If Onan's action inspired the use of the term *niddah* it would reinforce the view that the original meaning of the term is "expulsion, elimination," as Milgrom notes (745).

29. See Milgrom, *Leviticus 1–16*, 38.

30. See Chapter 1 on Lev 18:15.

ferent moves made by the lawgiver in Leviticus 18 and 20 in regard
to the brother's wife I account for by his procedure of following
through on the topic that he had under consideration, for instance,
that of bodily uncleanness (Sarah's and Onan's) in Lev 20:19–21.
The two rules about a brother's wife are differently expressed, and
my analysis readily accounts for this difference, for example, the
use of the term *niddah*, "impurity," in Lev 20:21.[31]

Leviticus 20:22–26

Ye shall therefore keep all my statutes and all my judgments, and do
them: that the land, whither I bring you to dwell therein, spue you
not out. And ye shall not walk in the manner of the nation, which I cast
out before you: for they committed all these things, and therefore I abhorred them. But I have said unto you, Ye shall inherit their land, and
I will give it unto you to possess it, a land that floweth with milk
and honey: I am Yahweh your God, which have separated you from
other peoples. Ye shall therefore put difference between clean beasts
and unclean, and between unclean fowls and clean: and ye shall not
make your souls abominable by beast or by fowl, or by any manner of
living thing that creepeth on the ground, which I have separated from
you as unclean. And ye shall be holy unto me: for I Yahweh am holy,
and have severed you from other peoples, that ye should be mine.

It is an obvious puzzle that rules about clean and unclean sources
of food should come after a rule prohibiting intercourse with a
brother's wife. The fact, however, that the topic of uncleanness surfaces in the latter incest prohibition suggests that the move from
one rule to the other may not have been haphazard. In Leviticus 11
and 12 rules about clean and unclean creatures are followed by rules
about the uncleanness of women after childbirth. Such similarity
in linkage for matters that seem quite unconnected (food and childbirth; incest and food) suggests that the conventional view that

31. On the marriage of Herodias to her brother-in-law, see Josephus, *Jewish Antiquities* 18.5.1.110, and Matt 14:4.

Leviticus 1—16 is a different document from Leviticus 17—27 (or 26) may not be accurate.

As a preamble to the rule about clean and unclean creatures, the lawgiver states that the Israelites must keep all the laws so that when they inherit the land of Canaan it will not "vomit" them out. The Israelites are not to do what the previous inhabitants (the Canaanites) did, abominable acts that caused God to cast them out. The preceding rule has as its focus Onan's action of expelling and destroying his seed on the ground so as to deny any heir to his deceased brother, Er. From the Priestly point of view, Onan also offended by conferring uncleanness on the land. If Onan, half-Canaanite himself, had produced offspring for his brother, he would have done so by a Canaanite woman. However much he abhorred it, from a Levitical lawgiver's perspective Onan's action with his seed is in some way correct because God moves to rid an Israelite family of Canaanite contamination.

The preceding law but one (forbidding a relationship with an uncle's wife) came out of Abraham's family history. In that history Abraham does not want his son, Isaac, to marry a Canaanite woman, and he takes steps to ensure that he does not (Gen 24:3). In the next generation Isaac's wife, Rebekah, expresses abhorrence at the thought of their son Jacob's marrying a Canaanite wife (Gen 27:46). The uncommon term *quṣ*, "to abhor," is used, and it is the one the lawgiver uses in Lev 20:23 about God's detesting the practices of the Canaanites. The Canaanite cultural backdrop to these recorded traditions inspired the lawgiver to set down his general statements about how the Canaanites are being cast out of the land and how the Israelites have to take it over but avoid Canaanite ways if their inheritance is to continue. The concern about intermarriage with Canaanites in succeeding generations makes it all the more understandable why Judah's life in Canaan plays such a major role in so many of the rules.

The rule about clean and unclean beasts states that because God has separated the Israelites from the surrounding peoples—not just from the Canaanites—they should make a distinction between these two kinds of animals. Why did the lawgiver choose this distinction to symbolize the need for the Israelites to separate themselves from other peoples? This is the only place in the Bible that mentions an explicit link between the Israelites' making a distinction between clean and unclean creatures and their separating themselves from other peoples.

As he typically did, the lawgiver searched out in a preceding generation an example parallel to Onan's unclean action (which was in focus for the preceding rule about the brother's wife). Onan furnishes an example of someone who, under an obligation to raise offspring to the dead, destroys his seed, and thereby deceives his father, to prevent the birth of offspring. It is a deliberate mixing of life and death: the living seed designed to give life but intentionally destroyed—the verb is *niphal shṭ*, "to spoil, ruin,"—so as to perpetuate his brother's death.[32] For both the Priestly and Deuteronomic lawgivers such a confusion of life and death is the essence of wrong-doing.[33]

A brother's perpetuating a deception against a brother, with the father also deceived, has a parallel in the immediately preceding generation. The incident, moreover, concerns the unclean use of an animal's blood. Joseph's brothers kill an animal and use its bodily fluid, blood this time—its life force—to suggest that Jacob's offspring, Joseph, is dead. As with Onan's action against his brother and father, there is a deliberate mixing of life and death because the brothers' action conveys to their father that the living Joseph is dead.

The deception perpetrated against Joseph is an earlier example than Onan's, and a more problematic one. Onan is partly Canaanite, and for the Levitical lawgiver his destruction because of his origin would have been welcome. No such clearcut solution to the problem of ethnic identity attaches to the brothers' deception about Joseph. Quite the reverse: Joseph becomes separated from his family and ends up in the foreign land of Egypt, where he takes on an Egyptian identity. The consequence of the brothers' unclean action

---

32. Compare this form of intensified death with the form signified by the talionic formula "life for life, eye for eye, tooth for tooth, hand for hand, foot for foot." See Carmichael, *Spirit of Biblical Law,* 107.

33. For this aspect of the Deuteronomic laws, see Calum Carmichael, "On Separating Life and Death: An Explanation of Some Biblical Laws," *HTR* 69 (1976), 1–7; "A Common Element in Five Supposedly Disparate Laws," *VT* 29 (1979), 129–42. Milgrom applies the insight extensively; *Leviticus 1–16,* 740–42, 767–68, 934.

with the animal's blood is that a true Israelite is forced to take on unacceptable foreign ways. Both the Joseph story and the Judah-Tamar story sharply pose the issue of, respectively, Israelite involvement with the Egyptians and with the Canaanites. This is an issue the lawgiver expresses concern about: "After the doings of the land of Egypt wherein ye dwelt, shall ye not do: and after the doings of the land of Canaan, whither I bring you, shall ye not do: neither shall ye walk in their ordinances" (Lev 18:3).

The switch in the language of the rule in Lev 20:22–26 from a reference to the nation—that is, Canaan—to the reference to "peoples" is one indication that the Egyptians were again included in the lawgiver's thinking. The major reason, however, that they came back into reckoning is that in light of Judah's move to Canaan, Joseph's move to Egypt provides an even more graphic illustration of how a member of the Israelite nation loses his native identity. As so many of the previous rules bring out (for example, the rules about forbidden mixtures in Lev 19:19), problems of identity were of central concern to the lawgiver.

The issue of Joseph's identity in Egypt is what prompted the lawgiver to work with the distinction between clean and unclean creatures and led directly to the issue of how food serves to separate one people from another. The link between food and Israelite identity as expressed in the rule is far from an obvious one and demands an explanation.

When Joseph's brothers come a second time to Egypt to obtain food for their family back in Canaan, Joseph, disguised in his Egyptian dress, cannot eat with them because the Egyptian laws of ritual purity prohibit it: "The Egyptians might not eat bread with the Hebrews; for that is an abomination unto the Egyptians" (Gen 43:32). The term *lehem*, "bread, food," has an inclusive meaning and can include, for example, the clean animals given as sacrifices by the priests in Lev 21:6, 8, 17, 21, 22. The last time the brothers ate together with Joseph in proximity, but not permitted to eat with them, was when he was in a pit and they plotted to be rid of him.

The Egyptians' stance that if they eat food with some foreign group they become ritually unclean inspired the lawgiver to focus on food as an indicator of ethnic identity for the Israelites. He did so by having the distinction—almost certainly one that derives from custom[34]—between a clean creature and an unclean one symbolize Israelite separation from other peoples. Joseph's adherence to the Egyptian food rules is, for two reasons, pertinent to the quite puzzling idea that one's ethnic identity is tied to a distinction between a clean animal and an unclean one. First, an Israelite, Joseph, adheres to an Egyptian custom regarding ritual purity, and such confusion of identity needs a response. Second, by sitting at table with his brothers but not eating with them, Joseph avenges himself upon them for their earlier treatment of him when they splashed animal blood on his special garment. That unclean use of an animal's blood had caused Joseph to become separated from his people in the first instance and led to his avoidance of eating with them because they were unclean foreigners.

Commentators all agree on the significance of the Egyptian custom for the Egyptians but rarely draw any attention to the fact that the Israelite dietary rules are analogous in their intent. G. C. Aalders (speculating about the Egyptian custom) and Claus Westermann state, respectively, "This [Egyptian] custom was based on a religious practice that did not permit Egyptians to eat the meat of certain animals that were commonly eaten by other peoples"; and "The brothers become aware of the Egyptian prohibition to eat at table with Canaanites." John Skinner shows some awareness: "The Egyptian exclusiveness in intercourse with foreigners, which would have been perfectly intelligible to the later Jews. . . . "[35] Milgrom makes no reference to the Egyptian custom when he attempts to make sense of the link between the food laws and the notion of Israel's separation from other peoples. He sketches a complicated explanation involving issues of sex, food, and idolatry.[36] Any attempt to understand how the Israelite food laws serve to signify their national identity has to deal first and foremost with the Egyptian custom (cp. Herodotus 2.41).

---

34. See David Wright's comments, "Observations on the Ethical Foundation of the Biblical Dietary Laws: A Response to Jacob Milgrom," in *Religion and Law: Biblical-Judaic and Islamic Perspectives*, ed. E. B. Firmage, B. G. Weiss, and J. W. Welch (Winona Lake, Ind., 1990), 193–96.

35. G. C. Aalders, *Genesis*, BSC (Grand Rapids, Mich., 1981), 233; Claus Westermann, *Genesis 37–50* (Minneapolis, Minn., 1986), 126; John Skinner, *Genesis*, ICC (Edinburgh, 1930), 482.

36. Milgrom, *Leviticus 1–16*, 725, 726.

The food laws in Leviticus 11 are more narrowly focused than in Lev 20:22–26 in that the concern is with an Israelite's eating an unclean creature and making himself separate from his fellow Israelites. In light of the link I am suggesting between clean and unclean creatures and the experience of Joseph's brothers in Egypt when they could not share a table with Joseph and the other Egyptians, it is noteworthy that the reason cited for observing the food rules in Leviticus 11 is: "For I am Yahweh that brought you out of the land of Egypt" (Lev 11:45). The reference to the Egyptian background is more significant than has been hitherto realized.

The link between food and Israel's identity in the rule in Lev 20:22–26 is not an isolated phenomenon in biblical material but is paralleled in the rule about uncircumcised fruit (Lev 19:23–25). That food rule, I argued, comes from the lawgiver's reflection on the history of Israel's involvement with the Canaanites at the time of Gideon and his half-Canaanite son, Abimelech.[37] The rule is intended to remind the Israelites how their identity is defined over against Canaanite identity. The move to relate Israelite eating habits to Israel's experience in Egypt is also not an isolated example. Other illustrations involving food are the rules about Passover (Exodus 12) and first-fruits (Deut 26:1–11). The single difference between these two examples and the one about clean and unclean creatures is that the former two, because they come from Moses' own experience, explicitly cited the links, whereas the latter, coming from a time before Moses lived, did not. The rule about leaving food at harvest time for the poor is, like the rule about clean and unclean creatures, also linked to Joseph's life in Egypt (Lev 19:9, 10; Deut 24:19–22), and hence neither has an explicit reference to that period of history. In all of the above examples customary practices have been given new significance in light of Israel's historical experiences.

Leviticus 20:27

A man or woman that hath a familiar spirit, or that is a medium, shall surely be put to death: they shall stone them with stones: their blood shall be upon them.

37. See Chapter 5 on Lev 19:23–25.

How did the lawgiver proceed to the topic of divination from that of clean and unclean creatures? Immediately after the incident when Joseph is unable to eat with his brothers because of the Egyptian rule against eating food with foreigners, he claims he has power to divine by means of his silver cup and, even in its absence because of theft, has other such powers available to him which enable him to "know" who has stolen it. Believing in his divinatory powers, Joseph's brothers respond by giving an account of their family history and, climactically, details about how their father thought that their brother Joseph had been torn to pieces by a wild beast (Gen 44:28). Since the lawgiver had already taken up the issue of Joseph's deceptive claim to foretell the future (in Lev 19:26 about divination and soothsaying)[38] he turned again to the brothers' deceptive use of an animal's blood to have their father think that Joseph is dead.

The brothers' deception plus Onan's—the two actions pertinent to the two preceding rules (clean and unclean creatures and the brother's wife)—are indeed about deceptive practices involving the dead. Onan deceives in order to avoid giving life in the form of offspring to his dead brother, and Joseph's brothers deceive with the animal blood in order to persuade Jacob that his son has died, the prey of a wild beast.

The lawgiver has just spelled out his concern to have the Israelites keep themselves separate from the surrounding peoples. Not surprisingly he proceeded to prohibit practitioners of foreign arts who consult with the dead. As with the similar rules in Lev 19:31 and Lev 20:6, what happens among the first generation of the Israelites is viewed as a harbinger of more fully developed deceptions to do with the dead among later generations of Israelites (1 Sam 28:3, 9; Isa 8:19; 19:3; 29:4; 2 Kgs 21:6; 23:24; 1 Chr 10:13).

The lawgiver's procedure explains the puzzle that Levine finds when he attempts to explain the problematic arrangement of the various rules: "The insertion of this verse [about familiar spirits and mediums] at the conclusion of chapter 20 is rather puzzling, since it seems to be an afterthought."[39] It is not an afterthought.

---

38. See Chapter 5 on Lev 19:26.
39. Levine, *Leviticus*, 140. I also do not think that we can speak of a conclusion at the end of chapter 20 as if the chapter divisions were original—which they were not—to the ancient authors.

The rule in question fits into the topics that the pertinent traditions raise, just as the next rule in Lev 21:1–6 about the defilement of the priests through contact with the dead follows on from the lawgiver's interest in a tradition that turns out to be related to the Judah story.

There is reference in the rule to a man or a woman who offends. The tradition in Genesis 38 presents both a male and a female example of deceptive practices in regard to the dead. Onan deceives his father into believing that his intercourse with Tamar has given seed to his dead brother Er, whereas he has destroyed it. The disguised Tamar, in turn, in luring Judah, deceives him into giving his seed on behalf of her dead husband, his son Er. The incident in 1 Samuel 28 furnishes, as we saw for the rule in Lev 19:31, an example in a later generation of a female expert in consulting with the dead.[40]

The Sequence of Topics in the Narratives
for the Laws in Leviticus 20

Joseph, when filling his brothers' sacks with grain, also secretly inserts the money they brought to Egypt to pay for it. The lawgiver saw his deed as an act of cheating in a transaction and set down a rule about giving correct weights and measure. The rule is the final one in Leviticus 19 (35–37). The lawgiver next moved to a similar topic but not to a similar rule. He noted how Tamar, seeking seed from Judah, deceives him when providing him with a prostitute's service. Judah does not go to any prostitute but to a Canaanite cult prostitute who is part of the Molech cult. Judah thereby gets himself involved in Molech worship indirectly. The rule the lawgiver set down has nothing to do with the topic of deceiving in a transaction: it concerns the sacrifice of children (human seed) to the Canaanite god Molech (Lev 20:1–5). Cheating in a transaction to do with seed is the issue shared by the two narratives. The dissimilarity in the two rules arises because the lawgiver, not surprisingly,

40. See Chapter 6 on Lev 19:31.

had no interest in giving a rule prohibiting prostitutes from cheating their clients. Rather he looked at a particular aspect of Tamar's deception. She acts the part of a cult prostitute to get a child for her dead husband, and this aspect leads to the rule prohibiting Israelite involvement with the Molech cult. There is confusion if we go from one rule to the next without observing how one narrative relates to the other.

The lawgiver stayed with Tamar's deception for his next rule about familiar spirits and mediums. In scrutinizing the same aspect of it he was led to his preceding concern with the Molech cult, a person's involvement with the dead. It is, therefore, not confusing that a rule about those who deal with the dead should follow a rule about Molech worship because Molech is an underworld deity whose cult requires the sacrifice of children. The narrative history is all-important for our understanding of how the lawgiver worked.

The next rule about respect for one's parents produces the usual bewilderment. Why should it follow a rule prohibiting resort to familiar spirits and mediums? But again the lawgiver proves consistent. He turned his attention from Tamar's deception aimed at producing a son for her dead husband to the different incident but similar deception by Joseph's brothers. Like Tamar, the brothers use a garment to deceive, and their aim is to convey that Jacob's favorite son is dead. A parent suffers terribly because of their action.

If we look at the contents of the two succeeding laws, concerning respect for parents and adultery, we are at a loss to account for the move from the one to the other. If, however, we fix our attention on the lawgiver's interest in an incident, we can anticipate what aspect of it he might have next focused on or found a parallel for in some other incident. The brothers' deception by means of a garment led to Joseph's becoming a slave in Potiphar's household. There Potiphar's wife deceived her husband into believing that Joseph had tried to commit adultery with her—and used Joseph's garment to do so. The lawgiver has gone from one incident involving a deception with Joseph's garment to another involving it. Each time the lawgiver looked at offenses in the narratives: contempt of a parent in one and adultery in the other. The move he made explains the puzzling juxtaposition of topics in the two rules.

The subject matter in the above five rules becomes intelligible because the lawgiver targeted deceptions that share similar features. The deceptions all involve cloth in some form or another: grainsacks, Tamar's guise as a prostitute, and Joseph's garments on two occasions (his blood-soaked garment and the garment he wore in Potiphar's household). Although it is not possible to say that one clear-cut topic dominated the lawgiver's interest, there are nonetheless sufficient common elements for us to claim that when laying out his rules he proceeded in an intelligible, not chaotic manner.

After the adultery rule comes a series of rules about sexual offenses, so that the lawgiver's common focus in each of them, sexual wrongdoing, is readily observable. We are, however, still faced with the task of explaining why the content of each rule should be as it is. Why should a rule about sexual relations with a father's wife follow the rule about adultery? The key to working out the precise moves the lawgiver made is again the related developments in the narrative histories.

A particular facet of Joseph's problem with Potiphar's wife explains why we go from the topic of adultery in one rule to the topic of sex with a father's wife in the next. Joseph's relationship to Potiphar's wife is that of a bondman to a freewoman. The difference in status between them is what the lawgiver focused on when he moved from her accusation that Joseph tried to seduce her to the incident in which Joseph's brother, Reuben, actually did lie with his father's bondwoman.

Reuben's brother, Judah, in turn, had intercourse with his daughter-in-law, Tamar. The lawgiver sets down a rule against just such a relationship, that is, intercourse with a son's wife. The arrangement of the two rules (intercourse with a father's wife and with a son's wife) causes no surprise in terms of their order. I wonder, however, if the question of status in the influencing narrative is what primarily determined the move. At the time of Tamar's sexual encounter with her father-in-law, her status is not straightforward. After her husband dies, Judah tells her to remain a widow in her father's house until his youngest son, Shelah, reaches maturity. When he does, Judah fails to require him to impregnate her. Intercourse between father-in-law and daughter-in-law occurs during this period when her status is ambiguous. The issue of status in the three narratives (Joseph and Potiphar's wife, Reuben and his father's concubine, and Judah and Tamar) may, then, have been the guiding one for the lawgiver. In each instance he sets down a rule for more straightforward relationships, where there is no complication involving status.

Homosexuality is the topic in the next rule, following the rule about intercourse with a son's wife. We are back to the problem of logical order. Again, however, we have to concentrate on the lawgiver's logic in working with the narratives. Judah's intercourse with Tamar is not just intercourse between a father and a son's wife but an Israelite's sexual involvement with a cult prostitute. True to form, the lawgiver zeroed in on that facet of the incident. For him, involvement in cultic prostitution began in the first family of Israel and became a major problem in the period of the monarchy. There are more numerous references to homosexual cultic activity than to heterosexual during this later period; the narratives presumably reflect a view, shared by the Priestly lawgiver, that cultic homosexuality stood out as the greater problem. The reflection has brought up for the lawgiver the issue of homosexuality in general.

A series of rules follows which, on the surface, lacks logical order: after the rule against homosexuality come rules prohibiting sexual relations with a woman and her mother, with beasts, with a half-sister, and with a menstruant. What accounts for this sequence is that the topic of harlotry engaged the lawgiver's attention in a number of narratives. Tamar's prostitution with Judah is in effect a sexual relationship with a man after she has had one with his son. The lawgiver sets down the equivalent male offense: no sexual relations with a woman and her mother. The Canaanite character of the Judah and Tamar episode has a parallel in the Canaanite Shechem's treating Dinah, Judah's sister, as a harlot. The two main Canaanites involved, Shechem and his father, Hamor, have names that refer to a donkey's shoulder and a donkey, respectively. Jacob, in turn, later describes his family's role in the incident in terms of the involvement of an ox. The use of animal names to refer to human beings caught up in a sexual offense prompted the lawgiver to take up the issue of humans who are involved sexually with beasts.

From the topic of harlotry in the incidents involving Tamar and Dinah, the lawgiver, going back through the generations, takes us to yet another incident that raises the issue of harlotry, Sarah's involvement with foreign royalty. Like Dinah's, Sarah's conduct is loose, and, like Dinah, Sarah gets involved sexually with a foreign noble. The lawgiver responded not with a ruling about some aspect of harlotry but with a rule about the issue in Sarah's life which is responsible for her behavior: she is both wife and (half-)sister to Abraham. The rule prohibits such a relationship.

The next topic in the rules is not that of incest but that of intercourse with a menstruant. The topic under scrutiny in the narratives, however, continues along the same track, Sarah's suspect conduct. When she is postmenopausal she learns that she will have a child. She will begin to menstruate again. The lawgiver dwelled on the implications of her response to what she hears. Sarah laughs and anticipates sexual pleasure with her husband. The rule reflects the lawgiver's negative reaction to a husband's having sexual relations during a woman's period because Sarah's resumption of menstruation and her anticipation of sexual pleasure might suggest that it is acceptable for a man to have intercourse then.

The rules return to the topic of incestuous unions, those of nephews with aunts. Again, the lawgiver followed through on events in the narrative he had under scrutiny. Sarah's resumption of conjugal relations with Abraham results in the birth of Isaac. But for the lawgiver Isaac is the product of an incestuous union. He is both a son and a nephew to each parent. Sarah is his aunt, his father's sister, and she is also his uncle's wife because Abraham is Sarah's brother. Just as he prohibits in his preceding rule but one Isaac's parents' relationship to each other (brother and half-sister), so he prohibits relationships between nephews and aunts (a father's sister and an uncle's wife) because he finds such unions actually presenting themselves for consideration in a later tradition about Moses's parents.

The preceding rule but one about intercourse during menstruation was tied into the theme of harlotry, the topic that the lawgiver was absorbed in when examining other incidents in the book of Genesis. The issue of menstruation came up because Sarah was childless. The issues of childlessness and the sexual activity directed at overcoming it next took up the lawgiver's attention. Isaac is born. His birth led the lawgiver to consider the complex relationships he has with Abraham and Sarah. In a later generation, Tamar is similarly childless, and a consequence is her brother-in-law's, Onan's, deliberate failure to give her conception to overcome her childlessness.

There seems to be an even more specific reason why the lawgiver moved from Sarah's childless state to Tamar's. In each instance the topic of unclean acts arose because of the sexual activity that may be or is engaged in by those who are in a position to remedy the problem of childlessness. The lawgiver saw the possibility that Abraham might have intercourse with a menstruating Sarah, and Onan spills his seed outside Tamar. A rule is set down prohibiting a brother (such as Onan) from having intercourse with a brother's wife (such as Tamar). The lawgiver observed that the relationship of brother to sister-in-law is the cause of Onan's offense.

The issue of uncleanness which arises because Sarah resumes menstruation became the topic of choice when the lawgiver scanned further narratives. It is given express mention in the three rules: intercourse with a menstruant, classifying as unclean a brother's intercourse with his sister-in-law, and consuming unclean creatures. The corresponding incidents are: Sarah's resuming sexual activity, Onan's spilling his seed with Tamar, and Joseph's inability to eat with his brothers in Egypt because he has come under the Egyptian restriction regarding unclean eating.

With the rule about the consumption of clean and unclean creatures we have left the subject of sex to approach that of food. The explanation is that the lawgiver turned from Onan's unclean sexual act to Joseph's brothers' use of animal blood to convince Jacob that Joseph had died—an act of impurity from a Priestly point of view. Their act is comparable to Onan's because each act has to do with a dead person, Joseph and Er. Joseph in fact had not died; instead, he had been forced to reside in Egypt and take on Egyptian ways. When eating with his brothers there he had to treat them as unclean by refusing to eat with them because of Egyptian ideas of impurity. This climactic event relates back to the time in Canaan when the brothers ate together. Immediately afterward—with Joseph imprisoned in the pit, and hence unable to share their meal—they engage in an act of impurity with the animal blood. The lawgiver, then, picked up the theme of food in the Joseph narrative and linked it to his own notions of what constitutes impurity.

To construct his final rule in Lev 20:27, the lawgiver looked at the brothers' unclean act again. It brought to his attention the issue of people who manipulate some medium, blood in the case of the brothers, to convey a message about the dead. He cites penalties for those who call up ghosts or spirits from the netherworld.

Conclusion

ONE of my primary aims has been to demonstrate why the biblical lawgiver sets down certain incest rules but not others, and certain other rules with few or no common themes. The key is his method of dealing with the legends and traditions about the history of his people. He was particularly concerned about the beginnings of a problem in an early generation of his ancestors. He zeroed in on it and followed up on comparable problems in succeeding generations.

A marked feature of all biblical law is that it was future oriented. Moses or, in the example of the decalogue, God, laid down rules that anticipate future problems in the life of the nation Israel. Frequently they pinpointed problems in the time of the monarchy but saw their beginnings in incidents in the book of Genesis (a book about beginnings). The narratives in Genesis were also future oriented in that they foreshadowed later developments in human and Israelite history. The legends about Adam and Eve, the Tower of Babel, Jacob and Esau, and Judah in Canaan are examples. The reality is that both the anonymous lawgivers and narrators in effect looked back on history, observed origins, and traced the course of problems.

There are in the history first-time developments involving incestuous relations in four different families. There is the first postdiluvian family of Noah and his sons, one of whom violates his father's privacy. There is the first of the patriarchal families: Abraham's, whose union of brother to half-sister produces a child, Isaac, who in turn has a complicated set of relationships to his parents. There is the first family of the nation Israel: Jacob's, furnishing the lawgiver with examples of unacceptable unions both incestuous and non-incestuous. There is the first family of the Judeans (who end up in exile in Babylon and from where the lawgiver is probably writing): Judah's, whose family history receives inordinate attention because he took up residence in Canaan. These four historical moments account for the setting down of the incest laws as well as the other laws in Leviticus 18—20. The particular problems that show up in these families explain why some problems but not others are taken up in laws.

Unlike the ancient Greeks, the ancient Israelites did set down rules about incest. They recorded in writing their claim to be different from surrounding cultures out of whose world of conventions and practices their ancestors had sprung. They perceived the influence of Egyptian and Canaanite cultures on their ancestors, claiming that the Israelites and their forebears had contracted incestuous liaisons when living among those foreigners. Their intent in setting down the incest rules was that later Israelites should define themselves over against the ways of foreign cultures.[1]

A major concern of the Levitical lawgiver was, then, to create rules that would shape the identity of the Israelites. This concern is an indication that he was not primarily taken up with the day-to-day functioning of the social order. He includes rules about nephews and aunts and about a half-brother and a sister because Abraham and Sarah produced a child, Isaac, who became a nephew to each of them, by a relationship, half-brother and sister, the lawgiver considered incestuous. If the guiding principle in setting down the rules is the ordering of Israel's social life, we would have expected rules about a full brother and a sister and about a father and his daughter; but they are to be inferred only.

---

1. Actually the Greeks themselves, while not having written rules on incest, nonetheless defined their own attitude to incest in a manner similar to the Israelites. They opposed their ways to those of the Persians. See Chapter 1, n. 41.

Many of the other (non-incest) rules in this section of Leviticus are also concerned with the issue of Israelite identity. Those about forbidden mixtures in Lev 19:19 furnish a prime example, as do the two food rules in Lev 19:23–25 and Lev 20:25, 26 about avoiding the fruit of newly planted trees and making a distinction between clean and unclean creatures. The many rules about the dead likewise reveal a concern with national identity. Most of them oppose Canaanite ways. It looks as if the Levitical lawgiver even opposed the levirate custom because of the Canaanite character of the Judah-Tamar story. The custom's intent is to do something for the dead, to raise up a son for a man who has died childless. It permits a relationship between a man and his deceased brother's wife but, because of the Judah-Tamar story, the Levitical lawgiver seems to have opposed even this exceptional relationship in his bar on a union between a man and his brother's wife (Lev 18:16; 20:21).

In Deut 25:5–10 the levirate custom is recognized. Does it follow that there is a clash between the Deuteronomic and the Levitical lawgivers? Not necessarily. The former simply had not explored the issues relating to the dead to the extent that the latter did because of priestly sensitivity to so many matters to do with the dead. If the former had pursued the matter further he might well have come to the same negative understanding of the levirate custom (should this in fact have been the Priestly lawgiver's position).

The major concern with ethnic identity in so many of the rules in Leviticus 18–20 may point to the lawgiver's own social reality: he and his fellow Israelites were probably living in a foreign land, Babylon. The laws would then have served the community's need to bolster a separate identity not just in sexual matters but in all matters in the face of pressure to conform to the ways of a foreign host nation. The lawgiver and his circle of adherents gave shape to who they were by immersing themselves in the history of their people and observing the occasions when their identity in the past had come under threat or been compromised.

Some of the incest rules suggest a concern with procreation not in terms of defective births but in terms of the inability to produce children by certain unions. The lawgiver prohibits certain unions involving a man with a woman relative of an older generation but not between a woman and an older male relative. The reason may have been the difficulty of conception. The interest in Sarah's situation when she becomes pregnant in her old age points in this direction. The lawgiver may not have been impressed with the miracle of her conception. Or if he was, he nonetheless rejected the possibility that similar miracles might occur in a comparable situation.

To evaluate the incest and other rules in the Bible, we must appreciate how the lawgiver formulated them. They are primarily products of his commentary on the traditions about his first ancestors. Idiosyncratic developments in the legends about them triggered the rules. However counterintuitive our rejection, one should not read the rules as direct responses to the economic, religious, social, and sexual issues articulated in them. The lawgiver would certainly have been aware of some of these in the society of his time, but their existence was not the primary reason why he set out his rules. There are, for example, problems in any society with those who cheat when using weights and measures. The rule in Lev 19:35, 36 (weights and measures), however, was not a response, at least not primarily so, to the societal problem; rather, Joseph's machinations with his brothers when he provides them with grain prompted its formulation. Again, the rule in Lev 19:32 to honor an elderly man is not just an articulation of what society requires in confronting the problem of how to treat the aged. The decidedly odd incident when King Saul bows down to the old man Samuel rising from the underworld triggered the rule.

The genesis of certain rules in legal cultures quite different from the literary legal culture I am sketching for the ancient Hebrews also indicates that an exceptional development, not a regularly experienced problem, may have prompted the rule. Consider the following four examples that, to be sure, do respond directly to real-life and not legendary or hypothetical problems.

(1) In 1975 the United States Congress reduced the legal automotive speed limit to fifty-five miles per hour in response not to the accidents that the higher limit caused, but to gasoline shortages brought about by an oil embargo. Recent arguments to retain the lower limit, however, stressed the problem of accidents at the higher

speed. This debate highlights what we would not have expected: a different motivation underlay legislating for a lower limit than for retaining it.

(2) Walter Weyrauch reminded me that Article II of the United States Constitution, limiting the presidency to natural-born citizens, may have come about because, among others, Thomas Jefferson opposed the potential candidacy of Alexander Hamilton. There may also have been a desire to exclude the controversial Swiss-born recent immigrant Albert Gallatin.[2] Like biblical rules in response to idiosyncratic developments, the rule adopts seemingly neutral, general language that would affect all future candidacies.

(3) More like the biblical development is an example from the Roman incest laws. For over three hundred years marriage to a brother's daughter was permitted but not marriage to a sister's daughter. The discrepancy had nothing to do with judgments that were made in response to problems of kinship and marriage in Roman society at large. Rather, a particular historical development, the marriage of the emperor Claudius to his brother's daughter Agrippina in 49 CE led to the toleration of a union between a man and his brother's daughter.[3]

(4) Roman law provides many examples. Alan Rodger points out how the comprehensive rule in Justinian's Digest of 533 CE, "Things are not considered to be 'given' which do not become the property of the recipient at the time when they are given" (D.50.17.167 pr., Paul *ad edictum*) conceals its original, narrow context.[4] If, as the result of construction on a neighbor's land, rainwater caused damage to one's own land, a remedy was available. In order to block such a legal action the neighbor may have gifted his land to someone—with a view to having it returned to him. It was consequently important for the litigant to determine whether full ownership had passed.

2. David Daube wonders whether the curious biblical provision in Deut 17:15 prohibiting the appointment of a foreigner to the kingship may have exerted some influence; "Ancestors in the Mist," *RJ* 7 (1988), 138–39.

3. See Alan Watson, *Society and Legal Change* (Edinburgh, 1977), 38: Tacitas and Suetonius stressed that until Claudius's passion for Agrippina, relations between uncle and niece were regarded as horrible incest.

4. Alan Rodger, "Roman Gifts and Rainwater," *LQR* 100 (1984), 77–85.

In regard to all societies, then, the more one examines a rule the more one realizes that it might not have been a direct response to the problem it addresses. From the background there may emerge some idiosyncratic or untoward development that prompted its formulation. Biblical rules are prime examples of this process of lawmaking; the laws of Leviticus 18–20 illustrate the biblical picture. To accept this feature of biblical law is to recognize how naive is the usual approach of reading the laws as windows through which one directly views the social and family structures of ancient Israelite society.

The wrong assumption that the incest rules necessarily furnish social data about how the ancient Israelites ordered their lives has been a powerful engine in the drive to explain not just the biblical incest rules but all incest rules in terms of how human beings think, feel, and function in relation to family members and other kin.[5] One can understand the need for such explanations, and there will always be scope for them. The Levitical lawgiver would certainly have known (as did the ancient Greeks) unwritten rules about incest current in his time. It does not follow that these rules are the ones he committed to writing in Leviticus 18 and 20.

Considerations similar to those I have advanced for understanding the biblical incest rules—they often did not directly reflect problems in social life, they took up mythical aspects of a culture, they have a fictional character because of their attribution to past authority—may also be pertinent to an understanding of the chaotic incest regulations that one finds in, for example, the United States. Florida prohibits and punishes relationships of close consanguinity but not of affinity—a man may marry his stepdaughter. In neighboring Alabama, however, such a marriage is prohibited as a form of incest and punishable. Even an affinal marriage to a deceased wife's sister was originally prohibited and punishable in Alabama. In Rhode Island an uncle may legally marry his niece if the couple is of the Jewish faith, while elsewhere in the United States such marriages are prohibited and void, possibly even if contracted validly in

---

5. In the Introduction I point out how modern theories about kinship and incest are really extensions of those current in the seventeenth and eighteenth centuries about the Levitical degrees.

Rhode Island. There is also an old federal case declaring an uncle-niece marriage, validly entered into in Russia among parties who were of the Jewish faith, void for purposes of immigration.[6] Yet in Florida an uncle-niece marriage, although prohibited and punishable by law, has been declared valid for inheritance purposes, after the parties had cohabited as husband and wife for many years.[7]

My interpretation of the approximately sixty rules in Leviticus 18–20 is in line with my method of explaining the presentation of other legal material in the Pentateuch. If my method has merit, some aspects of the composition of the Pentateuch require more emphasis than they ordinarily receive.

(1) The laws in the Pentateuch are embodied in a narrative history.[8] This integration of law and narrative is unique—comparative legal history provides no parallel[9]—and it explains the singular formulation of the biblical legal material that I have outlined. To be sure, the separation within the Pentateuch itself of the individual rules from the individual narrative accounts prompting their formulation points to a difficult problem. It is not obvious that all of the laws, as I claim, have to be read as issuing from matters arising in the narratives, although I should emphasize that some laws do explicitly direct attention to some of them, namely—and only—incidents in the life of Moses.[10]

We know very little about how the Pentateuch came to take the

6. *Devine v. Rodgers*, 109 F. 886 (D.C. E.D. Pa. 1901).

7. I am indebted to Professor Walter Weyrauch, College of Law, University of Florida, Gainsville, for drawing my attention to these bewildering features of contemporary United States law.

8. There is increasing recognition of the importance of this fact. See, for example, G. C. Chirichigno, "The Narrative Structure of Exod 19–24," *Bib* 68 (1987), 457–79; James W. Watts, "Rhetorical Strategy in the Composition of the Pentateuch," *JSOT* 68 (1995), 3–22.

9. See, however, R. H. Helmholz's discussion of the role of the Bible in the formation of canon law: "The Bible in the Service of the Canon Law," *Chicago-Kent Law Review* 70 (1995), 1573–81.

10. For example, those rules in Deut 23:3–8 about the creation of classes within Israelite society take up incidents recounted in the narratives about the Ammonites, Edomites, and Moabites. See Calum Carmichael, *Law and Narrative in the Bible* (Ithaca, 1985), 228–34. The structure of the book of Genesis is such that no attention is drawn to the fact that Laban's cheating Jacob is retribution for his cheating Esau. It is for the reader to spot the connection.

form that it does, and we have no historical information about its
intended audience. One thing is certain. The Pentateuch was not
intended for modern readers. When we instinctively feel that we
have to make sense of the rules in it by reading its contents as reflecting the social reality of the lawgivers' times, we are not paying
sufficient attention to what the texts plainly say. Modern interpreters substitute for the Moses of the biblical texts legislators
who—I simplify—responded to societal problems in their time by
borrowing and modifying rules known to the broader legal culture
of the ancient Near East. What these interpreters have not appreci-
ated is that the person of Moses is so constructed that he does what
even a great national lawgiver cannot do: he addresses the problems
of his people centuries later and responds to them with rules and
judgments. The issues and problems Moses takes up in his laws are
indeed, I am arguing, those contained in the history of his people,
and their precise source is the narratives in the biblical records.

If we define those who committed the Pentateuch to writing as a
scribal circle in a narrow sense and if we assume that the material
first circulated within it, then the members of this circle would
have been familiar with the relationship between the laws and the
narratives I describe. This is a reasonable assumption to make. I
cannot emphasize enough that the meaning of the rules I lay out is
their meaning at the time when they were committed to writing
against the background of the narrative histories.

(2) Before imposing modern methods of historical inquiry on the
Pentateuchal literature, scholars should consider the "historical"
methods of the biblical authors. Both the narrators of the histories
and the lawgivers exercised their historical imagination in creating
their material. They usurped the authority of the figure of Moses,
for example, and they reveal an intense interest in origins and recurring patterns of conduct throughout the generations.

The history that the lawgiver looked into when presenting his
rules is sometimes about Israel's struggle to attain the land of Canaan. The rule about uncircumcised fruit is an example because
it opens with the words "And when ye shall come into the land"
(Lev 19:23–25). Modern scholars err when they ignore such a historical notice in the text and pass over it as a mere device by which

a societal rule is ascribed to Moses. The notice constitutes a crucial key in letting us in on the lawgiver's historical method of setting out his rules. He reacted to the history he found in the traditions before him by setting down rules and practices, some of which would have existed in some form or another in his time, others of which would have been purely hypothetical constructions on his part. Where his knowledge of the rules and practices that existed in his time came from is, alas, but a matter of speculation.[11] Customary knowledge would have been one source. A familiarity with laws and practices of other cultures was possibly another.

The historical method of modern scholars cannot achieve the kind of historical knowledge they seek because the biblical lawgivers intertwined law and tradition. Modern historians—heirs to the sixteenth-century European legal humanists who worked initially in the area of Roman law—attempt to reconstruct the institutions of the past in order to interpret the actions, words, and thoughts of people who lived at that time.[12] Their method ran into serious problems in the study of Roman law, and it is not a method that works for the study of biblical law because it comes up against the fundamental fictional character of all biblical law. Just as I would not relate a law about the uncircumcised fruit to the actual time of the settlement in Canaan—although I cannot rule out that in historical reality some such law did come into existence then—so, for example, I would not relate the law about familiar spirits and mediums in Lev 20:6 to the reign of King Manasseh, as Milgrom and other scholars do.[13] No such easy correlation between institutions

11. The problem I describe has its parallel in our attempts to plot how human institutions develop. Extradition as a legal notion influenced the religious idea that God requires human communities to hand over offenders or face dire consequence—an idea we can read about in our literary sources, for example, in the book of Jonah and in Joshua 7 (Achan's offense), but not in any biblical legal source. (On extradition treaties in ancient Near Eastern sources for the return of fugitive slaves, see *ANET*, 531–32.)

12. See J. G. A. Pocock's excellent introductory chapter "The French Prelude to Modern Historiography," *The Ancient Constitution and the Feudal Law* (Cambridge, Eng., 1957), 1–29.

13. See Jacob Milgrom, *Leviticus 1–16*, AB 3 (New York: 1991), 26, 28; and Menachem Haran, "Behind the Scenes of History: Determining the Date of the Priestly Source," *JBL* 100 (1981), 329–33.

in the law codes and what may have happened in the history of ancient Israel is possible. All of the biblical rules have been filtered through the historical imagination of the Deuteronomic and Priestly lawgivers. In doing so they linked the laws to the history known to them in such a way that it is impossible for modern inquirers to do the kind of historical reconstruction that is so important to them today. In keeping with all ancient historiography, the biblical authors' aim was to conflate past, present, and future for didactic purposes. In regard to biblical laws and history I know of no way by which modern inquirers might undo the merging of law and legend, the most outstanding feature of biblical legal material, and pursue historical reconstruction.

(3) The study of biblical law is the study of law before it took on the institutionalized character so familiar in the contemporary world; this observation also applies to other ancient bodies of law. The modern features so familiar to us were lacking in the ancient world. There were no formal lawmaking bodies, no professional jurists, no professional judges or prosecutors, no police force, no forensic science. Scholars should not be surprised if the characteristics of ancient law and the creation of that law differ markedly from those of their modern counterparts. Ancient laws are more likely to partake of broader cultural features than our legal culture does. The use of national epics in the creation of a body of law, as I am suggesting is the origin of the biblical law codes, is not so strange in light of the nonformal nature of law in biblical times.

(4) It is rare in the study of ancient law that we can pick up so precisely the factors that have entered into the details of the rules we possess. More often than not we are left guessing as to what factors were at work in the ancient society that produced legal records. Biblical laws are different. Because of their intimate relationships to narrative histories available to us in other parts of the Bible, we have the data that enable us to work out exactly what motivated their construction and why they were arranged in such strange sequences.

Index of Sources

References are to the numbering in the English versions.

Subject Index